For Product Safety Concerns and Information please contact our
EU representative GPSR@taylorandfrancis.com Taylor & Francis
Verlag GmbH, Kaufingerstraße 24, 80331 München, Germany

EMBRACING THE AI FRONTIER

Perspectives on Business and Organizational Development

EMBRACING THE AI FRONTIER

Perspectives on Business and Organizational Development

Mihir Joshi, PhD
Mohsen Brahmi, PhD
Editors

AAP | APPLE ACADEMIC PRESS

First edition published 2026

Apple Academic Press Inc.
1265 Goldenrod Circle, NE,
Palm Bay, FL 32905 USA

760 Laurentian Drive, Unit 19,
Burlington, ON L7N 0A4, Canada

CRC Press
2385 NW Executive Center Drive,
Suite 320, Boca Raton FL 33431

4 Park Square, Milton Park,
Abingdon, Oxon, OX14 4RN, UK

Apple Academic Press exclusively co-publishes with CRC Press, an imprint of Taylor & Francis Group, LLC

Library and Archives Canada Cataloguing in Publication

CIP data on file with Canada Library and Archives

Library of Congress Cataloging-in-Publication Data

CIP data on file with US Library of Congress

ISBN: 978-1-77964-130-4 (hbk)
ISBN: 978-1-77964-131-1 (ebk)
DOI: 10.1201/9781779641311

About the Editors

Mihir Joshi, PhD
Assistant Professor, Marketing, Banasthali Vidyapith University, India

Mihir Joshi is working as an Assistant Professor of Marketing at Banasthali Vidyapith University. He completed his PhD in Emotional Intelligence and Consumer Decision-Making and received the prestigious Indian Council of Social Science Research (ICSSR) doctoral fellowship in 2016. His background includes a bachelor's degree in engineering and technology and a master's degree in business management. He is well versed in R and RStudio, Python for data analysis, and social media analytics. He has two published patents on artificial intelligence, in addition to publications on entrepreneurship, the Internet of Things (IoT), employee engagement, and biosciences analytics in Scopus-indexed journals. His areas of interest include strategic marketing, mindfulness, business intelligence, and technopreneurship. In addition to his academic career, he has several years of industrial experience.

Mohsen Brahmi, PhD
Lecturer, Faculty of Sciences and the Business Institute, India

Mohsen Brahmi received his PhD in Economics and ICT Management and is engaged in research and teaching at the Faculty of Sciences and the Business Institute as a lecturer. He has supervised research in management economics (Licenses L1 to L3) and teaches the Master Pro program in sustainable development and corporate social responsibility, as well as the Licenses Pro degree in human resource management and finance for small and medium enterprises (SMEs). His fields of research and publication include industrial innovation economics and management in sustainable development, corporate social responsibility, policy and management of human resources, social and organizational supervision, and the assessment of firm global performance. He is an Associate Editor for a Scopus-indexed journal and has authored several research articles and international conference papers.

Contents

Contributors

Fizza Asif
University of Chieti-Pescara, Chieti, Italy

Megha Bhatt
MBGE-CBSH, G. B. Pant University of Agriculture and Technology, Uttarakhand, India

Mohsen Brahmi
Faculty of Economics and Management (FEM), University of Sfax, Sfax, Tunisia

Elahe Hosseini
Department of Business Management, Faculty of Economics, Management and Accounting, Yazd University, Yazd, Iran

Kamran Jamshed
University of Chieti-Pescara, Chieti, Italy

Mihir Joshi
Faculty of Management Studies, Banasthali Vidyapith University, Rajasthan, India

Rabia Kishwer
Ulster University, London, United Kingdom

Faiza Liaqat
LUISS Guido Carli University, Rome, Italy

Kartik Lohani
College of Medical Sciences, Teerthanker Mahavir University, India

Pushpa Lohani
MBGE-CBSH, G. B. Pant University of Agriculture and Technology, Uttarakhand, India

Prachi Matolia
Banasthali Vidyapith, Rajasthan, India

Mohamed Saud Mira
Faculty of Management, Al Faisal University, Jeddah, Saudi Arabia

Rakia Nasir
University Polytechnic delle Marche, Ancona, Italy

Domenico Nicolò
Department of Law, Economics and Human Sciences (DIGIES),
University Mediterranea of Reggio Calabria, Reggio Calabria, Italy

Muhammad Nouman
LUISS Guido Carli University, Rome, Italy

Devesh Pathak
MBGE-CBSH, G. B. Pant University of Agriculture and Technology, Uttarakhand, India

Bahram Rahmani
Department of Tourism Marketing Management, Faculty of Management and Accounting, Allameh Tabataba'i University, Tehran, Iran

Syed Haider Ali Shah
Bahria University, Islamabad, Pakistan

Sogol Shahidi
Department of Tourism Marketing Management, Faculty of Management and Accounting, Allameh Tabataba'i University, Tehran, Iran

Shreshtha Sharma
FMS WISDOM, Banasthali Vidyapith University, Rajasthan, India

Ishita Shivpuri
FMS WISDOM, Banasthali Vidyapith University, Rajasthan, India

Pratibha Thakur
School of Business, Dr. Vishwanath Karad MIT World Peace University, Pune, Maharashtra, India

Muhammad Nawaz Tunio
University of Klagenfurt, Austria

Samreen Tunio
Department of Political, Economic and Social Sciences, University of Milan, Italy

Vandana
FMS-WISDOM, Banasthali Vidyapith, Rajasthan, India

List of Reviewers

Apoorva Bhatnagar
Balaji Institute, India

Priya Singh
CCS University, India

Megha Bhatt
G.B. Pant University of Agriculture and Technology, Uttarakhand, India

Tania Mittal
DBS Global University, India

Kirti Sharma
Chandigarh University, India

Erum Sheikh
University of Sindh, Pakistan

Karim Bensalem
Versailles University, France

Editorial Advisory Board

Abbreviations

ACE	Accelerator Contract for Equity
AI	artificial intelligence
ALS	adaptive learning system
AR	augmented reality
AVE	average variance extracted
BDA-AI	big data analytics-powered artificial intelligence
CAN	controller area network
CCPA	California Consumer Privacy Act
CFI	comparative-fit-index
CMFP	collaborative mining and filtering process
CO_2	carbon dioxide
ESDC	European debt crises
FAO	Food and Agriculture Organization
GDPR	General Data Protection Regulation
GFI	Goodness-of-Fit Index
GPRS	general packet radio service
HAL	hybrid assistive limb
HR	human resources
HRM	human resource management
IFI	Bollen's fit index
IoT	Internet of Things
LAI	leaf area index
LiDAR	light detection and ranging
ML	machine learning
NFI	normed-fit-index
NIR	near-infrared
NLP	natural language processing
PA	precision agriculture
RMSEA	root mean square error of approximation
RS	remote sensing
SaaS	software as a service
SAR	synthetic aperture radar
SBM	sustainable business model
SDG	sustainable development goal
TLI	Tucker-Lewis index
TPB	theory of planned behavior

UAV	unmanned aerial vehicle
UGV	unmanned ground vehicle
UNWTO	United Nations World Tourism Organization
VR	virtual reality
WLAN	wireless local area networks
WWAN	wireless wide area network

Foreword

In the annals of human progress, few technologies have demonstrated such transformative potential as artificial intelligence (AI). From revolutionizing healthcare to reshaping the way we conduct business, AI stands as a testament to our relentless quest for innovation. It is within this context that *Embracing the AI Frontier: Perspectives on Business and Organizational Development* emerges as an essential guide for those navigating the complexities of the modern business landscape.

This book arrives at a pivotal moment in history. As organizations around the globe grapple with unprecedented challenges and opportunities brought forth by rapid technological advancements, the need for insightful, forward-thinking perspectives has never been more critical. The integration of AI into the core functions of business is not merely a trend but a seismic shift that is redefining industries, job roles, and organizational structures. It is a frontier that promises to reshape the very essence of commerce and society.

Embracing the AI Frontier is not just a collection of papers and cases or a compendium of theories—it is a clarion call for leaders, managers, and entrepreneurs to recognize and harness the immense power of AI to drive innovation, efficiency, and growth.

The contributors to this volume are scholars and academicians, bringing a wealth of knowledge and diverse perspectives that span the spectrum of AI applications in business. Their collective insights provide a roadmap for navigating the complexities of AI integration, highlighting both the opportunities and the challenges that lie ahead. The narrative woven throughout *Embracing the AI Frontier* is one of optimism and pragmatism. It recognizes that while AI offers unparalleled potential for enhancing business performance, its deployment must be guided by thoughtful, strategic planning and an unwavering commitment to ethical standards. This balanced perspective is crucial in a world where the rush to adopt new technologies often overshadows the need for careful consideration of their broader impacts.

For those ready to embark on the journey of AI integration, this book serves as both a guide and a source of inspiration. It provides actionable insights, practical frameworks, and real-world examples that illuminate the path forward. Whether you are a seasoned executive, a mid-career professional, or an aspiring entrepreneur, the wisdom contained within these pages will equip you with the knowledge and confidence to embrace the AI frontier with foresight and purpose. As we stand on the brink of a new era defined by AI, it is clear that those who can adeptly navigate this complex landscape will be the leaders of tomorrow. *Embracing the AI Frontier* offers the tools and insights needed not only to survive but to thrive in this rapidly evolving world. It is a must-read for anyone seeking to understand and leverage the transformative power of AI in shaping the future of business and organizational development.

I congratulate the editors of this book—Dr. Mihir Joshi, Assistant Professor, Banasthali Vidyapith University, and Prof. Mohsen Brahmi, Associate Professor, University of Sfax, Tunisia—and the contributing authors from various universities for creating this title that benefits the academic fraternity.

—Pankaj Mittal, PhD
Secretary General, Association of Indian Universities;
Former Vice Chancellor, BPS Women University, Haryana, India

Acknowledgment

We are thankful to the authors, editorial board members, the Apple Academic Press (Taylor & Francis Group) team, and the reviewers who were involved in the production of this book. This work would not have been possible without their generous assistance. Most importantly, we are grateful to all chapter contributors—without them, this book would have remained only an idea. All chapter titles in the book were essential components, without which the book would not have been complete. We are also grateful to all our editorial board members and chapter reviewers for their diligent work and valuable time in helping us improve the quality of the content featured in the book. We extend our thanks to all authors who also contributed as reviewers during the course of the book's editing. Foremost, we are thankful to our families for their constant support, patience, and encouragement in enabling us to complete the book on time.

Preface

ॐ पूर्‌णमदःपूर्‌णमदिं पूर्‌णात्‌पुर्‌णमुदच्‌यते
पूर्‌णस्‌य पूर्‌णमादाय पूर्‌णमेवावशाषि्‌यते ॥ (Rigveda)

"If we remove infinity from infinity, what remains is still infinity."

In 1950, Alan Turing suggested that machines could be designed to perform complex decisions and solve real-life problems. The artificial intelligence (AI) behavior shown by these machines in the first generation was limited to the knowledge programmed into them. Initially, expert decision systems were developed. In the second generation, these machines could perform optimization and operate on the basis of statistical or stochastic models. However, in the third and fourth generations, AI gained the ability to create content similar to what the human brain can associate with. In the current generation, AI is becoming an integral part of everyday work, and in the coming years, it is likely to create a growing dependency for humans.

In the rapidly evolving landscape of technology, AI stands as a transformative force, reshaping the way we live, work, and conduct business. As organizations across the globe race to harness its potential, the need for strategic understanding and thoughtful integration becomes more crucial than ever. Over the past decade, we have witnessed AI transition from a futuristic concept to a tangible reality. Whether through automation, data analytics, machine learning, or robotics, AI's applications are vast and varied. This book examines these applications, focusing on how businesses can adopt AI to drive growth, efficiency, and innovation. The journey into AI's frontier is filled with opportunities, but it also comes with challenges and uncertainties.

Embracing the AI Frontier: Perspectives on Business and Organizational Development delves into the exciting and complex world of artificial intelligence (AI), offering insights, analysis, and practical strategies for individuals and organizations seeking to harness the power of this transformative technology. Through a collection of research articles and case study chapters, this book explores the many ways in which AI is being leveraged in industries ranging from finance, agriculture, and healthcare to marketing and human resources.

In the business world, AI is revolutionizing operations by enhancing decision-making processes, improving customer experiences, and streamlining supply chains. Companies are utilizing AI-driven analytics to gain insights into consumer behavior, optimize pricing strategies, and forecast market trends with unprecedented accuracy. This enables businesses to remain competitive and agile in an ever-changing market landscape.

In medicine, AI is making significant strides by enabling early disease diagnosis, personalizing treatment plans, and predicting patient outcomes. AI algorithms can analyze vast amounts of medical data, including imaging and genetic information, to identify patterns and correlations that might be overlooked by human practitioners. This leads to more accurate diagnoses, more effective treatments, and ultimately, improved patient care.

Agriculture is another sector experiencing profound changes due to AI. From precision farming techniques that optimize crop yields to autonomous machinery that reduces labor costs, AI is helping farmers increase productivity and sustainability. Predictive analytics can forecast weather patterns and pest infestations, enabling proactive measures that protect crops and strengthen food security.

The tourism industry is also benefiting from artificial intelligence (AI), with applications ranging from personalized travel recommendations to virtual tour guides. AI-powered chatbots and customer service agents provide travelers with instant assistance, while machine learning algorithms analyze travel preferences to suggest customized itineraries. These innovations enhance the overall travel experience, making it more convenient and enjoyable.

As we navigate this new frontier of AI, it is essential to embrace the opportunities it presents while also considering the ethical and societal implications of its adoption. This book offers a comprehensive overview of the benefits and challenges of integrating AI into business and organizational settings, as well as practical guidance on how to navigate this rapidly evolving landscape.

Moreover, the integration of AI into our daily lives represents not only a technological evolution but also a cultural and philosophical shift. The implications of AI extend beyond efficiency and productivity; they reach into the very essence of human interaction, creativity, and decision-making. As AI systems become increasingly autonomous, questions of accountability, transparency, and ethical usage grow ever more pressing. This book addresses these issues directly, providing a balanced perspective that underscores the importance of responsible AI deployment.

In addition, this text aims to equip readers with the knowledge needed to critically assess AI trends and developments. By understanding both the historical context and current advancements, businesses and individuals can better anticipate future shifts and prepare accordingly. The role of policymakers, educators, and technologists is also examined, highlighting the collaborative effort required to ensure that AI serves the greater good.

Through original research articles and reviews, *Embracing the AI Frontier* not only charts the trajectory of AI's growth but also provides a roadmap for sustainable and ethical AI integration. It is a call to action for all stakeholders to participate actively in shaping an AI-driven future that is equitable, innovative, and mindful of broader societal impacts.

Ultimately, this book highlights the extraordinary potential of AI and serves as a comprehensive guide for navigating its complexities. As we stand on the cusp of unprecedented technological advancement, it is our shared responsibility to guide this progress in a direction that benefits all of humanity. Embracing the AI frontier involves fostering a future where technology and human creativity work together harmoniously to create a more connected, efficient, and equitable world. Through thoughtful integration and ethical deployment, we can harness the power of AI to drive innovation and improve quality of life across various sectors, ensuring that the advancements we achieve today pave the way for a brighter tomorrow.

Chapter 1 examines the impact of AI on human resource management (HRM) and related practices. This chapter reviews the literature on artificial intelligence and HRM published over the past two decades and analyzes authorship, citations, contributing countries, and publication sources using VOSviewer. It also evaluates significant trends, identifies knowledge gaps, and suggests a future research agenda. The chapter draws on articles from leading databases spanning the years 2002 to 2023.

Chapter 2 investigates the contribution of AI to agricultural practices and the enhancement of these practices through AI tools. The integration of artificial intelligence (AI) with sustainable methods has emerged as a promising path forward in the rapidly evolving field of modern agriculture. This chapter explores the transformative potential of well-integrated AI applications in agriculture, as we stand at the intersection of technology and farming.

Chapter 3 focuses on major startups in the biotechnology and pharmaceutical industries. This study uses qualitative methodologies to select incubators in these sectors and to identify and describe the characteristics of the services they provide to incubated startups. The research selected the top 15 global incubators operating in the biotechnology and pharmaceutical sectors using multiple tools, expert rankings, the Google search engine, and two artificial intelligence bots: ChatGPT 3.5 and Google Bard (now Gemini). The characteristics of the incubation services were identified through a coding process. The practical implications of this study are both managerial and policy-related, as it provides a benchmark of excellence for the creation of specialized incubators in the biotechnology and pharmaceutical sectors.

Chapter 4 presents a bibliometric analysis of sustainable business practices within the context of their integration with artificial intelligence (AI). This investigation aims to elucidate the cumulative scholarly contributions at the intersection of sustainable business practices and AI, thereby offering valuable insights into the evolving landscape of sustainable and technologically advanced business strategies. The analysis provides scholars, decision-makers, and practitioners with a comprehensive understanding of the emerging fields of AI and sustainable business practices. With an ever-expanding body of knowledge and significant real-world impact potential, this research area is well-positioned for sustained growth and innovation as the international community works to address pressing sustainability concerns.

Chapter 5 examines the implementation of AI in the tourism sector and its advancements in the hospitality industry. AI enhances customer experiences, optimizes business processes, and promotes environmentally responsible travel. The integration of AI into European family-run hotels has significantly influenced the travel and tourism industry due to technological advancements. This qualitative study is based on secondary data, using literature, case studies, and statistical information from family-run hotel businesses in Europe.

Chapter 6 focuses on the e-learning and technology education sector. AI technologies such as machine learning, natural language processing models, and data analytics enhance the educational experience through personalized learning, adaptive assessment, automation of administrative tasks, chatbots, and predictive analytics. However, the integration of AI also introduces *technostress*—a psychological discomfort caused by technology use. Technostress can result from rapid technological changes, increased screen time, privacy concerns, and fear of job displacement. Ethical considerations are crucial for the responsible use of AI in learning environments. Understanding the challenges faced by educators and students can help in developing support systems and resources. This chapter contributes to the literature on balancing technological progress and technostress, both of which are essential for devising strategies to mitigate negative impacts and enhance the learning experience. The study examines the impact of AI on e-learning and technology education, highlighting its potential for improving accessibility and personalization while also raising ethical concerns about data privacy and application.

Chapter 7 presents a comprehensive and efficient model for sustainable tourism development based on blockchain technology, incorporating all factors that influence such a model. A meta-synthesis method with a qualitative approach was employed for this purpose. The research model was developed after reviewing 41 research papers on blockchain technology and tourism, published between 2017 and 2023. The findings indicate that blockchain technology can help achieve economic goals by increasing the number of tourists and ensuring the direct distribution of tourism revenue among local communities.

Chapter 8 applies the Theory of Planned Behavior and develops a modified model using quantitative methods. The analysis was conducted using SPSS version 25 and AMOS. After confirming, via the measurement model assessment, that the construct measures were reliable and valid, the structural model assessment was carried out to test the hypotheses.

Chapter 9 offers a thorough analysis of the obstacles, opportunities, and current developments in the application of artificial intelligence (AI) in medicine. The chapter begins by clarifying the many uses of AI in healthcare, including medication development, medical imaging analysis, predictive analytics, and personalized medicine. This study demonstrates the remarkable potential of AI algorithms to boost patient outcomes, optimize treatment plans, and increase diagnostic accuracy through the examination of multiple studies and real-world applications. Additionally, it addresses the challenges and limitations of implementing AI in clinical practice, including issues related to data privacy, algorithmic bias, legal barriers, and the need for interdisciplinary collaboration.

Chapter 10 examines how AI influences entrepreneurship, acting as an enabler for entrepreneurs within technological paradigms such as the

Internet of Things (IoT), augmented reality, and blockchain. Using a systematic literature review approach, this study analyzes and interprets closely related research on entrepreneurship and AI. The findings acknowledge that AI has significant implications for entrepreneurship, impacting it in three major ways: opportunity identification, decision-making, and performance improvement.

Chapter 11 identifies key AI technologies and their impact on enhancing customer engagement and personalization in today's digital landscape. The review highlights AI's important role in personalizing customer experiences, optimizing advertising campaigns, and automating marketing tasks. Researchers identify specific AI techniques—such as machine learning, natural language processing, and chatbots—as key drivers of these advancements. The chapter emphasizes the value of AI in creating targeted, data-driven marketing strategies that foster deeper and more meaningful customer relationships.

—Editors

CHAPTER 1

HR Revolution: Navigating the Era of Artificial Intelligence in Human Resource Management

PRATIBHA THAKUR*

School of Business, Dr. Vishwanath Karad MIT World Peace University, Pune, Maharashtra, India

*Corresponding author

ABSTRACT

In today's ever-changing business environment, technology has become an integral part of every organization, and the emergence of disruptive power has brought both challenges and opportunities for businesses. The advent of Artificial Intelligence (AI) has sparked a revolution in various industries, and Human Resource Management (HRM) is no exception. This chapter aims to present a critical review that addresses the profound impact of technology in reshaping HRM and discuss how organizations can leverage technology to drive growth and success in this competitive scenario. The main aim of this research is to review the literature on Artificial Intelligence and HRM that has been published over the past two decades and to analyze authorship, citations, countries, and publication sources using VOSviewer. The objectives of this chapter are to evaluate the significant trends, identify the knowledge gaps, and suggest a future research agenda. This chapter examines 208 articles from the Scopus database published in the English language from 2002–2023.

Embracing the AI Frontier: Perspectives on Business and Organizational Development. Mihir Joshiand and Mohsen Brahmi (Eds.)

DOI: 10.1201/9781779641311-1

1.1 INTRODUCTION

Modern technological breakthroughs, known as disruptive technologies, aim to replace conventional practices in this era [1]. They are considered business drivers, supporting functions of a business organization. The field of human resource management (HRM), sometimes referred to as a disruptive technology, is impacted by such emerging technologies [2]. According to Armstrong and Taylor, HRM is a strategic and comprehensive approach to manage an organization's human resources and enhance performance [3]. This field has given special consideration to the management of human resource management activities that support the system and performance in an effective manner [4]. This emphasis urges organizations to reassess and envision the structure and execution of HRM for enhanced performance and efficiency. This can be achieved either through streamlined processes or by incorporating technological advancements. Rather than relying on conventional HR systems, organizations are now turning to digitalization of processes and the integration of artificial intelligence (AI) applications. This chapter focuses on the power of artificial intelligence on HR systems.

According to Bhave et al., AI can be defined as computer programs that imitate or simulate intelligent behaviors that are similar to human behavior, even though they behave differently [5]. The term AI encompasses various technological advancements that empower computers to perform tasks typically associated with human cognition, such as making adaptive decisions [6]. Technological developments are substantially changing the way employees work and are managed in organizations, with a focus on HRM [7, 8]. AI is regarded as one of the most advanced digital technologies with the greatest potential for disruption [9]. There is an increasing interest in academic research about the various AI tools and techniques and whether or not businesses might benefit from them [10, 11]. For instance, the challenges brought about by the COVID-19 pandemic have presented unprecedented hurdles for HR managers, particularly in the realms of recruitment, orientation, and skills development [12]. Consequently, there has been a rapid uptake of AI solutions in HR management. Compelling indications suggest that the forthcoming trends in HR practices will be marked by extensive digitization and heightened reliance on virtual platforms, facilitated by AI advancements. These strategies are geared towards attaining sustainable competitive edge by optimizing human capital [13].

Researchers have also suggested that utilizing AI has become common in various facets of the hiring and recruitment process, encompassing selection, interviewing, training, development, workforce planning, diversity, and inclusion initiatives, performance management, and succession planning [14]. Consequently, acquiring the essential competencies necessary for effectively integrating AI into HRM practices can offer significant advantages to organizations. Through leveraging data and analytics, HR departments can delve into employee behavior, attitudes, and performance, empowering them to make informed decisions regarding talent management, workforce planning, and overarching organizational strategy [15]. In this context, prominent HRM journals have given special attention to the recent demand for academic research on AI in HRM.

AI is a technological breakthrough that is ready to launch the next wave of organizational digital transformation [16]. AI is defined as "making a machine behave in ways that would be called intelligent if a human were so behaving" [17]. The impact of technology on the global economy, businesses, and society is growing exponentially, enabling unprecedented innovation. With the advent of artificial intelligence, experts anticipate substantial changes in the nature of employment over the next decade [18]. AI technology is introducing new functions to human resource management and altering how human resources are managed in an organization [19]. AI is used progressively in the field of HRM because of its potential to provide value for customers, employees, and organizations. By assisting HR managers in making decisions and anticipating employee behavior at the workplace, AI contributes to reducing the tedious administrative duties that are to be performed by HR managers. The Human Resources (HR) department is still unable to implement AI-based tools, despite the fact that several departments of various organizations have adopted or integrated them [20]. While numerous HR professionals in companies recognize the significance of leveraging AI, they also highlight that they have not undertaken any specific measures in this regard.

Around 71% of the Indian workforce is using AI in 2022, which indicates that AI has been adopted by the majority of employees [21]. Existing HRM studies have investigated the applicability of AI, the projected advantages, and the influence on human workers and organizations [22]. HRM has identified a way to navigate past breakthroughs like the computer and the internet to electronically enhance production, cost-effectiveness, and competitiveness [23]. Yet, recent studies have indicated that, despite spending time, effort, and resources, organizations have failed to realize the predicted benefits of AI adoption. The significance of advanced technologies and innovation for humans are getting increasingly complicated, with machines shifting from being efficient tools for production or utilization to serve a significant role in several sectors of organizational and economic life [24].

Bibliometric analysis is regarded as an advanced [25] and scientifically rigorous methodology for gaining a comprehensive understanding of any field of study [26]. Garfield initially articulated this valuable approach, emphasizing its utilization of various statistical and mathematical tools for the analysis and scrutiny of publications [27]. The importance of bibliometric evaluation has surged in recent years, primarily because of its capacity to offer thorough insights into a given subject [28]. Bibliometric analyses serve to illuminate the advancements within a topic, providing insight into past trends within the field, and thereby paving the way for further research opportunities [29]. This bibliometric analysis helps the readers in identifying the highly cited journals, authors, year wise publication trend and the countries publishing maximum papers in the field of AI and HRM. The present study not only highlights gaps in existing literature but also puts forth a novel approach for future research. This approach has the potential to stimulate advancement in the realm of AI in HRM, serving as a catalyst for academic exploration and practical application by HR managers. The research aims to contribute to the generation of new knowledge, fostering a deeper understanding of techniques and procedures involved in the implementation of AI in HRM.

1.2 RESEARCH METHODOLOGY

Since Scopus is regarded as a reliable database with an adequate number of search parameters, we have designated it as the data repository from which to collect pertinent documents [30]. It is commonly known that one of the noteworthy techniques for evaluating and projecting the research trends of particular subjects is bibliometric analysis [31]. The combination of words in the search query are: "(TITLE-ABS-KEY ("""HUMAN RESOURCE MANAGEMENT""") OR TITLE-ABS-KEY ("""HRM""") AND TITLE-ABS-KEY OR TITLE-ABS-KEY ("""ARTIFICIAL INTELLIGENCE""") OR TITLE-ABS-KEY ("""AI""")) AND PUBYEAR > 1999 AND

PUBYEAR < 2023 AND (LIMIT-TO (SUBJAREA , “““BUSI”“) OR LIMIT-TO (SUBJAREA , “““SOCI”“)) AND (LIMIT-TO (DOCTYPE , “““ar”“)) AND (LIMIT-TO (PUBSTAGE , “““final”“)) AND (LIMIT-TO (SRCTYPE , “““j”“)) AND (LIMIT-TO (LANGUAGE , “““English”“))” (Figure 1.1).

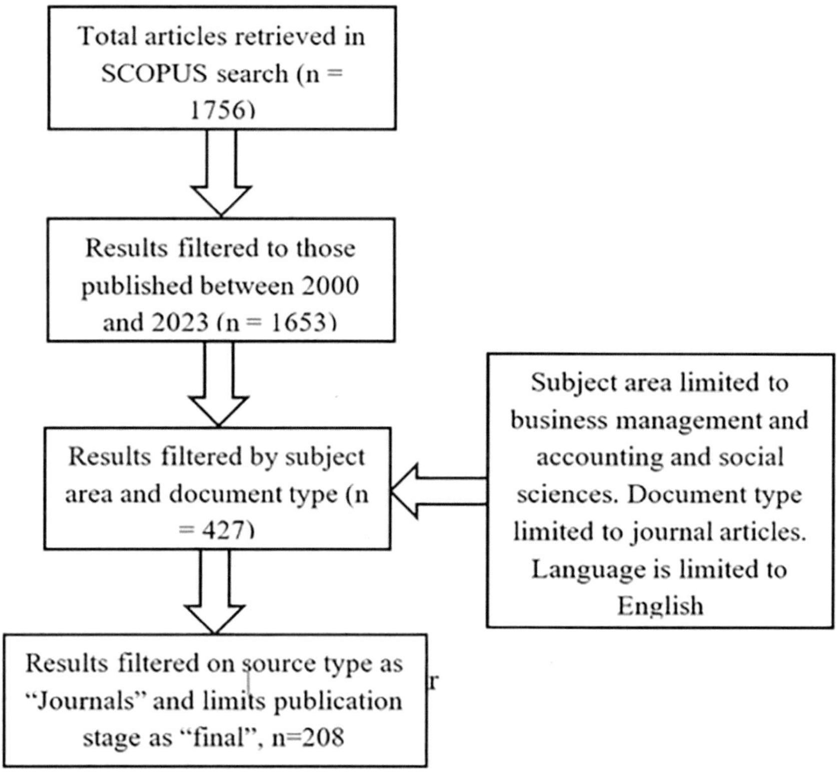

FIGURE 1.1 Search query in flowchart form.

Source: Author.

The study utilizes a five-step process to choose and analyze research articles in order to find the answer to the research questions related to citations of authors and journals, publication trends, and countries.

The articles are assessed over a span of two decades (2002–2023); this timeframe is selected due to the significance and nature of the topic under review are discussed as:

1. Step 1 is related to the selection of the time duration. The decision to review articles over a two-decade period is driven by the scope and nature of the topic under examination (2002–2023). Since the major research studies were carried out after 2007, the actual review starts after 2007. The purpose of the study and the accessibility and accuracy of the data determined the time frame for the bibliometric analysis.
2. Step 2 covers the validation for choosing the Scopus database in the present research. Elsevier's Scopus Core Collection was the source of the articles on AI and HRM used in this review. Due to its comprehensive coverage of articles on AI and HRM from diverse sources, the Scopus database was employed for the bibliometric review. The Scopus database has been widely used in earlier studies and provides bibliometric researchers with a single source of information [32].
3. Step 3 covers the inclusion and exclusion criteria for the selection of papers. 208 articles were selected on the basis of inclusion criteria related to keywords, language, publication stage, publication year, subject area, and document type.
4. Step 4 presents the usage of VOSviewer for analyzing the selected articles. The analysis of the present paper covers the categories related to journals, authors, citations, countries, and keywords.
5. Step 5 is related to the gap identification and scope and agenda for future research in AI and HRM.

1.3 RESULTS

1.3.1 PUBLICATION TREND AND CITATIONS

There are 208 publications in the selected database (Scopus) that are related to AI and HRM from 2002–2023. The maximum number of citations was received in the year 2021, followed by 2017 and 2023. The trajectory graph of the publications related to AI and HRM and their citations is presented in Figure 1.2. The upward trend and the growing body of published research in the field of AI and HRM, especially in the last few years, indicates the growing interest and awareness of this subject among academics.

FIGURE 1.2 Year wise growth in publications.

Source: Author.

1.3.2 CO-OCCURRENCE ANALYSIS (KEYWORDS)

Keyword and term co-occurrence analysis was conducted to explore common patterns in research related to AI and HRM. Using VOSviewer, a co-occurrence analysis of all keywords—including author and index keywords—was carried out to determine the focus [28]. Out of 1612 sources, 69 met the threshold value of four (minimum number of occurrences of a keyword are four). The most frequently used keywords in AI and HRM studies are "Artificial Intelligence" (135 occurrences), "Human Resource Management" (114 occurrences), "innovation" (10 occurrences), "decision support system" (14 occurrences), "learning system" (11 occurrences), "Machine Learning" (21 occurrences), "Decision Making" (21 occurrences), and "information management" (13 occurrences). The strength of the connection between keywords is indicated by the thickness of the lines connecting each node, which stands for a keyword. This relationship was established based on how frequently keywords emerged together in articles that were published (Figure 1.3).

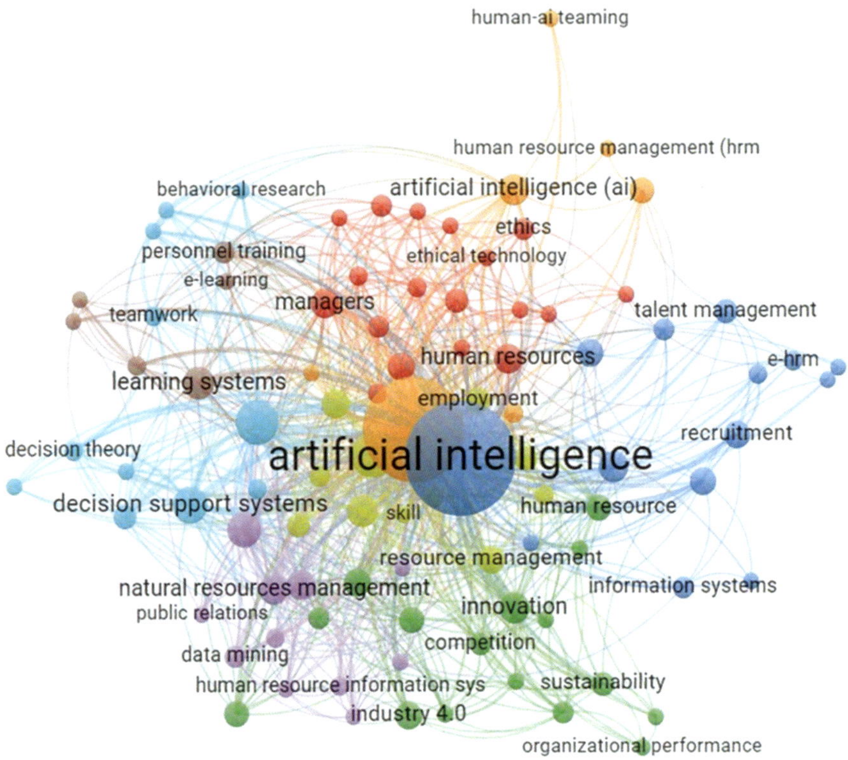

FIGURE 1.3 Co-occurrence analysis (keywords).

Source: Author.

1.3.3 CO-CITATION ANALYSIS (AUTHORS)

Out of 23,543 authors, 67 met the threshold of a minimum of 20 citations. Table 1.1 provides a summary of the top 10 authors who have made significant contributions to the literature on AI and HRM. According to the table, Malik has received the greatest number of citations, with a total link strength of 3043. The second highly cited author is Cooke, having 77 citations and 2232 total link strength, followed by Budhwar, having 68 citations with 2186 total link strength. Mcneese and Demir have 60 citations each, with total link strengths of 1970 and 1940.

TABLE 1.1 Top 10 Authors on the Basis of Citations

SL. No.	Author	Citations	Total Link Strength
1	Malik A.	99	3043
2	Cooke N.J.	77	2232
3	Budhwar P.	68	2186
4	Mcneese N.J	60	1970
5	Demir M.	60	1940
6	Pereira V.	57	1493
7	Strohmeier S.	50	1074
8	Salas E.	39	1065
9	Cappelli P.	54	1014
10	Sarstedt M.	47	901

1.3.4 CO-CITATION ANALYSIS (SOURCES)

Out of 6697 sources, 66 met the threshold value of 20 (minimum citations are 20). The five different clusters are presented in Figure 1.4. From the analysis, it can be concluded that the top most cited journals

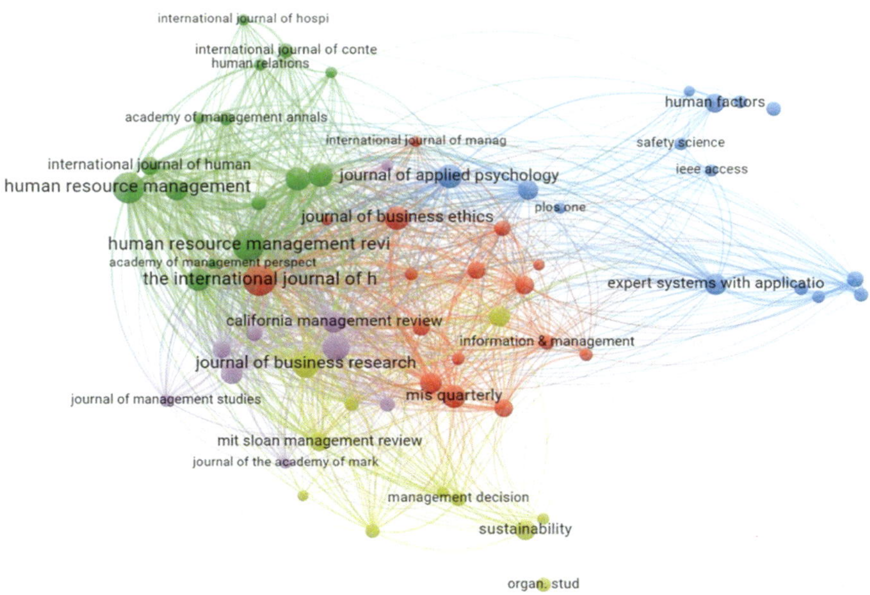

FIGURE 1.4 Co-citation analysis (Sources).

Source: Author.

are "International Journal of Human Resource Management" (179 citations), "Human Resource Management Review" (169 citations), "Human Resource Management" (167 citations), "Journal of Business Ethics" (98 citations), "Journal of Business Research" (126 citations), "MIS Quarterly" (88 citations), and "Journal of Applied Psychology" (98 citations).

1.3.5 CITATIONS (COUNTRIES)

Using the VOSviewer software, an analysis of the citation networks of the various countries was done, and the results showed which countries had the most citations. The network has the countries with a minimum of five documents, whereas the minimum number of citations is 10, and six different clusters are formed. From the 62 countries, 17 met the threshold. From the visualization in Fig. 5, it can be concluded that the United States has the maximum documents, 52, and 1307 citations (96 total link strength). Second is France, having 23 documents and 943 citations (110 total link strength), followed by the United Kingdom, having 26 documents and 826 citations (71 total link strength), then India, having 22 documents with 410 citations (Figure 1.5).

FIGURE 1.5 Citation analysis (Countries).

Source: Author.

1.3.6 CITATION ANALYSIS (DOCUMENTS)

Important statistics were generated and examined from the citation analysis report that the Scopus database developed. Citations are used to acknowledge the contributions made by earlier researchers. It emphasizes how significant the work is. Using the VOSviewer software, an analysis of the citation networks of the various authors was conducted, and the results present the documents with the most citations. From 208 documents, 63 met the threshold with a minimum of 20 citations. Figure 1.6 shows the documents with maximum citations. The results clearly indicate that the document by [6], published in *California Management Review*, has received the maximum number of citations (328), followed by [20], having 207 citations published in the *International Journal of Human Resource Management*. The next highly cited document was by Pillai (2020), published in *Benchmarking* with 94 citations, and Caputo (2019), having 94 citations, was published in *Management Decision*.

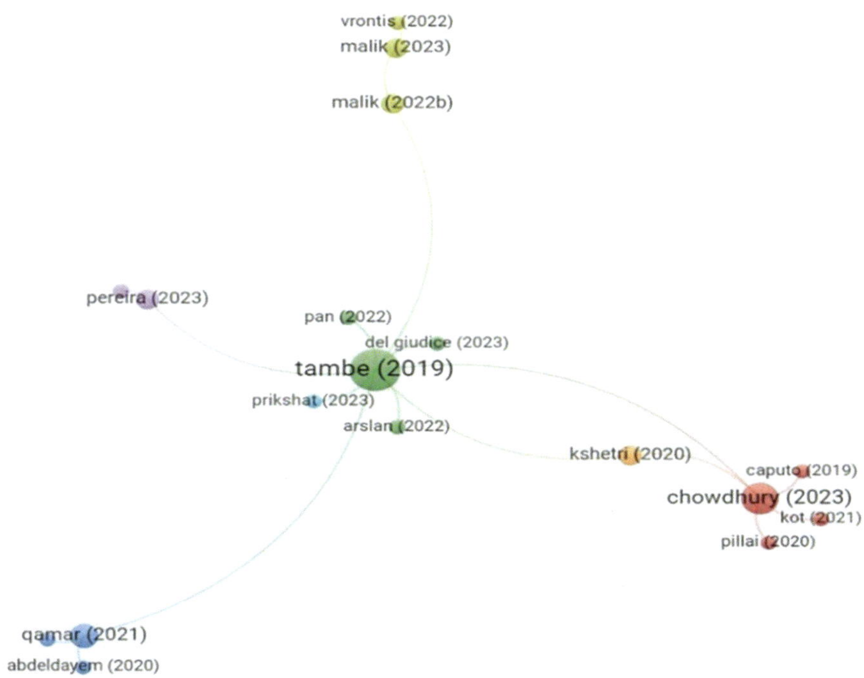

FIGURE 1.6 Citation analysis (Documents).

Source: Author.

Studies conducted by Chowdhury (2023), Del Giudice (2023), and Peiera (2023), published in the *Human Resource Management Review* journal with 52, 29, and 57 citations, are some of the highly cited recent publications in 2023. Studies by Korzynski (2023) and Malik (2023) have 25 and 20 citations and are also in the list of highly cited publications in the *Central European Management Journal* and *Human Resource Management* journal.

1.4 DISCUSSION

To explore the full potential of Artificial Intelligence, organizations have invested in robust HR technology infrastructure, upskilled HR professionals, and ensured alignment between technology adoption and business goals. According to data from the Scopus database, this study sheds light on bibliometric analysis of the studies conducted on AI and HRM between 2002 and 2023. Our paper offers a thorough analysis of the research work carried out on AI and HRM in order to identify popular issues and research trends. In order to develop conceptual and theoretical models, this study offers guidance to scholars who are interested in investigating the association between AI and HRM. It also presents previous research, present circumstances, and potential advancements in the field. Firstly, the paper offers a trend analysis which presents that the research on AI and HRM has gained substantial development after 2017. Secondly, the keywords that have been widely used in the studies apart from AI and HRM are innovation, decision support system, machine learning, decision making, and information management. The three highly cited journals publishing articles in the area of AI and HRM are "International Journal of Human Resource Management," "Human Resource Management Review," and "Human Resource Management." From the results, it can be seen that The United States has published the maximum number (52 documents, 1307 citations) of highly cited documents. Second is France, having 23 documents and 943 citations, followed by the United Kingdom, having 26 documents and 826 citations, and then India, having 22 documents with 410 citations. However, if their researchers can establish and foster closer collaboration with researchers in the United States, France, or The United Kingdom, this concentration creates new opportunities for a stronger development of this research field in different nations. In the case of the highly cited authors, Malik, Cooke, and Budhwar are found to be the most cited authors. The document by [6] has received the highest citations, followed by [20], having 207 citations.

AI is essential to evolving HRM procedures so they can become innovative in the age of digitization [33]. Emerging digital technologies like AI, networks, and robotics have an impact on HRM practices as well, since technology is pervasive and changing how businesses operate [7]. The results indicate that it concentrates on a small number of countries, publications, and authors. Consequently, most of the research conducted on the subject to date has concentrated on only a limited number of countries, publications, and authors. In broad terms, the bibliometric analysis yielded significant findings regarding AI and HRM studies. Important themes, well-known authors, and recently developed fields are identified by the analysis. Researchers, practitioners, and policymakers will find this analysis useful in comprehending the latest developments in this dynamic and constantly changing field. The present review provides insights into the main themes and potential future research directions by shedding light on categories of keywords, authors, or documents associated with the concept of AI and HRM.

1.5 RESEARCH IMPLICATIONS

Technological advancements indeed represent an interesting domain, with AI interventions showcasing transformative potential capable of reshaping the business landscape. This study adds to the existing literature by uncovering the prevalent topics in HRM studies through an analysis of the most frequently utilized keywords. Citation analysis results provide a more precise understanding of the most frequently cited authors and documents, offering valuable insights into the scholarly landscape. While there are many advantages to integrating AI into HRM, there are drawbacks as well, including the need to carefully analyze ethical, legal, and human factors. This resource will prove beneficial for emerging researchers as they advance and enrich the study's content. Additionally, it can be advantageous for HR professionals seeking to investigate, explore, and evaluate the present landscape of the field. HR professionals need to adapt themselves with the rapid advancements in technology and use AI tools to improve employee experience and organizational effectiveness.

1.6 MANAGERIAL IMPLICATIONS

This study can be valuable as a practical guide for obtaining a broad comprehension of HRM research. As indicated by García-Lillo et al., conducting citation and co-citation analyses aids researchers in discerning the diverse research areas and trajectories constituting the intellectual framework of the subject [34]. The analysis would aid HR practitioners in the creation of prospective models for businesses as well as the shaping of present ones. On the basis of literature review, it can be concluded that the infusion of AI into HRM intensely shapes data-driven decision-making processes. HR professionals can identify the power of predictive analytics to strategically plan their workforce and identify high-potential employees. Moreover, AI extends its impact to the employee realm by adopting a more personalized experience. This includes the provision of tailored learning opportunities and instant resolutions through the implementation of chatbots. As a holistic influence, the integration of AI in HRM not only streamlines operational efficiency but also elevates the quality of decision-making, thereby enriching the experiences of both employees and candidates within the contemporary workplace. The chapter offers valuable insights to assist managers and policymakers in grasping the significance of artificial intelligence within their specific domains of expertise and employment.

1.7 CONCLUSION AND LIMITATIONS

This bibliometric analysis carries substantial implications for AI and HRM research as it aids in gaining a deeper understanding of the current level of awareness in this field of study. In this domain, bibliometric research proves valuable in pinpointing knowledge gaps and identifying emerging research trends. The chapter presents an analysis of previous AI and HRM research using publications, authors, journals, citations, countries, and keywords. Through an examination of the citation trends and keyword occurrence, scholars can gain insight into the dissemination and practical implementation of concepts. Scholars who are interested in studying AI and HRM or developing new research avenues in the field will find the data presented in this chapter to be of concern. Since 2002, the field of AI and HRM has experienced tremendous growth, particularly in the last few years, which has had a significant influence on the literature.

In conclusion, AI is a topic that has emerged recently and is now very significant for both business and academia. However, there are limitations on the aforementioned results. Firstly, the research is based on documents that have been published on the Scopus database only. In order to discover more about this field, researchers should think about conducting a bibliometric analysis using additional databases like Web of Science and Google Scholar.

KEYWORDS

- **artificial intelligence**
- **bibliometric analysis**
- **citations**
- **human resource management**
- **publication trend**
- **Scopus database**
- **VOSviewer**

REFERENCES

1. Buhalis, D., Harwood, T., Bogicevic, V., Viglia, G., Beldona, S., & Hofacker, C. (2019). Technological disruptions in services: Lessons from tourism and hospitality. *Journal of Service Management, 30*, 484–506.
2. Gupta, A., & Saxena, S. (2013). Electronic human resource management (e-HRM): Growing role in organizations. *Management Insight, 8*, 60–66.
3. Armstrong, M., & Taylor, S. (2021). *Armstrong's Handbook of Human Resource Management Practice*. Kogan Page Publishers, London.
4. Boxall, P., & Purcell, J. (2011). *Strategy and Human Resource Management* (3rd ed.). Palgrave, Macmillan, UK.
5. Bhave, D. P., Teo, L. H., & Dalal, R. S. (2020). Privacy at work: A review and a research agenda for a contested terrain. *Journal of Management, 46*, 127–164.
6. Tambe, P., Cappelli, P., & Yakubovich, V. (2019). Artificial intelligence in human resources management: Challenges and a path forward. *California Management Review, 61*, 15–42.
7. Van Esch, P., Black, J. S., & Ferolie, J. (2019). Marketing AI recruitment: The next phase in job application and selection. *Computers in Human Behavior, 90*, 215–222.

8. Yamin, M. A. Y. (2020). Examining the effect of organizational innovation on employee creativity and firm performance: Moderating role of knowledge sharing between employee creativity and employee performance. *International Journal of Business Innovation and Research, 22*, 447–467.
9. Bhattacharyya, S. S., & Nair, S. (2019). Explicating the future of work: Perspectives from India. *Journal of Management Development, 38*, 175–194.
10. Aouadni, I., & Rebai, A. (2017). Decision support system based on genetic algorithm and multi-criteria satisfaction analysis (MUSA) method for measuring job satisfaction. *Annals of Operations Research, 256*, 3–20.
11. Castellacci, F., & Viñas-Bardolet, C. (2019). Internet use and job satisfaction. *Computers in Human Behavior, 90*, 141–152.
12. Prikshat, V., Islam, M., Patel, P., Malik, A., Budhwar, P., & Gupta, S. (2023). AI-augmented HRM: Literature review and a proposed multilevel framework for future research. *Technological Forecasting and Social Change, 193*, 122645.
13. Mefi, N. P., & Asoba, S. N. (2021). Sustainable human resource practices for organizational competitiveness post the COVID-19 pandemic. *Academy of Entrepreneurship Journal, 27*, 1–7.
14. Deepa, R., Sekar, S., Malik, A., Kumar, J., & Attri, R. (2024). Impact of AI-focused technologies on social and technical competencies for HR managers–A systematic review and research agenda. *Technological Forecasting and Social Change, 202*, 123301.
15. Verma, S., Rana, N., & Meher, J. R. (2024). Identifying the enablers of HR digitalization and HR analytics using ISM and MICMAC analysis. *International Journal of Organizational Analysis, 32*, 504–521.
16. Queiroz, M. M., Pereira, S. C. F., Telles, R., & Machado, M. C. (2019). Industry 4.0 and digital supply chain capabilities: A framework for understanding digitalization challenges and opportunities. *Benchmarking: An International Journal, 28*, 1761–1782.
17. McCarthy, J., Minsky, M. L., Rochester, N., & Shannon, C. E. (2006). A proposal for the Dartmouth summer research project on artificial intelligence, August 31, 1955. *AI Magazine, 27*, 12–12.
18. Davenport, T. H., & Kirby, J. (2016). Just how smart are smart machines? *MIT Sloan Management Review, 57*, 21–25.
19. Dhamija, P., & Bag, S. (2020). Role of artificial intelligence in operations environment: A review and bibliometric analysis. *The TQM Journal, 32*, 869–896.
20. Vrontis, D., Christofi, M., Pereira, V., Tarba, S., Makrides, A., & Trichina, E. (2022). Artificial intelligence, robotics, advanced technologies and human resource management: A systematic review. *The International Journal of Human Resource Management, 33*, 1237–1266.
21. Jaiswal, A., Arun, C. J., & Varma, A. (2022). Rebooting employees: Upskilling for artificial intelligence in multinational corporations. *The International Journal of Human Resource Management, 33*, 1179–1208.
22. Chowdhury, S., Dey, P., Joel-Edgar, S., Bhattacharya, S., Rodriguez-Espindola, O., Abadie, A., & Truong, L. (2023). Unlocking the value of artificial intelligence in human resource management through AI capability framework. *Human Resource Management Review, 33*, 100899.

23. Hmoud, B. I., & Várallyai, L. (2020). Artificial intelligence in human resources information systems: Investigating its trust and adoption determinants. *International Journal of Engineering Management Sciences, 5*, 749–765.
24. Coupe, T. (2019). Automation, job characteristics and job insecurity. *International Journal of Manpower, 40*, 1288–1304.
25. Markoulli, M. P., Lee, C. I., Byington, E., & Felps, W. A. (2017). Mapping human resource management: Reviewing the field and charting future directions. *Human Resource Management Review, 27*, 367–396.
26. Bouyssou, D., & Marchant, T. (2011). Bibliometric rankings of journals based on impact factors: An axiomatic approach. *Journal of Informetric, 5*, 75–86.
27. Garfield, E. (1955). Citation indexes for science. *Science, 122*, 108–111.
28. Van Eck, N., & Waltman, L. (2009). Software survey: VOSviewer, a computer program for bibliometric mapping. *Scientometrics, 84*, 523–538.
29. Durieux, V., & Gevenois, P. A. (2010). Bibliometric indicators: Quality measurements of scientific publication. *Radiology, 255*, 342–351.
30. de Oliveira, O. J., da Silva, F. F., Juliani, F., Barbosa, L. C. F. M., & Nunhes, T. V. (2019). Bibliometric method for mapping the state-of-the-art and identifying research gaps and trends in literature: An essential instrument to support the development of scientific projects. In *Scient Metrics: Recent Advances* (pp. 1–25). IntechOpen.
31. Zupic, I., & Čater, T. (2015). Bibliometric methods in management and organization. *Organizational Research Methods, 18*, 429–472.
32. Pham-Duc, B., Tran, T., Huu Hoang, D., & Bao Do, C. (2022). Global scientific literature on human resource development: A bibliometric analysis using Scopus database. *European Journal of Training and Development, 47*, 846–861.
33. Joshi, M. (2019). Burnout and stressors as influencers on work engagement among law enforcement agents in selected cities. In *Management Techniques for Employee Engagement in Contemporary Organizations* (pp. 268–283). IGI Global.
34. Abdeldayem, M. M., & Aldulaimi, S. H. (2020). Trends and opportunities of artificial intelligence in human resource management: Aspirations for public sector in Bahrain. *International Journal of Science and Technology Research, 9*, 3867–3871.
35 García-Lillo, F., Úbeda-García, M., & Marco-Lajara, B. (2017). Organisational ambidexterity: A literature review using bibliometric methods. *International Journal of Bibliometric Business Management, 1*, 3–25.

CHAPTER 2

Seeding Sustainability: An Introduction to the Synergy of AI and Agriculture

ISHITA SHIVPURI[1] and MEGHA BHATT[2]

[1]FMS WISDOM, Banasthali Vidyapith University, Rajasthan, India

[2]G.B. Pant University of Agriculture and Technology, Uttarakhand, India

*Corresponding author

ABSTRACT

The rapid advancement of technologies like robotics and sensor technology, automated decision-making, and predictive analytics powered by artificial intelligence, will probably alter how people, communities, governments, and private actors view and react to climate and ecological change. Several artificial intelligence-based research sectors, like environmental monitoring and climate change research, are already utilizing these methods. Investments in using these technologies for forestry, agriculture, and marine resource exploitation also appear to rise quickly.

The combination of artificial intelligence (AI) and sustainable practices has become a ray of hope for the future in the rapidly evolving field of modern agriculture. This chapter explores the revolutionary possibilities embodied in the well-integrated application of AI in agriculture, as we stand at the nexus of technology and agriculture.

2.1 AGRICULTURE AND SUSTAINABILITY

The European Commission has officially declared 2021 to be the start of the era of "Industry 5.0," thanks to ongoing industrial innovation.

Embracing the AI Frontier: Perspectives on Business and Organizational Development. Mihir Joshiand and Mohsen Brahmi (Eds.)

DOI: 10.1201/9781779641311-2

The industrial world—which includes the agriculture sector—is beginning to move closer to automated and digital technologies. Although agriculture originated in the Copper Age, following the Neolithic era, when humans first began cultivating land and domesticating animals, it was transformed by applying metallic tools for crop cultivation, a period known as the first and second agricultural revolutions. Agriculture had access to robotics, machinery, genetic sequencing, telecommunications, and other innovations throughout the third and fourth industrial revolutions. The cloud and artificial intelligence (AI) are the foundations of the fifth and current revolution [1].

The growing advancements in technology in recent years have drawn more attention to the idea of "sustainable agriculture." According to Rocchi et al.'s Burst analysis of 2020 keywords for the ecological modernization approach, "sustainable agriculture" continuously exhibits a very high citation burst in both historical and contemporary literature [2].

Owing to its great popularity among scholars, more recently published bibliometrics studies in the field of sustainable agriculture examine how big data in sustainable agriculture, agriculture systems modernization approach, and the economy, society, and policy making interact with sustainable agri-food systems. Regarding artificial intelligence in agriculture, recent studies offer bibliometric analyses of the convergence of modern information and communication technology in agriculture, global trends in precision agricultural technology, and the use of remote sensing technologies to agriculture [3–7].

For the purposes of this review, sustainable agriculture is described as those farming methods that ensure that the current and future generations' food and nutrition needs are satisfied while optimizing the net advantage towards the environment, society, and planet when all costs and benefits are considered [8]. For the sake of this research, AI is defined in the rational approach as a system that uses computer programming to automate intelligent behavior or develop intelligence over time, and then generates logical outputs to carry out specific tasks with little assistance from humans. John McCarthy coined the term AI in 1956, and since then, a number of meanings have arisen [9].

An efficient and sustainable agriculture sector ensures food security and safety, which is required by the growing global population, climate change, and sustainable development goals. The Food and Agriculture Organization (FAO) estimates that, in light of the growing demand for wholesome, ecologically friendly food, existing agricultural production must rise by 70% by 2050 [10].

These days, precision agriculture (PA) is regarded as a crucial technological advancement that makes it possible to use agricultural resources more effectively. Increasing harvest and/or quality yields while lowering input costs is one of PA's main objectives. Another is to lessen the detrimental effects of farming on the environment, which include overuse of fertilizers and pesticides and ineffective irrigation.

To increase farm yield and reduce risks from weeds, pests, and diseases, farmers can now adopt a data-driven approach by gathering and analyzing vast amounts of data about the current state of their fields. This is made possible by the emergence of new technological trends like AI. Intelligent sensors, instrumentation, and machinery are starting to become increasingly important in agricultural systems. These systems are impacted by a variety of factors, including environmental factors, soil properties, water availability, harvesting techniques, plant diseases, weeds, and other pests. Advanced tools for PA will soon be available thanks to the integration of AI algorithms, decision assistance tools, and automated data collecting and analysis. Additionally, robotic systems—both terrestrial and aerial—will play a significant part in introducing PA and digitalization to the field for tasks like data collecting, pest control, and harvesting, to mention a few [11].

2.2 METHOD

We considered a qualitative research method, and studies utilizing a quantitative method were also considered for this research work. Our goal was to incorporate content from a wide range of academic journals, from well-known to obscure databases. Our goal was to incorporate content from a wide range of academic journals, from well-known to obscure databases.

2.3 AGRI TECH SERVICES

The term "advanced agriculture" describes the application of state-of-the-art tools, creative methods, and contemporary approaches to maximize farming's benefits and improve farming's efficiency, sustainability, and productivity. This phrase highlights how technological innovations in the agricultural industry, such as robotics, digital farming, biotechnology, precision agriculture, and data analytics, can be combined to overcome obstacles and create new opportunities. The goal of advanced agriculture is to minimize resource consumption and environmental impact while meeting the growing demand for food by utilizing scientific knowledge and technical innovation. At the moment, the adoption of several wireless and Internet of Things sensors opens the door to numerous innovations for agricultural enhancement. Numerous customary agricultural concerns, such as disease control, efficient irrigation, and cultural Modern technologies like the Internet of Things and unmanned aerial vehicles (UAVs) have transformed and combined all of the conventional methods. At the moment, the adoption of several wireless and Internet of Things sensors opens the door to numerous innovations for agricultural enhancement. These new, developing technologies are currently addressing a number of conventional crop challenges, such as disease management, efficient irrigation, cultural practices, and drought responses [12].

2.3.1 AGRICULTURAL REMOTE SENSING

Agricultural remote sensing is a highly helpful tool that enables us to synoptically, remotely, and non-destructively observe crops on a big scale. Typically, it requires a sensor placed atop a platform, which could be an unmanned ground vehicle (UGV), satellite, or RPA, vehicles, or a robot in the field. The electromagnetic radiation that plants emit or reflect is detected by the sensor, and it is subsequently processed to yield valuable data and products. The characteristics of the agricultural system and how they change over time and space are included in this data. The biochemical, morphological, phenological, physiological, and structural physiognomies that control an organism's (plant's) performance or fitness are known as functional characteristics [13].

These characteristics differ between plants and between locations. Based on their individual characteristics, they can be classified as typological, biological, physical, structural, geometrical, or chemical. RS offers an efficient relationship between a plant's radiance and its corresponding attributes to derive information that is valuable, such as the soil moisture content, chlorophyll content, and leaf area index (LAI). However, a lot of variables must be understood in order to heterogeneously produce reliable information from RS products. These variables include the crop phenological stage, crop type, soil type, location, wind speed, precipitation, humidity, sun radiation, and nutrient availability. Among the important informational items that RS provides are plant density, organ computing, LAI, green cover fraction, leaf biochemical content, leaf orientation, height, soil, and vegetation temperature, and soil moisture [14].

2.3.2 SENSORS

The sensors that supply all the fundamental data for both the environment and crops are the foundation of remote sensing (RS). A few examples of the variables that have a significant impact on plant quality and yield are temperature, humidity, light, and carbon dioxide (CO_2) levels. [6] Sensors make it simple to measure these elements and a wide range of additional properties [7]. Sensors can be airborne, space-borne, or ground-based depending on their capabilities and are typically used for narrow band hyperspectral or broadband multispectral data collecting usage in fields or laboratories, RPAs, and satellites, respectively [15].

Nowadays, light detection and ranging (LiDAR), fluorescence spectroscopy, near-infrared (NIR), and synthetic aperture radar (SAR) are the most often utilized sensors in agricultural RS, using visible RGB (VIS), multispectral, and image sensors; then analyzing a range of parameters based on requirements.

2.3.1.1 LIST OF AGRICULTURAL SENSORS

1. **Air Temperature and Humidity Sensor:** The agricultural planting environment's variations in air temperature and humidity can be tracked by the air temperature and humidity sensor. The standard monitoring ranges for temperature and humidity are -40°C–+80°C and 0%RH–100%RH, respectively. Wall-mounted enclosures can be used in greenhouses and other similar spaces; a location for shade with good environmental air circulation; it can be erected in a solar radiation shield for outdoor weather monitoring in conjunction with the agrometeorological station during outdoor monitoring.

2. **Soil Moisture Sensor:** One of the most crucial agricultural sensors is the soil moisture sensor. Crop water supply is determined by the moisture content of the soil. Crops will not grow normally above ground if the soil moisture content is too high or too low. Root water absorption, leaf transpiration, and soil moisture levels must all be appropriate for a balanced condition to be reached, which encourages crop root growth [16].

Rapid research and development in the areas of digital circuits, radio frequency technologies, and smaller sensing devices has also been brought about by the fifth industrial revolution. The primary distinction between WSN and RFID is that while RFID devices do not offer cooperative capabilities, WSN allows multi hop communication and network topologies. These days, WSNs serve as the foundation for precision livestock and poultry husbandry in addition to precision agriculture. These days, RFID—which was primarily created for identifying purposes—is being used to create new wireless sensor gadgets. These systems are made up of a small number of sinks and several tiny sensor nodes, which are made up of three main components: sensing, processing, and communication. Every wireless sensor node can be used in the intended crop field; they are connected by a gateway unit and can communicate with other computer systems via LANs and wireless local area networks (WLANs), Internet, wireless wide area network (WWAN), or controller area network (CAN), utilizing common protocols (e.g., global system for mobile communication (GSM) or general packet radio service (GPRS) [17].

2.3.3 ARTIFICIAL INTELLIGENCE (AI) IN SUSTAINABLE AGRICULTURE

Aspects of farming such as image sensing for yield mapping, yield prediction, skilled, and unskilled labor, raising yield, and decision-support for farmers and producers could all be transformed by the application of AI in sustainable agriculture [18]. In order to make agriculture more sustainable, AI is being widely used in a number of ways, according to a 2019 article by Alreshidi. These include predictive analysis, fully automated climate-controlled greenhouses, crop quality monitoring, livestock management, and climate monitoring [19]. Customers with backgrounds in sustainable agriculture are particularly interested in chatbots for informational support on farming techniques, digital plant health diagnostic apps, remote sensing devices, and irrigation management systems [20].

In order to achieve sustainable agriculture through the use of AI techniques, [28] presented an optimization strategy for drip irrigation system optimization [21]. But [29] focused on material science and informatics to use AI and nanotechnology to discover sustainable solutions in sustainable agriculture [22]. [30] posited that technology can aid in precision farming and explored the applications of AI and the internet of things (IoT) in agriculture to evaluate water needs, humidity levels, fertilizer requirements, and other factors [23]. By using a design science methodology, [31] evaluated the problems with food security and suggested an AI strategy as a solution [24]. [32] used an applied technology acceptance model to study the obstacles to AI adoption in agricultural [25].

2.3.4 MACHINE LEARNING IN SUSTAINABLE AGRICULTURE

The 2018 book "Foundations of Machine Learning" defines machine learning as computational procedures that make use of historical data and prior experiences to adjust, enhance, fix, and forecast future performance with accuracy [26]. The most recent applications of machine learning in sustainable agriculture include supply chain optimization [27], in-field monitoring [28], prediction of soil temperature [29], and sustainable soil management [30]. Various machine learning technologies, such as decision trees, neural networks, polynomial prediction algorithms, and K-nearest neighbors [31], can be employed to promote sustainable production [32]. For large-scale land suitability assessments, machine learning technologies are becoming more and more popular. Traditional methods of assessing the suitability of the soil for sustainable agriculture can prove to be costly and time-consuming, particularly in remote areas where data about the properties of the soil is unavailable [33].

2.3.5 ROBOTICS IN SUSTAINABLE AGRICULTURE

In agriculture, robotics is mostly used to expedite monotonous and repetitive processes such as spraying, mowing, sowing, harvesting, controlling weeds, picking, and ultimately sorting goods and packaging. Fresh produce supply chains have found use for the automation that robotics, cloud computing, blockchain, and big data can give. In the context of sustainable farming, field robots are utilized for precision farming to manage weeds instead of treating crops and soil with toxic and excessive amounts of chemical sprays [34]. The phrase "Agriculture 5.0," which refers to integrating robotics and artificial intelligence into data-driven farming systems, has been gaining traction [35].

2.4 FUTURE RESEARCH

Since sustainable agriculture and sophisticated technologies constantly intersect with the market's thirst for newer breakthroughs, there is a great deal of room for future research in these areas. For more in-depth bibliometric study of older literary works, advanced R bibliometrix programming can be used for features like co-occurrence analysis, co-citation analysis, cluster, and stream analysis, and so forth. More technologies, like supply-chain solutions, cloud computing, blockchains, and the Internet of Things, which are widely employed in the agriculture sector, can be added to the dataset used for the study. To extract a larger dataset, future research might also include academic papers and reviews from many index sources, such as Scopus and Web of Science. However, additional processes will be necessary to remove redundant and duplicate information from this type of collection.

2.5 IMPLICATIONS

It is necessary to offer new ideas for soil and plant sample retrieval based on intelligent and autonomous robots in order to get more high-quality plant data faster and with less human labor. As a result, networks of diverse, clever, and independent agricultural systems are needed. It is necessary to build UAVs and ground robots (UGVs) that can recognize, approach, manipulate, sample, collect, carry, and deliver soil and plant samples needed for inspection. Robots will be able to collect high-quality sampling data, which will enable the creation of innovative DDS. This will then make it easier to make judgments about the precise location, amount, and mode of input usage that will optimize output and ensure sustainable resource use. When used, the idea will significantly improve farming processes' accuracy and caliber.

Future developments of this work will include applying AI algorithms to the idea of smart farming, which would include efficient management of cattle. For instance, automated video tracking of animal behavior to identify certain occasions, such as calving. Farmers and breeders are interested in finding ways to increase the effectiveness of their professional activities, and this includes studying heat waves or other physiological phenomena. An automated system has the ability to help around-the-clock, every day of the week, anticipate alerts, make reporting easier, guarantee traceability, and lessen the strain on farmers while also taking care of the animals' health. Progressively more sophisticated functions based on AI and sensing that are kept non-invasive for animals will be included to the livestock monitoring system.

The study's conclusions have the potential to have a big influence since they offer scholars, readers, and researchers who are interested in sustainable agriculture and artificial intelligence a thorough overview of past research on the subject. The findings suggest that there is a growing interest in investigating the many uses of AI in sustainable agriculture. Prominent writers with backgrounds and experiences spanning multiple disciplines are drawn to fusing it with other global theme fields.

Since the corpus of literature is smaller than in other bibliometric studies, it also suggests that there is room for more literary and research pieces to be published. Additionally, by drawing readers' attention to this underutilized potential, this chapter may inspire them to close this research gap. Additionally, the study architecture may offer a more efficient means of developing relevant academic research subjects in this specific thematic area [36].

2.6 CONCLUSION

In order to show the already obtained results, the ongoing studies, and the unresolved technical issues, this study presented the most recent research activities in the form of research projects executed and validated by the authors in many European nations. Two examples of current German projects that deal with the availability of agricultural data and its potential use in DT to provide insights into such complex systems have been described. Agriculture has always relied on accurate and low-cost monitoring of crop and soil health. On the one hand, the expansive NaLamKI project will oversee the integration of sensor data from machines, remote sensing (drones and satellites), soil, weather, and other available data sources to create a dataset that will enable the application of advanced AI methodologies for the optimization of agricultural processes while overcoming the current data availability limitation. Additionally, the integration of semantic agricultural models and explainability—two ongoing research concerns in AI—will be addressed. However, even though it is still in its early phases, the use of DT in agriculture may soon result in a breakthrough in technology. To offer valuable perspectives on intricate agricultural systems, the DEAL project has integrated geographic ML and DL algorithms to autonomously extract plant items from 3D point clouds, overcoming model-based abstractions and heuristic-based reconstructions, as well as explicit geographic modelling. Consequently, agricultural DT may be fully automated to model, plan, analyze, and enhance crop production in order to maximize yields, lessen impact on water resources and soil quality, and turn agriculture into a sustainable industry.

Second, farmers are employing AI in agriculture to help them change their management tactics to precision cultivation in order to achieve greater crop quality and production while utilizing fewer resources. Applications of AI in agriculture, such as irrigation, weeding, and spraying, reduce the need for excessive amounts of water, pesticides, and herbicides while preserving soil fertility, which raises output and improves the quality of items produced. It is indisputable that the average age of farmers is rising, and younger generations are less likely to take their place, raising concerns about labor shortages in the agricultural sector. Lastly, robotics agriculture will not only make agriculture more precise but also a sustainable business.

All facets of life on Earth will be governed by sustainability as we move forward. Making sure food is available and safe for everyone will be the biggest challenge posed by climate change. The capacity to produce food has increased dramatically during the industrial and green revolutions, but these movements have also placed unsustainable strain on the environment, natural resources, and agricultural areas, with unavoidable and lasting consequences. With its high-tech capabilities, the fourth industrial revolution offered sustainable alternatives to conventional agricultural methods that might prevent or slow down the depletion of the planet's resources [37].

KEYWORDS

- **agriculture**
- **artificial intelligence**
- **climate change**
- **digitalization**
- **governments**
- **precision agriculture**
- **private sector**
- **sustainability**

REFERENCES

1. Commission, E. (2021). Industry 5.0: Towards more sustainable, resilient and human-centric industry. https://ec.europa.eu/info/news/industry-50-towards-more-sustainable-resilient-and-human-centric-industry-2021-jan-07_en (accessed on 29 August 2025).
2. Rocchi, L., Boggia, A., & Paolotti, L. (2020). Sustainable agricultural systems: A bibliometrics analysis of ecological modernization approach. *Sustainability, 12*, 1–16.
3. Bilali, H., Strassner, C., & Hassen, T. (2021). Sustainable agri-food systems: Environment, economy, society, and policy. *Sustainability, 13*, 1–67.
4. Kharel, T., Ashworth, A., Owens, P., & Buser, M. (2020). Spatially and temporally disparate data in systems agriculture: Issues and prospective solutions. *Agronomy Journal, 112*(5), 4498–4510.
5. Bai, B., Wang, J., Tian, S., & Peng, X. (2021). Analysis on the competitiveness of global agricultural remote sensing research based on artificial intelligence technology. *Journal of Physics: Conference Series, 1852*, 1–8.
6. Armenta-Medina, D., Ramirez-delreal, T., Villanueva-Vásquez, D., & Mejia-Aguirre, C. (2020). Trends on advanced information and communication technologies for improving agricultural productivities: A bibliometric analysis. *Agronomy, 10*(12), 1–24.
7. FAO. (2021). cb1000es.pdf. https://www.fao.org/3/cb1000es/cb1000es.pdf (accessed on 29 August 2025).
8. Tilman, D., Cassman, K., Matson, P., Naylor, R., & Polasky, S. (2002). Agricultural sustainability and intensive production practices. *Nature, 418*(6898), 671–677. pmid:12167873
9. Russell, S., & Norvig, P. (1995). *Artificial Intelligence: A Modern Approach*. Prentice Hall.

10. Linaza, M. T., Posada, J., Bund, J., Eisert, P., Quartulli, M., Döllner, J., & Lucat, L. (2021). Data-driven artificial intelligence applications for sustainable precision agriculture. *Agronomy, 11*(6), 1227.
11. Khan, N., Ray, R. L., et al. (n.d.). Current progress and future prospects of agriculture technology: Gateway to sustainable agriculture.
12. Weiss, M., Jacob, F., & Duveiller, G. (2020). Remote sensing for agricultural applications: A meta-review. *Remote Sensing of Environment, 236*, 111402.
13. Ahonen, T., Virrankoski, R., & Elmusrati, M. (2008). Greenhouse monitoring with wireless sensor network. In *Proceedings of the 2008 IEEE/ASME International Conference on Mechatronic and Embedded Systems and Applications*, Beijing, China, 12–15 October 2008; pp. 403–408.
14. Joshi, M. (2019). Burnout and stressors as influencers on work engagement among law enforcement agents in selected cities. In *Management Techniques for Employee Engagement in Contemporary Organizations* (pp. 268–283). IGI Global.
15. Joshi, M., & Brahmi, M. S. (2023). A mediation-based analysis of emotional intelligence effect on cognition and consumer decision-making. *International Journal of Public Sector Performance Management, 12*(1, 2), 223–251.
16. Joshi, M. (2023). A qualitative assessment of inter-organizational networks, organizational ecosystems, and joint venture associations. In *Exploring Business Ecosystems and Innovation Capacity Building in Global Economics* (pp. 1–25). IGI Global.
17. Joshi, M., Joshi, G., & Pathak, S. (2020). Awareness, entrepreneurial event theory and theory of planned behaviour as antecedents of student entrepreneurial intentions: An Indian perspective. *International Journal of Business and Globalization, 25*(2), 170–184.
18. Joshi, M. (2018). Workforce trends and challenges: A peek into the future. In *Management Techniques for a Diverse and Cross-Cultural Workforce* (pp. 39–53).
19. Dawar, G., Singh, S., Joshi, M., & Kumar, P. (2021). Effective corporate social responsibility in small and medium enterprises. In *Organizing Entrepreneurship and MSMEs Across India* (pp. 231–246).
20. Esposito, L., Brahmi, M., & Joshi, M. (2023). The importance of innovation diffusion in the renewable energy sector. In *Exploring Business Ecosystems and Innovation Capacity Building in Global Economics* (pp. 283–302). IGI Global.
21. Astill, J., Dara, R. A., Fraser, E. D., Roberts, B., & Sharif, S. (2020). Smart poultry management: Smart sensors, big data, and the internet of things. *Computers and Electronics in Agriculture, 170*, 105291.
22. Huang, Y., Chen, Z. X., Tao, Y., Huang, X. Z., & Gu, X. F. (2018). Agricultural remote sensing big data: Management and applications. *Journal of Integrative Agriculture, 17*, 1915–1931.
23. Agriculture sensors such as air, soil, and moisture sensors. (n.d.). https://www.renkeer.com/agriculture-sensors-list/#:~:text=Agriculture%20sensors%20such%20as%20air,to%20monitor%20water%20and%20fertilizer (accessed on 29 August 2025).
24. Lary, D. J., Alavi, A. H., Gandomi, A. H., & Walker, A. L. (2016). Machine learning in geosciences and remote sensing. *Geoscience Frontiers, 7*, 3–10.

25. Talaviya, T., Shah, D., Patel, N., Yagnik, H., & Shah, M. (2020). Implementation of artificial intelligence in agriculture for optimization of irrigation and application of pesticides and herbicides. *Artificial Intelligence in Agriculture, 4*, 58–73.
26. Alreshidi, E. (2019). Smart sustainable agriculture (SSA) solution underpinned by internet of things (IoT) and artificial intelligence (AI). *International Journal of Advanced Computer Science and Applications, 10*(5), 93–102.
27. Partel, V., Kakarla, S., & Ampatzidis, Y. (2019). Development and evaluation of a low-cost and smart technology for precision weed management utilizing artificial intelligence. *Computers and Electronics in Agriculture, 157*, 339–350.
28. Klyushin, D., & Tymoshenko, A. (2021). Optimization of drip irrigation systems using artificial intelligence methods for sustainable agriculture and environment. In *Artificial Intelligence for Sustainable Development: Theory, Practice and Future Applications* (pp. 3–17).
29. Zhang, P., Guo, Z., Ullah, S., Melagraki, G., Afantitis, A., & Lynch, I. (2021b). Nanotechnology and artificial intelligence to enable sustainable and precision agriculture. *Nanotechnology for Agriculture, 7*, 1–13.
30. Aggarwal, N., & Singh, D. (2021). Technology assisted farming: Implications of IoT and AI. In *IOP Conference Series: Materials Science and Engineering, 1022*(1).
31. Spanaki, K., Karafili, E., Sivarajah, U., Despoudi, S., & Irani, Z. (2021). Artificial intelligence and food security: Swarm intelligence of AgriTech drones for smart AgriFood operations. *Production Planning & Control*, 1–19.
32. Mohr, S., & Kühl, R. (2021). Acceptance of artificial intelligence in German agriculture: An application of the technology acceptance model and the theory of planned behavior. *Precision Agriculture*, 1–29.
33. Mahto, A. K., Alam, M. A., Biswas, R., Ahmad, J., & Alam, S. I. (2021). Short-term forecasting of agriculture commodities in context of Indian market for sustainable agriculture by using the artificial neural network. *Journal of Food Quality*, 1–13.
34. Mohri, M., Rostamizadeh, A., & Talwalkar, A. (2018). *Foundations of Machine Learning*. The MIT Press.
35. Sharma, R., Kamble, S., Gunasekaran, A., Kumar, V., & Kumar, A. (2020). A systematic literature review on machine learning applications for sustainable agriculture supply chain performance. *Computers and Operations Research, 119*, 1–17.
36. Li, K. Y., Yang, M. D., de Lima, R., Peciña, M., Sepp, K., Cabral Pinheiro, V., et al. (2021). An automated machine learning framework in unmanned aircraft systems: New insights into agricultural management practices recognition approaches. *Remote Sensing, 13*(3190), 1–24.
37. Zeynoddin, M., Ebtehaj, I., & Bonakdari, H. (2020). Development of a linear based stochastic model for daily soil temperature prediction: One step forward to sustainable agriculture. *Computers and Electronics in Agriculture, 176*, 1–24.
38. Motia, S., & Reddy, S. (2021). Exploration of machine learning methods for prediction and assessment of soil properties for agricultural soil management: A quantitative evaluation. *Journal of Physics: Conference Series, 1950*, 1–15.
39. Balducci, F., Impedovo, D., & Pirlo, G. (2018). Machine learning applications on agricultural datasets for smart farm enhancement. *Machines, 6*(38), 1–22.

40. Taghizadeh-Mehrjardi, R., Nabiollahi, K., Rasoli, L., Kerry, R., & Scholten, T. (2020). Land suitability assessment and agricultural production sustainability using machine learning models. *Agronomy, 10*(573), 1–20.
41. Mohri, M., Rostamizadeh, A., & Talwalkar, A. (2018). *Foundations of Machine learning*. The MIT Press.
42. Linaza, M. T., Posada, J., Bund, J., Eisert, P., Quartulli, M., Döllner, J., Pagani, A., Olaizola, I. G., Barriguinha, A., Moysiadis, T., et al. (2021). Data-driven artificial intelligence applications for sustainable precision agriculture. *Agronomy, 11*, 1227. https://doi.org/10.3390/agronomy11061227 (accessed on 29 August 2025).

CHAPTER 3

Best Practices in Startup Incubation Services in the Biotech and Pharmaceutical Sectors: The Use of GPT-3.5 and Google Bard AI Bots in the Sample Selection

DOMENICO NICOLÒ

Department of Law, Economics and Human Sciences (DIGIES), University Mediterranea of Reggio Calabria, Reggio Calabria, Italy

*Corresponding author

ABSTRACT

In this chapter, we focus on the main services provided to startups by the main global incubators specialized in the biotech and pharmaceutical sectors. To this end, we use qualitative methodologies both to select incubators in these sectors and to identify and describe the characteristics of the services they provide to incubated startups. We have selected the top 15 global incubators operating in the biotechnology and pharmaceutical sector with different tools, expert rankings, the Google search engine, and two artificial intelligence BOTs: ChatGPT 3.5 and Google Bard (now Gemini). The identification of the characteristics of the incubation services was carried out through a coding process. Therefore, this study contributes to filling a gap in the scientific literature. The practical implications of this study are both managerial and for policymakers, as it provides a benchmark of excellence for the creation of specialized incubators in the biotechnology and pharmaceutical sectors.

Embracing the AI Frontier: Perspectives on Business and Organizational Development. Mihir Joshiand and Mohsen Brahmi (Eds.)

DOI: 10.1201/9781779641311-3

3.1 INTRODUCTION

This study examines the services provided to startups by leading incubators operating in the biomedical and pharmaceutical sectors. Therefore, it provides best practices as a reference for incubating startups, especially those operating in these sectors.

The useful practical implications of this research are obvious. By highlighting "how" the world's leading incubators operating in the biotech and pharmaceutical sectors make services and infrastructure ("what") available to startups, this study provides best practices as a useful benchmark to create incubators that can aspire to excellence in the biotech and pharmaceutical sectors. Implications also arise for policymakers who can take on these models of incubation excellence to sustain the emergence of business incubators specializing in these sectors.

We selected the most relevant incubators operating in the biomedical and pharmaceutical sectors through both the Google search engine and generative artificial intelligence bots, ChatGPT 3.5 and Google Bard. By comparing the search results of these two bots with those provided by Google and with the rankings of the best incubators specializing in the biotech and pharmaceutical sectors compiled by experts, we also checked whether the search results provided by the artificial intelligence bots confirm, and to what extent, those provided by the Google search engine and the experts.

First, we selected the 10 "most relevant" incubators with the highest number of mentions in the first 10 positions of the search result returned by Google. Then, we selected 10 incubators present in at least three of those 10 rankings. Finally, to these, we added five others indicated as "the most relevant in these industries" by the Google search engine (4) and the two generative artificial intelligence bots consulted (1): ChatGPT 3.5 and Google Bard (now Gemini), if they had at least one citation in one of the 10 expert-provided rankings considered in this study. We placed this additional condition to "correct" any bias in the answers provided by the AI bots.

For each of the 15 selected incubators, based on the information on their websites, we analyzed the services they provide to startups: mentorship, consulting, networking, coworking spaces, operating locations, labs, cloud, equity participation, loans, donations, cash prizes, and other services.

3.2 LITERATURE REVIEW AND RESEARCH QUESTION

Biotech startups are not fundamentally different from other technology startups [1–4]. Typically, they are started by highly qualified researchers from universities or research institutes who have high expertise in specific technology areas. They start a business to commercialize their research results [5]. Many of these startups are university spin-offs, that is, "new, initially small, high technology or knowledge-intensive companies whose intellectual capital has its origin in a university or a public research institution" [6].

Although the scientific expertise of the founding team is critical to achieving success, like all businesses, biotech startups must also have adequate management skills. Founders of biotech startups often have a high level of expertise in their scientific field, but they often lack adequate skills in business management [5–7] and the personality traits typical of entrepreneurs (entrepreneurial intuition, risk tolerance, charisma, interpersonal skills, ability to build and lead teams, etc.). Developing skills through training, therefore, becomes critical to success [5]. To this end, incubators can play an important role for startups through mentors and coaches [8].

Adequate commercial expertise is a prerequisite for the survival and development of pharmaceutical startups as well. The latter are even more vulnerable than biotech startups, as the payback time of investments in this sector is very long and many drug and drug development projects fail [9].

Biotechnology and pharmaceutical startups also require expensive laboratory space and equipment, must comply with stringent regulations, and often find it difficult to obtain funding, given the reduction in public investment in scientific research and long payback times. Biotech incubators/accelerators play a crucial role in this regard because they can help reduce these difficulties [10].

Incubators also play the valuable function of connecting incubating startups with biotechnology and pharmaceutical industries and universities [7, 11]. Large, mature companies look with great interest at startups and, rather than risk investing substantial resources in research, invest in these young companies, which demonstrate that they can successfully introduce radical innovations. [12] carried out a systematic literature review on the value-adding services delivered to startups by technology-focused university business incubators (shared office space, business support, access to capital, business networks, and rent breaks). Previous literature has examined value-added services in technology incubators [13–17].

However, there is a lack of specific studies examining the services provided by incubators specializing in biotechnology and pharmaceuticals. The present study is part of this line of research to fill this gap in the literature.

To this end, it aims to answer the following research question: *What are the characteristics of the incubation services provided by the most relevant startup incubators specializing in the biotech and pharmaceutical sectors?*

3.3 TOP STARTUP INCUBATORS OPERATING IN THE BIOTECH AND PHARMACEUTICAL SECTORS

As we have already highlighted, there is a lack of research in the literature that focuses on the distinctive features of the services delivered to startups by the most successful startup incubators in the biotech and pharmaceutical sectors. This chapter aims to fill this gap by examining the services provided by the world's leading incubators specializing in these sectors. The type of services (what) and the way they are provided to startups (how) are undoubtedly best practices to be considered as a positive reference for other incubators aspiring to success.

To this end, it was necessary to identify leading startup incubators operating in the biomedical and pharmaceutical sectors. To this end, we performed a two-step process. First, we identified the top 10 global Google rankings with the question: Which are the best biotech and pharmaceutical incubators and accelerators? From these 10 rankings (*see* Table 3.1), in the second step, we selected 50 incubators. The most relevant in the world as they are present in at least one of these 10 rankings. Of the latter, we selected the 10 most relevant incubators because they were mentioned in at least three of the 10 rankings considered in this study (*see* Table 3.2).

To these 10 incubators (most relevant by number of mentions in the expert rankings), we added others derived from the responses obtained from the Google search engine and the generative AI BOTs Chat GTP 3.5 and Google Bard, to the following question: Which are the most relevant startup incubators in the biotech and pharmaceutical sectors?

To give robustness to the selection, we considered the following condition: to supplement the list, the indicated incubators had at least one citation in the rankings in Table 1. The following four indicated by the Google search engine were added to this list because they had at least one place in the 10 rankings selected: Y Combinator, UCSF Rosenman Institute, Pennsylvania Biotechnology Center, and Portland State University.

TABLE 3.1 Top 10 Startups' Incubators Rankings

Sl. No.	Rankings	Sector	Website
1.	GEN- genetic engineering e biotechnology news – Top 20 biotech accelerators and incubators	Biotech	www.genengnews.com
2.	Failory – Top 97 Biotech Accelerators and Incubators	Biotech	www.failory.com
3.	Incubator list - Top biotech Startup Accelerators, Incubators, and VCs (2023)	Biotech	www.incubatorlist.com
4.	Startupsavant – 16 Best Biotech Accelerators and Incubators for Startups	Biotech	www.startupsavant.com
5.	Kolabtree blog – Top 15 Biotech Incubators and Accelerators in the USA	Biotech	www.kolabtree.com/blog
6.	Excedr – 17 Incubators for US-Based Biotech Startups	Biotech	www.excedr.com/blog
7.	Labiotech – 25 Best Biotech Incubators Hatching Startup Stars in Europe	Biotech	www.labiotech.eu
8.	Kolabtree blog – Top 10 European biotech startup incubators	Biotech	www.kolabtree.com/blog
9.	Bubble – Top Pharma and Biotech Accelerators of 2023	Biotech and pharmaceutical	www.bubble.io/blog
10.	Failory – Top 17 Pharmaceutical Accelerators and Incubators	Pharmaceutical	www.failory.com

Source: Google search engine.

TABLE 3.2 The List of Top-Cited (In the Rankings) Biotech and Pharmaceutical Startups' Incubators Rankings

Sl. No.	Incubators/Accelerators	No. of Citations
1.	Johnson and Johnson Innovation: JLABS	5
2.	IndieBio	5
3.	Bio City	4
4.	MBC BioLabs	4
5.	StartX	4
6.	Alchemist	3
7.	Bayer Collaborator	3
8.	Sequoia Capital China Intelligent Healthcare Genomics Incubator by Illumina accelerator and Sequoia Capital China	3
9.	LabCentral	3
10.	Bakal labs by QB3	3

Source: Our Elaboration.

With the same criterion, that is, at least one quote in the rankings referred to in Table 1, another incubator has been added, MassChallenge Health-Tech, indicated by chat GTP 3.5 in the list of 10 incubators returned in response to the question: Which are the most relevant start-up incubators in the biotech and pharmaceutical sectors? Adopting the same criterion, no additional incubator has been added to the list, because seven of the eight incubators indicated by Google Bard were already on the list of the 10 most relevant by the number of citations in the rankings by experts, while the Calibs incubator was not selected because it had not reported any mention in the 10 rankings considered.

Finally, we collected and analyzed the information present on the websites of the 15 incubators selected using the above criteria.

This is the context of analysis of the present study: the case study [18] of the main incubators specialized in the biotech and pharmaceutical sectors.

3.4 METHODOLOGY

We carried out the empirical analysis by acquiring information from the websites of these incubators regarding the services ("what") they provide and the methods ("how") with which these services are provided to startups.

Based on the various empirical sources used, we identified the following nine categories as main aspects of the incubation process of the 15 incubators examined: (i) application and selection criteria; (ii) mentoring; (iii) infrastructure and equipment; (iv) training; (v) consultancy; (vi) networking; (vii) financing/capital contribution/other financial services; (viii) other incubation services; and (ix) post-incubation services.

We then aggregated the service categories into the following three macro-categories corresponding to as many phases of the startup incubation process: (i) pre-incubation: application and selection criteria; (ii) incubation: mentoring, training, consultancy, networking, financing/equity/other financial services, other incubation services; and (iii) post-incubation.

We coded the information collected from the websites by category and macro-category to accurately understand the peculiarities of the services provided to startups by the incubators examined. This coding procedure is divided into the following three sub-processes: information reduction, analysis, and interpretation [19]. It allows us to focus on the aspects that emerge most, and which appear relevant in the cases observed and to examine their properties. As argued by [20], the coding procedure allows us to examine the specificities of the data, not only in a descriptive sense but also in an analytical sense, since it allows comparisons between the properties of the different conceptual meanings and categories that they want to identify.

The empirical material thus codified was used to investigate which services the selected incubators provide to startups ("what") and "how" these services are delivered to the incubated enterprises.

3.5 DISCUSSION

Below, we present the analysis of the services provided to startups by the 15 incubators selected as most relevant in the biotech and pharmaceutical fields.

3.5.1 PRE-INCUBATION

Pre-incubation activities (coded as a macro category) precede the incubation process. These activities are:

1. "Scouting" of new ideas and startups, "application," and "selection."
2. Johnson and Johnson (JLABS) is always scouting for new ideas and startups. No information regarding this activity was found on the websites of the other 14 incubators examined.
3. The incubation process is preceded by an application and follows the selection. Johnson and Johnson also welcomes seeds, that is, companies not yet established, if they have a potentially high impact on innovation in the field of health.
4. The application is online. It is necessary to provide details of the business idea, the proposed product/service, the team, and the reference market, and other elements deemed useful for evaluating the startup that intends to apply to the incubation program.
5. Sequoia Capital China Healthcare Genomics Incubator of Illumina Accelerator and Sequoia Capital China, an incubator specialized in genomics, provides a selection mechanism based

on a competition in which founders present their startups. This incubator allows participation in the competition only for startups specializing in genomics.

6. Bakal Labs, founded by the QB3 research institute of the University of California Berkeley, affiliated with three campuses of the University of California in the San Francisco Bay Area: Berkeley, San Francisco, and Santa Cruz, welcomes only startups based in California or willing to move to California.
7. Some incubators publish on their website the selection criteria for startups applying to the program. Johnson and Johnson, for example, indicates the following criteria: financial strength, team quality, innovativeness, business model, compatibility with the areas of interest of the JLABS ecosystem, originality of the idea, impact on human life, identification of key resources and project feasibility, presence of data or research to support projects.
8. IndieBio particularly considers the business idea, market potential, technical feasibility, team, and potential impact of the project.
9. MBC Biolabs and Alchemist evaluate the potential of startups through an interview.
10. Bayer evaluates and selects startups through its own research and development sector and the personnel sector of Leaps, Bayer's venture capital partner fund.
11. During the selection process, LabCentral acquires useful information to choose the best destination for startups among its laboratories: "LabCentral 610," a laboratory with a strong scientific impact; "LabCentral 238," which supports companies from the research and development phase up to the production of preclinical and then biomedical materials; "Blavatnik Harvard Life Lab Longwood," which puts the founders in contact with structures affiliated with Harvard hospitals and institutions to identify the most suitable resources for the research and development of therapeutic discoveries.

3.5.2 INCUBATION

The companies or business ideas (seeds) that pass the selection begin the incubation process, in which they benefit from valuable services (mentoring, coaching, training, consultancy, networking, other services, etc.) and the use of infrastructures (laboratories, equipment, offices, coworking, and event space, etc.). Many of the incubators reviewed provide loans and other financial services to startups. Some contribute equity capital.

We now describe the salient characteristics of these services based on the information purchased from the institutional websites of the incubators examined.

3.5.2.1 INFRASTRUCTURE, EQUIPMENT, AND CAPITAL ASSETS

1. JLABS rents labs and instrumentation for molecular biology, chemistry, cell culture, data analytics, prototyping, and more, as well as office space for incubated startups.
2. IndieBio allows startups to use equipment and labs but charges for reagents and other consumables.
3. MBC BioLabs charges a fee for the use of laboratory benches and provides consumables free of charge. Startups do not make long-term commitments and are not required to incur fixed costs. They rent only what they need (offices, conference rooms, common spaces, basic equipment, cold rooms).
4. BioCity provides startups with the use of laboratories, coworking spaces, and offices, for a total value of 185,000 euros, as well as cutting-edge technologies such as mass spectrometry, nanobio-engineering, and nanoelectronic beams. In collaboration with the Fraunhofer Institute for Cell Therapy and Immunology, it provides startups with the so-called GMPs, that is, the clean rooms necessary for laboratory experiments.
5. Some incubators, such as StartX and Alchemist, grant discounts and credits that entitle incubated startups to use resources provided by partners for free or at advantageous prices.
6. To reduce capital expenditure, Bayer leases startups with complete labs and state-of-the-art offices with shared equipment. There is a unique Bayer Co. Lab in Cambridge, designed specifically to support cell and gene therapy startups.
7. Sequoia Capital China Intelligent Healthcare Genomics Incubator provides startups with laboratories in Shanghai specialized in genomics and DNA sequencing systems.

8. LabCentral has a network of well-equipped laboratories and offices to accommodate up to 125 start-ups and approximately 1,000 scientist-entrepreneurs, with 54 individual laboratory benches, 11 "pods" for 3–4 scientists in a shared laboratory, 15 suites of private laboratories, conference rooms, and event spaces.
9. Incubators at the Pennsylvania Biotechnology Center and Portland State University provide startups with turnkey access to private and co-working office spaces, wet labs, and prototyping facilities.
10. MassChallenge HealthTech provides free workspace to startups incubated in offices in Austin, Boston, Houston, Dallas, and Providence.

3.5.2.2 MENTORING

1. JLABS, BioCity, and StartX assign a mentor to each startup to assist with product development, marketing, and supply chain optimization.
2. Alchemist believes in mentoring customized to startups' needs and offers startups the opportunity to choose from more than 3,000 teachers and mentors. The Pennsylvania Biotechnology Center also offers startups the ability to choose from a broad network of mentors.
3. IndieBio provides startups with five mentors who are experts in the specific sector in which each of them operates, who assist them whenever they need it, even daily. Their philosophy is based on the continuous interaction between startups and experts, considered fundamental for their evolution as a successful startup.
4. Bakal Labs by QB3 mentors mainly deals with the following topics: drafting the business plan, adapting the technology to the market, managing intellectual property, free consultations with legal affiliates up to the first round of financing, team building, and fundraising strategy. The program pairs startup founders with experienced executives. The mentorship service lasts a maximum of six months. The mentor receives shares in exchange for their work, according to the following scheme: pre-startup, none; if newly established, 1% will accrue in months 4–6 of the program; if seed funded, it would receive 0.5%; if series A financing, 0.25%.

5. At Y Combinator, mentors are experts who have built successful businesses in the startup industry they mentor. They provide business advice on areas such as innovation, business models, fundraising, and industry trends. Experience is also a hallmark of UCSF Rosenman Institute mentors.
6. MassChallenge HealthTech mentors work with startups through personalized consultations, both in-person and online. One-on-one mentorship is also provided.

3.5.2.3 TRAINING

All the incubators examined consider the training of startuppers strategic and dedicate a lot of time and resources to this activity. They organize workshops, seminars, and webinars. In addition to training in business management, financing, and team building, they train startuppers in healthcare, laboratory use, and hazardous waste management compliance.

3.5.2.4 ADVICE

JLABS experts provide strategic guidance to incubated startups, who have access to internal experts operating in Johnson and Johnson group companies.

1. MBC BioLabs advises startups on EH&S protocol compliance, business strategy, data, and market analysis. Their team of consultants can help with chemical handling, safety training, medical waste disposal, shipping, and so forth.
2. Alchemist makes experts available to its startups for targeted consultancy on specific topics.
3. Bayer experts provide ongoing advice on key issues, such as manufacturing and early access to leadership and technology.
4. Sequoia Capital China Intelligent Healthcare Genomics Incubator (by Illumina accelerator and Sequoia Capital China) offers startups the "Illumina for Startups Grant" program under which it provides business consultancy and coaching on go-to-market and financing strategy, team building, and corporate consultancy.

5. In addition to administrative consultancy, LabCentral supports incubated startups with services for laboratory operations and the processing of laboratory and healthcare waste.
6. QB3's Bakal Labs offers startups various consultancy services, including through partners. In addition to the scientific advice of over 20 professors and experts from UC Berkeley, UCSF, and UC Santa Cruz, thanks to the collaboration with Startup Legal Garage it offers startups free legal services worth between $15,000 and $30,000. They can also benefit from corporate business transactions and technology advice, privacy, and data protection compliance, regulatory affairs, and litigation. Finally, banking partners provide advice on financing and investments.
7. The Pennsylvania Biotechnology Center also offers its startups the opportunity to benefit from business consulting and scientific services. Specifically, consultancy services concern legal, banking, life sciences, and clinical studies aspects.
8. The UCSF Rosenman Institute offers free legal consulting services to its startups.

3.5.2.5 NETWORKING

All incubators take care of startup networking such as:

1. JLABS promotes networking events to connect incubated startups with experts and research institutes and encourages the creation of commercial partnerships with investors through its Investor Hub.
2. BioCity promotes collaboration with professors from six departments of the University of Leipzig and with non-university institutes aimed at research and development.
3. To accelerate the building of innovation pipelines by startups, MBC BioLabs encourages the building of relationships, alliances, and collaboration opportunities between startups and pharmaceutical companies, research centers, and equipment manufacturers.
4. StartX networks startups with entrepreneurs, venture capitalists, and professors from Stanford's Med School.
5. Bayer highlights on its website the key role in networking played by the strategic location of the headquarters near the world's most important academic centers in the field of healthcare, university

hospitals, and testing centers, as well as the networking events organized with entrepreneurs, global investors, and local and scientific communities.

6. Sequoia Capital China Intelligent Healthcare Genomics Incubator implements a specific networking program between startups and financiers called "Illumina for Startups Network."
7. MassChallenge HealthTech helps incubate startup networks by connecting them to a global expert community of nearly 3,000 successful entrepreneurs, industry-leading experts, and other professionals.
8. The UCSF Rosenman Institute connects entrepreneurs and investors at the Rosenman Symposium.

3.5.2.6 FINANCING, EQUITY CONTRIBUTION, FUNDRAISING SUPPORT, AND OTHER FINANCIAL SERVICES

The guiding idea of JLABS is that each startup has specific financing and investment needs. For this reason, they customize each financing and investment operation to everyone's needs. IndieBio invests in startup capital a package of $275,000 for an 11.2% equity position after debt. $200,000 is in cash and $75.00 is in kind. This investment is regulated by an ACE (Accelerator Contract for Equity). They also offer an additional $250,000 from Genesis Consortium during the program, which startups may not accept. With the program "Smile," BioCity helps startups to raise funding and equity. MBCBiolabs does not participate in the venture capital of startups but promotes the collection of equity investments by investors. Enter the acceleration program, start-ups give Alchemist Accelerator a percentage of their shares, which is around 5% and cannot exceed 9.99%. Alchemist supports them in fundraising by connecting them with over 5,500 venture investors in its network. Sequoia Capital China Intelligent Healthcare Genomics Incubator with the "Illumina for Startups Grant" program provides a 6-month scholarship to founders of startups entering the incubation program. The "China Genomics Incubator" program, specializing in genomics, supports the acquisition of funding by Sequoia Capital China. LabCentral only supports start-ups in raising equity. Silicon Valley Bank provides QB3 Startup companies with current accounts without having to deposit money and without commissions. Startuppers have access to the Y Combinator database which contains profiles and reviews for over 50,000 investors. Y Combinator offers up to $500k in exchange for 7% Equity. The UCSF Rosenman Institute supports startups in accessing funding and investors, through the MedTech Venture Partners venture fund. The Pennsylvania Biotechnology Center provides investment opportunities to startups, including Ben Franklin Technologies (VC), BioAdvance, Delaware Crossing, and JP Morgan. Organize events to promote the collection of investments by startups.

3.5.2.7 OTHER STARTUP SERVICES WITH DISCOUNTS, CREDITS, AND SO FORTH

Biocity provides incubated startups with an online platform for collaboration and knowledge sharing. Alchemist Weekly Gathering and Alchemist's Feedback Summits are two programs through which startups compare, share milestones achieved, and compare topics they consider relevant. Alchemist also gives credits and discounts on numerous services provided by partners, including cloud computing, legal consulting, marketing, and other services, for a total value of about $450,000. Bayer provides a hazardous waste disposal service for startups. Lab Central takes care of the maintenance of the startup equipment and takes care of the cleaning and waste disposal services. It also provides startuppers with access to the kitchen. Bakal Lab by Q3 through the fully funded QWEST program is dedicated to developing the startup workforce. In the summer months, The Bakal lab selects Berkeley UC undergraduate students for training and work experience in incubation startups. The six-month internship is entirely funded by QB3. There is also the opportunity to select students from the graduate internship program. In Y Combinator, every incubated startup gets free credits or significant discounts on hosting, banking, back-office services, and so forth. Leading software companies offer YC startups over 1000 deals worth over $500,000. The Pennsylvania Biotechnology Center also has several strategic sponsors that provide startups with quality services at discounted prices.

3.6 LIMITATIONS AND FUTURE RESEARCH PROSPECTS

This study has the limitation of considering too limited a sample of incubators, only 15, and of not having taken into consideration successful incubators operating in nations other than the United

States and Europe, such as those in South-East Asia, Australia, South America, and so forth. Another limitation is that biotech startups are overrepresented compared to pharmaceutical ones. Future research may achieve better results by expanding the sample geographically. In this way, incubation services not examined by this study, but important for the success of startups specialized in the sectors of interest in this study, could be identified.

3.7 CONCLUSION

This study contributes to the literature on the incubation of startups, particularly those operating in the biotech and pharmaceutical industries. It also has significant practical implications. Since it highlights the services and infrastructures offered by the main incubators operating in the biotech and pharmaceutical sectors (what) and how they are made available to startups (how), the analysis carried out constitutes a useful reference for incubators operating in these sectors.

To carry out the analysis, we selected the most relevant startup incubators in the biotech and pharmaceutical sectors by consulting the top 10 rankings drawn up by experts returned by the Google search engine to the question: "What are the main biotech and pharmaceutical incubators and accelerators in the world?" We have thus selected 10 incubators with the highest number of citations in the rankings (at least 3). Then we "checked" and at the same time "expanded" this list by asking the same question to the AI ChatGPT 3.5 and Google Bard (now Gemini) bots. In this way, another five incubators were added, with at least one mention in the 10 rankings drawn up by the experts. Therefore, the overall list used for this study consists of 15 startup incubators, which can be considered the most important in the biotech and pharmaceutical sectors.

The generative artificial intelligence bots consulted therefore contributed significantly to the selection of the sample. Based on the specified criteria, ChatGPT 3.5 allowed four incubators to be added to the list of the 10 incubators with the most citations in the rankings drawn up by experts, while Google Bard essentially confirmed the list of the 10 incubators with the most citations in the rankings drawn up by experts, given that it allowed only one incubator with at least one mention in the aforementioned rankings to be added to the list.

After selecting the sample, we consulted the websites of these 15 incubators to collect and codify information on the services they offer to startups, namely: use of infrastructures (plants, machinery, equipment), both offices and laboratories, mentoring, consultancy, networking, training, financial services and equity capital provision, other services.

The use of laboratory infrastructure is a fundamental service in the incubation of startups operating in the biotech and pharmaceutical sectors. All the incubators examined provide startups with the use of cutting-edge laboratories and the consumables necessary for research and experimentation. In some cases, these laboratories are shared, to reduce the costs borne by the startups.

Additionally, incubators/accelerators provide training for users working inside in laboratory operations, maintenance, technical support, housekeeping, and hazardous waste management and disposal such as:

1. The offices are made available fully furnished. They can be for shared use, to reduce costs.
2. Startups can also take advantage of meeting rooms, conference rooms, and community spaces.
3. All incubators provide mentorship. Startups can be followed by mentors who assist groups of companies or have a dedicated mentor.
4. The consultancy is provided by teams of experts or individual consultants, on a periodic basis or at the request of the startups and concerns multiple issues: corporate (access to credit and the capital market, marketing, etc.), legal, scientific (related to the development, testing, and distribution of products).
5. The incubators examined carry out many activities to encourage the networking of startups with investors, entrepreneurs, and the scientific community.
6. The training includes participation in seminars, webinars, and workshops, organized to help improve the startup's product and business idea. It can also be delivered via e-learning platforms.
7. Incubators/accelerators also offer other types of services, making discounts and credits available to startups for the acquisition of internet services, cloud space, and software.
8. Regarding accommodation or canteen services, little information is available on the websites of the incubators examined.

ACKNOWLEDGMENT

This research was supported by Project CAL.HUB.RIA funded by the Ministry of Health, Project CUP: F63C22000530001. Local Project CUP: C33C22000540001.

KEYWORDS

- **artificial intelligence**
- **biotechnology**
- **google bard**
- **pharmaceutical startups**
- **policy makers**
- **startup incubation**
- **startup incubation services**

REFERENCES

1. Huayamares, S. G., Lokugamage, M. P., Sanchez, A. J. D. S., & Dahlman, J. E. (2022). A systematic analysis of biotech startups that went public in the first half of 2021. *Current Research in Biotechnology, 4*, 392–401.
2. Rathmann, G. B. (2020). Biotechnology startups. In *Biotechnology—The Science and the Business* (pp. 47–58). CRC Press.
3. Lebret, H. (2018). *Are Biotechnology Startups Different?* arXiv:1805.12108.
4. Galvagno, M., & Pisano, V. (2012). Le caratteristiche dell'impresa biotech dotata di capacità dinamiche (The characteristics of a biotech firm with dynamic capabilities). In *Capacità Dinamica E Imprese Biotech. Strategie e Assetti Competitivi* (pp. 1–41). Giappichelli.
5. Gurdon, M. A., & Samsom, K. J. (2010). A longitudinal study of success and failure among scientist-started ventures. *Technovation, 30*(3), 207–214.
6. Yagüe-Perales, R. M., & March-Chordà, I. (2012). Performance analysis of research spin-offs in the Spanish biotechnology industry. *Journal of Business Research, 65*(12), 1782–1789.
7. Niosi, J. (2003). Alliances are not enough: Explaining rapid growth in biotechnology firms. *Research Policy, 32*, 737–750.
8. Nätterlund, L., & Sigerud Lärkert, J. (2014). Business incubation success in biotechnology: How should bio-incubator performance be assessed? https://www.

diva-portal.org/smash/record.jsf?dswid=581&pid=diva2%3A732054 (accessed on 29 August 2025).
9. Rasmussen, B. (2007). Response of pharmaceutical companies to biotechnology: Structure and business models. https://vuir.vu.edu.au/15946/ (accessed on 29 August 2025).
10. Grifantini, K. (2015). Incubating innovation: A standard model for nurturing new businesses, the incubator gains prominence in the world of biotech. *IEEE Pulse, 6*(6), 27–31.
11. George, G., Zahra, S. A., & Wood, D. R. (2002). The effects of business–university alliances on innovative output and financial performance: A study of publicly traded biotechnology companies. *Journal of Business Venturing, 17*(6), 577–609.
12. Mian, S. A. (1996). Assessing value-added contributions of university technology business incubators to tenant firms. *Research Policy, 25*(3), 325–335.
13. Allen, D. N., & Rahman, S. (1985). Small business incubators: A positive environment for entrepreneurship. *Journal of Small Business Management, 23*, 12–24.
14. Hisrich, R. D., & Smilor, R. W. (1988). The university and business incubation: Technology transfer through entrepreneurial development. *Technology Transfer*, Fall, 14–19.
15. Allen, D. N., & Bazan, E. J. (1990). Value-added contribution of Pennsylvania's business incubators to tenant firms and local economies. Report prepared for Pennsylvania Department of Commerce. Pennsylvania State University, University Park, PA.
16. Lichtenstein, G. A. (1992). The significance of relationships in entrepreneurial development: A case study of the ecology of enterprise in two business incubators (Unpublished doctoral dissertation). University of Pennsylvania, PA.
17. Bergek, A., & Norrman, C. (2008). Incubator best practice: A framework. *Technovation, 28*, 20–28.
18. Yin, R. K. (2017). *Case Study Research and Applications: Design and Methods*. Sage Publications.
19. O'Dwyer, B. (2004). Qualitative data analysis: Illuminating a process for transforming a 'messy' but 'attractive' 'nuisance.' In *The Real-Life Guide to Accounting Research* (pp. 391–407). Elsevier.
20. Strauss, A., & Corbin, J. (1998). *Basics of Qualitative Research: Techniques and Procedures for Developing Grounded Theory*. Sage Publications, Inc.

SITOGRAPHY

1. GEN–Genetic Engineering & Biotechnology News. (n.d.). Top 20 biotech accelerators and incubators. https://www.genengnews.com (accessed on 29 August 2025).
2. Failory. (n.d.). Top 97 biotech accelerators and incubators. https://www.failory.com (accessed on 29 August 2025).
3. Incubator List. (2023). Top biotech startup accelerators, incubators, and VCs [2023]. https://www.incubatorlist.com (accessed on 29 August 2025).

4. StartupSavant. (n.d.). 16 best biotech accelerators and incubators for startups. https://www.startupsavant.com (accessed on 29 August 2025).
5. Kolabtree Blog. (n.d.). Top 15 biotech incubators and accelerators in the USA. https://www.kolabtree.com/blog (accessed on 29 August 2025).
6. Excedr. (n.d.). 17 incubators for US-based biotech startups. https://www.excedr.com/blog (accessed on 29 August 2025).
7. Labiotech. (n.d.). 25 best biotech incubators hatching startup stars in Europe. https://www.labiotech.eu (accessed on 29 August 2025).
8. Kolabtree Blog. (n.d.). Top ten European biotech startup incubators. https://www.kolabtree.com/blog (accessed on 29 August 2025).
9. Bubble. (2023). Top pharma & biotech accelerators of 2023. https://www.bubble.io/blog (accessed on 29 August 2025).
10. Failory. (n.d.). Top 17 pharmaceutical accelerators and incubators. https://www.failory.com (accessed on 29 August 2025).

CHAPTER 4

Bibliometric Analysis on AI and Sustainable Business Practices: Mapping the Research Landscapes

VANDANA[1] and PRACHI MATOLIA[2,*]

[1]*FMS-WISDOM, Banasthali Vidyapith, Rajasthan, India*

[2]*Banasthali Vidyapith, Rajasthan, India*

*Corresponding author

ABSTRACT

This research endeavor seeks to provide an extensive and enduring bibliometric analysis of Sustainable Business Practices within the context of their integration with Artificial Intelligence (AI). Sustainable Business Practices refer to the strategic and operational activities adopted by organizations to minimize their environmental impact, promote social responsibility, and ensure long-term economic viability. In parallel, Artificial Intelligence represents a cutting-edge technological domain that comprises the development and application of algorithms and computational systems capable of simulating human-like intelligence, learning, and problem-solving. This investigation aims to elucidate the cumulative scholarly contributions to the intersection of Sustainable Business Practices and AI, thereby offering valuable insights into the evolving landscape of sustainable and technologically advanced business strategies. A total of 703 scholarly articles were extracted from the Scopus database, utilizing a set of carefully chosen keywords. Our search was further refined by limiting the scope to the subject areas of "Business," "Management," and "Accounting." The VOSviewer software was employed to perform a comprehensive analysis of the dataset, facilitating the visualization and exploration of the

Embracing the AI Frontier: Perspectives on Business and Organizational Development. Mihir Joshiand and Mohsen Brahmi (Eds.)

DOI: 10.1201/9781779641311-4

research landscape. This bibliometric analysis offers scholars, decision-makers, and practitioners a thorough understanding of the developing fields of artificial intelligence and sustainable business practices.

4.1 INTRODUCTION

Artificial intelligence (AI) can help humans tackle environmental issues by providing unbiased and comprehensive solutions with sufficient information. It can help avoid oversimplified explanations and personal biases that might hinder effective decision-making. Studies show that AI can contribute to ecological, social, and economic sustainability by offering holistic solutions and important information. Therefore, AI has the potential to advance sustainability initiatives and aid in the creation of long-term solutions [1].

As per a report by McKinsey and Company, the integration of artificial intelligence in business operations has increased twofold since 2017. The reason behind this growth is that AI technology can be tailored to the specific requirements of an organization. McKinsey's survey also found that 63% of respondents anticipate higher investment in AI technologies over the next three years [2]. According to IDC's 2019 projections, this investment will reach 77.6 billion dollars in 2022.

AI has the potential to impact the production and consumption patterns in businesses, which can lead to the development of sustainable business models (SBMs) that align with the Sustainable Development Goals (SDGs) outlined in the UN 2030 Agenda. By integrating AI into business practices, companies can establish a link between innovation and sustainability, thereby contributing towards the achievement of the SDGs [4].

Big data analytics-powered artificial intelligence (BDA-AI) has the potential to improve supply chain performance and promote sustainable manufacturing practices, which can lead to the development of circular economy capabilities. Many manufacturing firms adopt BDA-AI to address the need for high-quality decision-making in a dynamic business environment [5].

4.1.1 BUSINESS DEVELOPMENT THROUGH ARTIFICIAL INTELLIGENCE

AI has the potential to revolutionize marketing by providing faster, more accurate, and cost-effective ways to reach audiences. By utilizing self-learning systems like data mining and natural language processing, AI can identify trends, enhance customer service, and analyze large amounts of data for compliance violations. This can give businesses a competitive edge and increase response rates from their target audience [6]. AI refers to a range of technologies including machine learning, automation, predictive analytics, and facial recognition that can help businesses optimize their operations and increase profitability by reducing costs. Whether you're a large corporation or a small to mid-size business, AI can benefit you by increasing automation, reducing errors, and predicting consumer behavior [7].

Burnout and occupational stressors critically undermine work engagement, as evidenced in law enforcement contexts. Within business practices, AI offers a strategic mechanism to alleviate these challenges through workload optimization, predictive analytics, and personalized interventions, thereby fostering sustainable employee engagement, enhancing organizational performance, and supporting resilient workforce development [8]. For e-commerce and AI-enabled platforms, integrating emotional intelligence insights can help predict consumer decisions more accurately. Businesses must adopt holistic consumer behavior models that integrate emotional and cognitive dimensions, which AI can help analyze at scale [9]. Leveraging AI in inter-organizational collaborations improves efficiency, coordination, and adaptability in both domestic and international markets. IONs are essential in fostering relationships and collaborations between organizations, particularly in cross-cultural associations. In AI-driven business practices, IONs can be enhanced through data-driven insights and predictive analytics to reduce risks in alliances [10]. Enablers are being augmented through AI technologies—where awareness is scaled via digital platforms, feasibility is strengthened by data-driven insights, desirability grows through AI-enabled innovation, and planned behavior is supported by intelligent systems [11]. AI is transforming business practices by automating processes, enhancing decision-making, and reshaping workforce demands. It streamlines recruitment, boosts efficiency, and fosters innovation while reducing costs. Though routine jobs face automation risks, AI creates new opportunities requiring adaptability, creativity, and emotional intelligence, making human–machine collaboration vital for sustainable competitiveness [12]. AI enables novel business models like energy-as-a-service, dynamic pricing, and grid flexibility services, which support both the financial viability of clean technologies and their diffusion into broader markets [13].

4.1.2 ARTIFICIAL INTELLIGENCE FOR SUSTAINABLE BUSINESS PRACTICES

AI is a significant technology that supports business processes by providing a deeper understanding of the market, consumers, and competitors, and forecasting forthcoming changes [14]. AI can have a substantial influence on sustainable business practices by enhancing efficiency and promoting innovation. It is essential to provide funding to AI firms to boost their innovation performance. Additionally, social investment and institutional intermediaries can play a critical role in influencing policy decisions and increasing the chances of receiving public funding [15].

4.2 METHODOLOGY

The present study employs a rigorous bibliometric analysis methodology to investigate the literature on the use of artificial intelligence in sustainable business practices. The study covers the period of 2013–2023 and includes 703 articles selected from the Scopus database. The articles were carefully filtered to ensure the accuracy and relevance of the derived conclusions. Scopus is widely recognized as a preferred source index by the academic community due to its ability to facilitate streamlined keyword searches across titles, citations, abstracts, and publication keywords within its extensive database.

Bibliometric analysis is a trustworthy method for conducting empirical research and gathering existing literature from various disciplines. The term "bibliometrics" was first used by Pritchard in 1969 to refer to the comprehensive examination of books, written materials, articles, and media communication using statistical and mathematical techniques. Broadus gave a concise definition in 1987, describing bibliometrics as "the quantitative study of physical published units or their surrogates" [16]. This approach is highly beneficial for systematically evaluating the scholarly landscape and identifying patterns within published works.

4.3 BIBLIOMETRIC ANALYSIS

The procedure followed in this study was standard comprehensive Bibliometric analysis, which starts from keyword search in the Scopus search syntax as shown in Figure 4.1. The keywords indicate that articles and publications containing "Artificial Intelligence" OR "Machine Learning" OR "Deep Learning" OR "Cognitive Computing" OR "Automation" AND "Sustainable Business Practices" OR "Business" OR "Sustainable Business Models" OR "Sustainable Business" in their titles, keywords, or abstracts. The search was run, and the total number of articles obtained between 2013 and 2023 and before any type of filtration was 41,057. Any redundant information was then removed from the output. Thereafter, using filters between 2013 and 2023, the total number of articles was brought to 703.

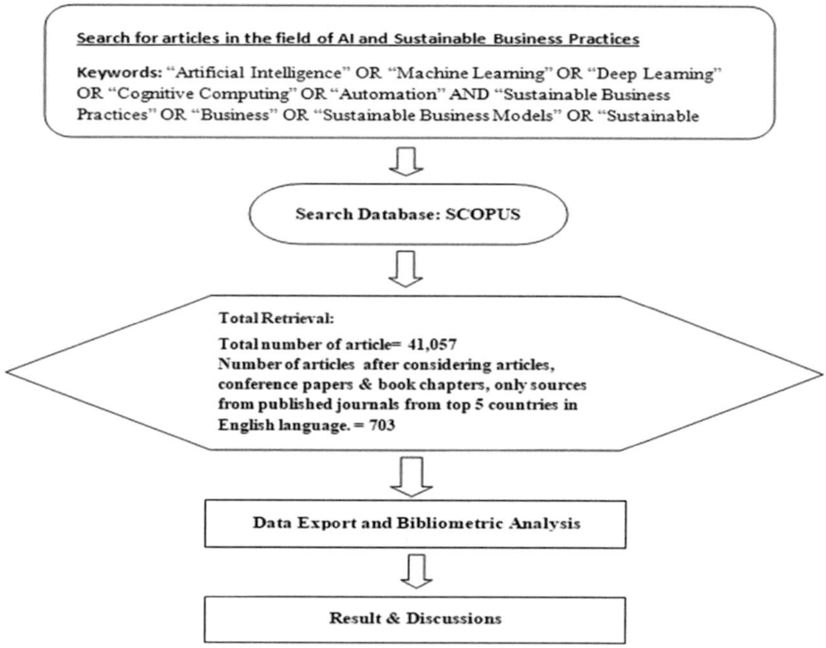

FIGURE 4.1 Bibliometric procedure.

4.4 RESULTS

4.4.1 PUBLICATION GROWTH RATE

Figure 4.2 shows the annual frequency distribution of publications that indicate a significant growth trend in the field of Artificial Intelligence and Sustainable Business Practices from the years 2013–2023, with an average growth rate of 69.76%. Notably, the year 2023 has the highest number of publications, with 153 publications that account for 21.76% of the total records. The year 2022 also made a substantial contribution with 149 publications, which constitutes 21.19% of the dataset, while 2021 maintained a noteworthy presence with 120 publications, making up 17.06% of the total publications during the given period. This trend shows the increasing scholarly interest and research activity in the intersection of Artificial Intelligence and Sustainable Business Practices over the specified temporal domain.

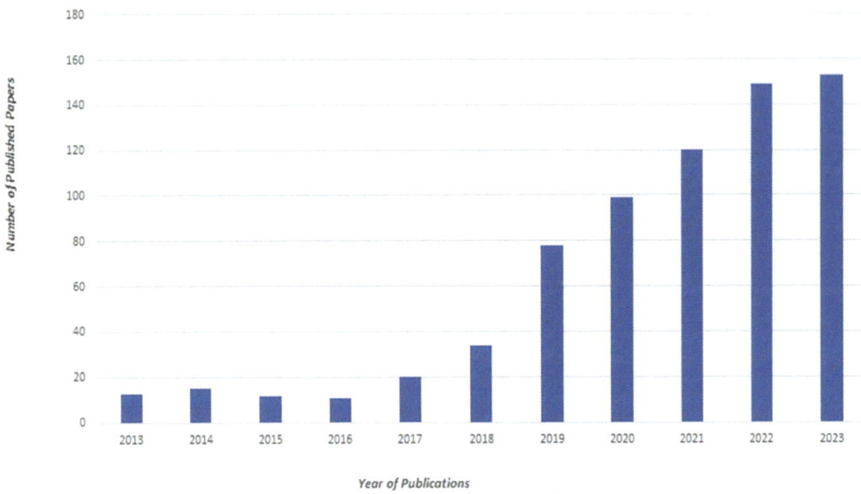

FIGURE 4.2 Publication count by years.

4.4.2 PUBLICATIONS BY COUNTRY

Table 4.1 presents a comprehensive overview of the incorporated literary works categorized based on their distribution across different countries. Notably, the United States emerged as the primary contributor, constituting approximately 38.12% of the total literary works (268 out of 703). Subsequently, India held the second position, contributing 21.9% (154 out of 703), closely followed by the United Kingdom at 21.1% (149 out of 703). Additionally, China and Germany were also notable contributors, albeit to a lesser extent, in the context of the examined literary corpus.

TABLE 4.1 Publication Distribution by Top Five Countries

Publications by Country		
Ranks	**Countries**	**Number of Published Papers**
I	United States	268
II	India	154
III	United Kingdom	149
IV	China	119
V	Germany	115

4.4.3 SOURCE OF PUBLICATIONS

Table 4.2 delineates the preeminent journals at the forefront of disseminating scholarly contributions in the intersection of Artificial Intelligence and Sustainable Business Practices. The data, extracted from the comprehensive "Document Support System," underscores its prominence as the leading source, accounting for a notable 4.4% (31 out of 703) of the total publications. Subsequently, the "Journal of Business Research" emerges as a significant contributor, constituting 3.5% (25 out of 703) of the corpus. Additionally, "Technological Forecasting Social Change" assumes a noteworthy position, with 3.2% (23 out of 703) of the total articles and conference papers in this domain. These findings offer valuable insights into the distribution of scholarly output across prominent journals in the field, shedding light on the key platforms shaping the discourse on the amalgamation of artificial intelligence and sustainable business practices.

TABLE 4.2 Publications Distribution by Top Five Journals

Source of Publications	
Source	**Number of Published Papers**
Decision Support Systems	31
Journal of Business Research	25
Technological Forecasting and Social Change	23
International Journal of Information Management	15
Journal of Cleaner Production	15

4.4.4 DOCUMENT CITATIONS

Table 4.3 presents a comprehensive compilation of the 10 most cited documents within the realm of Artificial Intelligence in Sustainable Business Practices, showcasing pertinent details such as authors, sources, and corresponding citation counts. The dataset utilized for this analysis was extracted from a CSV file obtained from the Scopus database. Notably, three of the top 10 cited articles originated from the "International Journal of Information Management." Noteworthy is the article titled "A survey on opinion mining and sentiment analysis: Tasks, approaches, and applications," which commands a substantial total citation score of 929. Following closely is the publication titled "AI Multidisciplinary perspectives on emerging challenges, opportunities, and agenda for research, practice, and policy," accruing a total of 789 citations. These findings underscore the prominence of specific journals and highlight key contributions that have significantly impacted the field of Artificial Intelligence in the context of sustainable business practices.

TABLE 4.3 Top 10 Highly Cited Articles

Title	Authors	Year	Source Title	Cited by
A survey on opinion mining and sentiment analysis: Tasks, approaches, and applications	Ravi K.; Ravi V.	2015	Knowledge-Based Systems	929
Artificial Intelligence (AI): Multidisciplinary perspectives on emerging challenges, opportunities, and agenda for research, practice, and policy	Dwivedi Y.K.; Hughes L., et al.	2021	International Journal of Information Management	789
Building dynamic capabilities for digital transformation: An ongoing process of strategic renewal	Warner K.S.R.; Wäger M.	2019	Long Range Planning	786
DeepAR: Probabilistic forecasting with autoregressive recurrent networks	Salinas D.; Flunkert V.; Gasthaus J.; Januschowski T.	2020	International Journal of Forecasting	644
Setting the future of digital and social media marketing research: Perspectives and research propositions	Dwivedi Y.K.; Ismagilova E.; Hughes D.L.;et.al.	2021	International Journal of Information Management	543
Impact of COVID-19 pandemic on information management research and practice: Transforming education, work, and life	Dwivedi Y.K.; Hughes D.L.; et.al.	2020	International Journal of Information Management	514
Machine learning and deep learning	Janiesch C.; Zschech P.; Heinrich K.	2021	Electronic Markets	497
Predicting the performance of online consumer reviews: A sentiment mining approach to big data analytics	Salehan M.; Kim D.J.	2016	Decision Support Systems	429
Frontiers: Machines vs. humans: The impact of artificial intelligence chatbot disclosure on customer purchases	Luo X.; Tong S.; Fang Z.; Qu Z.	2019	Marketing Science	363
Developing and validating a service robot integration willingness scale	Lu L.; Cai R.; Gursoy D.	2019	International Journal of Hospitality Management	323

4.4.5 SUBJECT AREAS PUBLICATIONS

In accordance with the Scopus subject categories, the research domains of the articles under investigation were delineated, as outlined in Table 4.4. Notably, the examination revealed that the preeminent scholarly contributions pertaining to the subject of Artificial Intelligence in Sustainable Business Practices emanated predominantly from the field of Business, Management, and Accounting, for a substantial proportion of 703 articles, constituting 41.1% of the entire corpus. This specific category was deliberately chosen to serve as the focal point for the ensuing bibliometric analysis, thereby affording a comprehensive understanding of the scholarly landscape surrounding the intersection of Artificial Intelligence and Sustainable Business Practices.

TABLE 4.4 Publications Distribution by Top Five Research Domains

Subject Area Publications		
Rank	**Subject**	**Percentage**
I	Business, Management, and Accounting	41.1%
II	Decision Sciences	12.2%
III	Computer Science	11.8%
IV	Engineering	9.2%
V	Social Sciences	8.4%

4.4.5 VISUALIZATION OF AUTHOR'S KEYWORDS

In Figure 4.3, the co-occurrence patterns of authors' keywords are elucidated by employing the full count method, wherein each instance of a keyword within the document is systematically tallied. The analysis encompassed 2298 keywords, with the network visualization selectively highlighting keywords that manifested at least five occurrences. This filtering yielded a discernible arrangement of 71 keywords, organized into eight distinct clusters as visually represented in the network diagram. The diagram is comprised of variably colored and sized circular fields, interconnected at varying distances. The color scheme denotes membership within specific groups or clusters, facilitating the identification of topics characterized by high interconnectivity. Furthermore, the size of each circle is indicative of the respective keyword's frequency of use within the document, with larger circles denoting more prevalent keyword usage. This comprehensive visualization provides insights into the thematic clustering and prominence of keywords, enhancing our understanding of the document's subject matter.

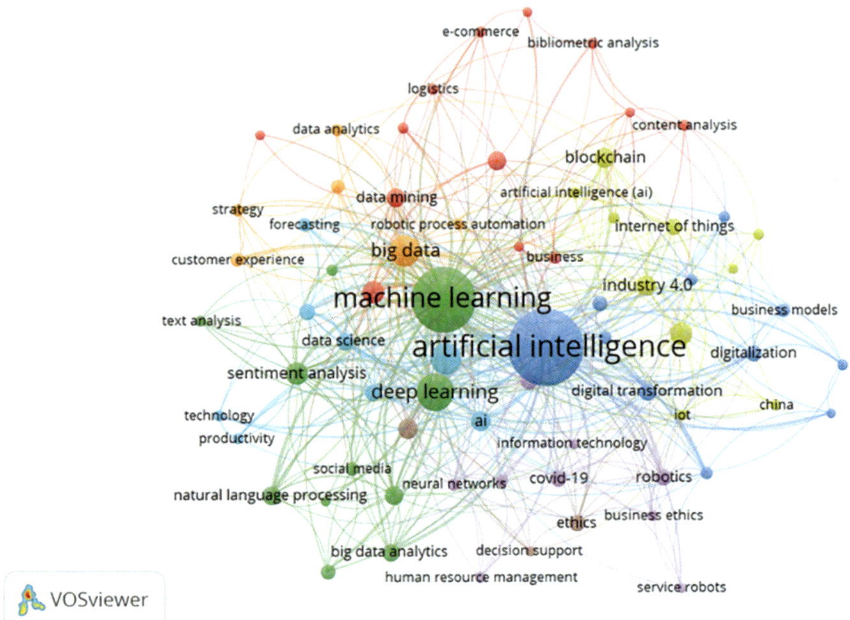

FIGURE 4.3 Co-occurrence of authors' keywords.

Source: Generated from VOSviewer.

As delineated in the schematic representation titled "Artificial Intelligence," the paradigms of "Machine Learning" and "Deep Learning" emerge as predominant methodologies within the domain of Artificial Intelligence, often employing key terms as integral components. The synergistic intersection of "Business" and "Business Analytics" is showcased to underscore the pivotal role played by Artificial Intelligence in fostering Sustainable Business Practices. Broadly, salient descriptors such as "Robotic Process Automation," "Automation," "Business Ethics," "Big Data," "Industry 4.0," and "Data Mining" encapsulate some of the most widely acknowledged and frequently referenced keywords within the discourse of Artificial Intelligence research. These terms collectively contribute to the foundational lexicon shaping discussions and advancements in the field.

4.5 DISCUSSION

The current study considered bibliometric data to analyze published works in Artificial Intelligence in Sustainable Business Practices. The findings are discussed further. Out of 703 documents retrieved, 700 of them are journal articles and three of them are conference papers that were published during 2003–2023. Papers produced in and after 2017 constitute 92.88% of included studies. The top five countries with the maximum number of publications were included in the study. The subject area "Business Management and Accounting" was considered. The papers that are fully published in only English language were customized.

The integration of AI-powered software in marketing can enhance conversion rates, customer comprehension, marketing decision-making, data analysis, and overall efficiency. AI empowers businesses to provide better services, maximize customer satisfaction, and increase return on investment. Organizations can leverage AI to gain insights into their practices, challenges, and opportunities.

4.6 CONCLUSIONS

Artificial Intelligence has been used for a variety of purposes. This concept is evolving and becoming widespread in the field of business area. AI is an integral part of the fourth industrial revolution and has the potential to transform business development. This study examines the trends in Sustainable business practices related to Artificial Intelligence research that were indexed in the Scopus dataset. In the included year range, the rate of publication has grown immensely. The main factor in increased publications has been the increased adoption of Artificial Intelligence in transforming Sustainable Business Practices. In this context, the study can assist scholars, business practitioners, and others to better understand the evolution of Sustainable Business Practices embraced by Artificial Intelligence.

4.7 LIMITATIONS

The Scopus database is large enough to provide a diversity of publications necessary for this analysis; however, future studies will use other databases, such as WOS, to examine more papers. The author did not include gray literature, that is, papers written in languages other than English. Therefore, relevant studies conducted in different languages may be overlooked.

KEYWORDS

- **artificial intelligence**
- **bibliometric analysis**
- **deep learning**
- **machine learning.**
- **problem-solving**
- **sustainable business practices**

REFERENCES

1. Sipola, J., Sunila, M., & Ukko, J. (2023). Adopting artificial intelligence in sustainable business. *Journal of Cleaner Production, 426*, 139197.
2. Vazquez, C. Q., & Goodwin, M. (2024). What is artificial intelligence (AI) in business? *IBM.* https://www.ibm.com/topics/artificial-intelligence-business (accessed on 29 August 2025).
3. Di Vaio, A., Palladino, R., Hassan, R., & Escobar, O. (2020). Artificial intelligence and business models in the sustainable development goals perspective: A systematic literature review. *Journal of Business Research, 121*, 283–314.
4. Bharadiya, J. P., Thomas, R. K., & Ahmed, F. (2023). Rise of artificial intelligence in business and industry. *Journal of Engineering Research and Reports, 25*(3), 85–103.
5. Bag, S., Pretorius, J. H. C., Gupta, S., & Dwivedi, Y. K. (2021). Role of institutional pressures and resources in the adoption of big data analytics powered artificial intelligence, sustainable manufacturing practices and circular economy capabilities. *Technological Forecasting and Social Change, 163*, 120420.
6. Joshi, M. (2019). Burnout and stressors as influencers on work engagement among law enforcement agents in selected cities. In *Management Techniques for Employee Engagement in Contemporary Organizations* (pp. 268–283). IGI Global.

7. Joshi, M., & Brahmi, M. S. (2023). A mediation-based analysis of emotional intelligence effect on cognition and consumer decision-making. *International Journal of Public Sector Performance Management, 12*(1–2), 223–251.
8. Joshi, M. (2023). A qualitative assessment of inter-organizational networks, organizational ecosystems, and joint venture associations. In *Exploring Business Ecosystems and Innovation Capacity Building in Global Economics* (pp. 1–25). IGI Global.
9. Joshi, M., Joshi, G., & Pathak, S. (2020). Awareness, entrepreneurial event theory and theory of planned behaviour as antecedents of student entrepreneurial intentions: An Indian perspective. *International Journal of Business and Globalization, 25*(2), 170–184.
10. Joshi, M. (2018). Workforce trends and challenges: A peek into the future. In *Management Techniques for a Diverse and Cross-Cultural Workforce* (pp. 39–53).
11. Joshi, M., Joshi, G., & Pathak, S. (2020). Awareness, entrepreneurial event theory and theory of planned behavior as antecedents of student entrepreneurial intentions: An Indian perspective. *International Journal of Business and Globalization, 25*(2), 170–184.
12. Joshi, M. (2018). Workforce trends and challenges: A peek into the future. In *Management Techniques for a Diverse and Cross-Cultural Workforce* (pp. 39–53).
13. Esposito, L., Brahmi, M., & Joshi, M. (2023). The importance of innovation diffusion in the renewable energy sector. In *Exploring Business Ecosystems and Innovation Capacity Building in Global Economics* (pp. 283–302). IGI Global.
14. Sestino, A., & De Mauro, A. (2022). Leveraging artificial intelligence in business: Implications, applications and methods. *Technology Analysis & Strategic Management, 34*(1), 16–29.
15. Xiong, Y., Xia, S., & Wang, X. (2020). Artificial intelligence and business applications, an introduction. *International Journal of Technology Management, 84*(1–2), 1–7.
16. Broadus, R. N. (1987). Toward a definition of "bibliometrics." *Scient Metrics, 12*, 373–379.

CHAPTER 5

Artificial Intelligence and Tourism Development: How Family Business Hotels in Europe Are Transforming

KAMRAN JAMSHED,[1,*] FIZZA ASIF,[1] SYED HAIDER ALI SHAH,[2] and RAKIA NASIR[3]

[1]*University of Chieti-Pescara, Chieti, Italy*

[2]*Bahria University, Islamabad, Pakistan*

[3]*University Polytechnic delle Marche, Ancona, Italy*

*Corresponding author

ABSTRACT

The hotel industry is recovering, with family-owned hotels balancing traditional customs and modern conveniences. AI enhances customer experiences, optimizes business processes, and promotes environmentally responsible travel. The integration of AI in European family-run hotels has significantly impacted the travel and tourist industry due to advancements in technology. This is a qualitative study based on secondary data where the literature, case studies, and the stats of the family businesses hotels of Europe are used. By examining the historical significance of these hotels, their present issues, and the ways in which they are applying AI to preserve their past while remaining relevant today, this chapter explores the benefits, problems, and potential ramifications of incorporating AI into these esteemed organizations using case studies, data analysis, and ethical considerations.

Embracing the AI Frontier: Perspectives on Business and Organizational Development. Mihir Joshiand and Mohsen Brahmi (Eds.)

DOI: 10.1201/9781779641311-5

5.1 INTRODUCTION

Imagine living in a world where your dream vacation is planned and executed with ease by a highly intelligent assistant that can predict and fulfill all desires. A place where busy airports are transformed into places of efficiency, with the assistance of artificial intelligence that streamlines procedures and speeds you through security. Since 1991, there has been an increasing trend in AI research in the hospitality and tourism sector, with an emphasis shifting from technology to client attitudes and willingness to accept AI [1]. The tourism business is the canvas that artificial intelligence is painting on, and the brushstrokes are as daring as they are nuanced with their depth. However, it is possible for it to have both positive and negative connotations in the tourism industry, which can have an impact on the creation of values and assist organizations in becoming ready for the future of AI-facilitated experiences [2]. An increase in the use of artificial intelligence in tourism is anticipated, and research priorities include the development of AI that is useful, the facilitation of adoption, the evaluation of impacts, and the creation of a sustainable future with AI [3]. The tourist sector is undergoing a rapid transformation brought about by AI, which is bringing forth great chances for expansion.

The use of artificial intelligence in the tourism sector has the potential to change the industry by boosting customer experience and providing personalized services [4]. According to Ferràs et al.'s [35] research, artificial intelligence-enabled smart tourism boosts customer happiness by providing individualized experiences and activities. This, in turn, leads to the creation of services that are both automated and cost-efficient. Although artificial intelligence and robots have the potential to improve the tourism sector by delivering personalized services and making the booking process more efficient, they are not yet capable of replacing the human touch [5]. A tremendous quantity of user data is analyzed by AI algorithms to gain an understanding of individual preferences. These algorithms then make recommendations for flights, destinations, activities, and lodgings that are a great match for the user's interests. This results in highly tailored travel experiences, which go above and beyond expectations and generate loyalty towards the brand. Booking confirmations, itinerary management, and fraud detection are just some of the repetitive processes that may be automated by artificial intelligence, which saves tourist organizations both time and resources. The software also does an analysis of trends and industry data in order to forecast demand and make recommendations for appropriate pricing strategies for flights, hotels, and tours. This enables businesses to optimize income while also providing travelers with competitive costs. Personalization is at the forefront, with artificial intelligence algorithms diving into your travel DNA to find preferences that you may have been hiding. Itineraries that are predetermined and predetermined in every way are no longer the norm; instead, artificial intelligence conjures up experiences that genuinely resonate, from off-the-beaten-path trips that inspire your wanderlust to hidden gem restaurants.

According to Ferràs et al.'s [35] research, AI in conjunction with open innovation has the potential to create new opportunities in the tourist industry by providing personalized experiences and activities that are based on the individual's qualities and motivations. Chatbots that have been imbued with human-like empathy become tireless travel companions, providing answers to questions, resolving concerns, and making recommendations in a variety of languages. According to Melián-González et al.'s research from 2021, the various factors that influence the intention to use chatbots in the travel and tourism industry include expected performance, habit, hedonic component, self-service technology preferences, social influences, and chatbot behavior that is similar to that of a human. According to Jamshed et al. [6], the hospitality sector in Europe is the biggest and accounts for about half of the worldwide hospitality market. The purpose of this chapter is to study the fascinating process of AI adoption in family-run hotels in Europe, as well as the significant consequences that this process has had on the travel and tourism industry. Typically, a single family or a small group of families operate family tourism firms, offering their customers outstanding, personalized solutions [6]. In terms of worldwide turnover and social impact due to their large employment base, family firms account for a significant portion of the global economy [7]. However, family businesses are very important to the tourism industry economically and fall into four categories: innovation performance, marketing orientation, sustainability, competitiveness, and capabilities, strategy, and economic performance, and entrepreneurship [8].

5.2 OBJECTIVES

The purpose of this chapter was to study how family business hotels in Europe have transformed with the usage of AI and NLP-based digitalization.

This qualitative study is based on the stats, case studies, and the literature on the transformation of family business hotels in Europe. In this chapter, the historical significance of these family businesses of Europe hotels is also discussed in depth, along with their present issues and the methods in which they are integrating artificial intelligence to preserve their heritage while being relevant in the modern world. Further, this chapter investigates the advantages, disadvantages, and potential consequences of incorporating artificial intelligence into these highly regarded organizations, carried out using secondary literature. As we proceed with our investigation, it becomes abundantly clear that hotels in Europe that are owned and operated by families are utilizing artificial intelligence to modernize the tourism industry while simultaneously preserving their cultural heritage. This is evident as we move forward with our investigation.

5.3 LITERATURE REVIEW

Millions of people from all over the world travel to Europe every year to take advantage of the continent's rich cultural legacy, amazing natural scenery, and stunning locations. Europe's hotel chains are incredibly inefficiently structured. About two-thirds of the rooms are found in the greatest 10% of chains, whilst only 0.5% of the rooms are found in the smallest 10% of chains. Family business hotels possess a special chance to leverage AI for sustainable operations, customized brand interaction, sustainable product development, and international partnerships in aid of the UN Sustainable Development Goals [9]. As a result, the use of AI technology in family-owned hotels has improved client experiences, increased efficiency, and improved performance [10]. For instance, IHG has reduced food waste in its hotels by 30% by implementing Winnow Vision AI technology. To analyze ingredients and kitchen waste, the solution makes use of an intelligent camera, smart scales, and an AI-based smart meter. In the EMEAA region, it has been successfully installed in seven IHG hotels, and 30 more are anticipated to follow [11].

In the world of tourism, there is a rich tapestry of experiences, and hotels that are owned and operated by families have been an essential part of that collection. The hospitality provided by these hotels is friendly, and they provide tailored attention as well as a one-of-a-kind look into the way of life in the region. These enterprises, which have traditionally been handed down from one generation to the next, have carved out a place in the hearts of tourists who are looking for more than just a place to sleep, since they offer a home away from home. In contrast, these hotels that are owned by families are confronted with a double difficulty in the tourism scene of today, which is always shifting and evolving. To maintain the ancient, time-honored rites and values while also satisfying the demands of modern tourists for seamless experiences and convenient modern facilities, they need to find a way to strike a balance between the two. In another example, Iberostar is implementing Winnow AI-based technology in its hotels to reduce food waste, a significant portion of the company's waste. The technology, which has already been installed in five Iberostar hotels since 2021, has saved 618,000 meals per year and 1,065 tons of CO_2e per year. The company is now rolling out the technology globally, with pilot programs in Europe, the Caribbean, and Latin America [12].

AI has been included into the management of family-run hotels across Europe because of the confluence of these two variables, which has led to a substantial shift in the industry. AI technologies make it possible for organizations to integrate on a global scale, thereby improving their strategic skills and electronic human resource management. This allows them to acquire a competitive advantage and connect with economies and links throughout the world [13]. It improves competitiveness, gives workers more autonomy, and facilitates the customization of procedures. It influences the relationships between stakeholders, the calculation of return on investment, the enhancement of sustainability, and the regulation of ethical data use. The use of artificial intelligence helps networks, modifies distribution methods, and improves customer service [14]. As a result of its capacity to enhance customer experiences, streamline business processes, and encourage environmentally responsible tourism, artificial intelligence has emerged as an indispensable resource for family-owned businesses operating in the hospitality industry.

The emergence of artificial intelligence technologies such as chatbots, data analytics, and automation has provided these hotels with access to new opportunities for success in an environment that is experiencing rapid transformation. These hotels now have access to fresh prospects for achievement. Even though artificial intelligence and robotics are causing a revolution in the restaurant business, its use is still in its infancy [15]. The European Accommodation Barometer Summer 2023 reveals that only 8% of businesses in the accommodation industry in Europe use applications powered by AI, while 23% of those businesses intend to implement these applications within the next six months. This indicates that the number of AI business users in the sector is expected to quadruple.

This COVID-19 pandemic has changed the entire industry's concepts, and several hotels have revived their products and protocols and redesigned them to be able to deal with any pandemic that may occur in the future. The technology is getting more advanced every day, and we have seen that pandemics are not new to the hospitality industry [16]. As a result of its ability to change travel through the provision of travel assistants, tailored services, chatbots, and data analysis, artificial intelligence is currently being utilized often through the hospitality business. The client experience, dynamic pricing, sentiment analysis, hospitality, and luggage handling are all improved as a result of this function. In the present day, the tourism and hospitality business has the potential to contribute to the achievement of sustainability and local autonomy, two objectives that have recently gained a lot of attention [17]. Tourism makes a positive contribution to the growth of areas in Europe, with places with high levels of education enjoying the largest growth benefit from the presence of tourists [18]. Inventory solutions that are powered by artificial intelligence can update prices, identify the emotion of customers, and humanize responses. On the other hand, cloud-based AI tools can improve data management and security. In addition, if there is a lack of appreciation and application of environmentally friendly strategies for managing human resources, it can be beneficial to hotels in terms of both their finances and their impact on the environment [19]. The reason for this is because artificial intelligence is poised to change the tourism sector, particularly for members of Generation Z and Millennials, by upgrading travel experiences and providing better services. AI is being utilized in a variety of applications, including travel agents, operations optimization, sentiment analysis, customer segmentation, personalization, and luggage handling, even though there are issues around data privacy and cyberattacks. As a result of the proliferation of Internet of Things devices, artificial intelligence and travel have been able to successfully combine. For example, FlightBeat monitors heart rate, and British Airways tracks emotions. The optimization of artificial intelligence voice search is also in great demand, and tourist applications are making use of virtual reality and augmented reality techniques. For improving artificial intelligence in areas such as payments, smart contracts, transparency, luggage management, and loyalty programs, blockchain technology is being utilized.

5.3.1 ARTIFICIAL INTELLIGENCE (AI) AND TOURISM

Regarding the future of artificial intelligence in the tourism industry, it is anticipated that substantial investments will be made in the fields of data science, deep learning algorithms, biometric identification, natural language processing, artificial intelligence technologies, artificial intelligence of things, and hyper-personalization. A worldwide survey of travel companies was conducted by STATISTA, which revealed that AI influenced 21% of revenue in 2021, which is an increase from 9% in 2018. It is anticipated that this percentage will reach 32% by 2024, indicating a significant growth in sales that are influenced by AI. A tremendous revolution is currently taking place in the tourism sector, which was traditionally dominated by paper maps and helpful local guides. This transformation is being fueled by the rise of AI. With personalized recommendations and automated tasks, artificial intelligence is becoming increasingly integrated into the traveler experience, presenting travelers with both exciting potential and challenging obstacles. A categorization method that is based on deep learning has been shown to increase personalized travel suggestions by 64.2%, resulting in services that are both more accurate and more convenient than those provided by standard methods [20]. Artificial intelligence systems analyze large amounts of traveler data in order to generate personalized suggestions for flights, destinations, activities, and lodgings that are tailored to fulfill the preferences of each individual traveler. Imagine an artificial intelligence system that, based on your fascination with regional wines, suggests a tour to a hidden gem vineyard, or that, if you are looking for peace and quiet, suggests a wonderful homestay nestled in the countryside.

Chatbots that are driven by artificial intelligence provide service in multiple languages around the clock, answering inquiries, resolving problems, and providing recommendations. In addition to guaranteeing that travelers have access to immediate support whenever and wherever they need it, this frees up human staff to focus on more complex jobs. The introduction of machines that are powered by AI and robotics technologies has already had a significant impact on the hospitality industry. The questions regarding the effects of these machines' replacement on the human workforce have been the subject of a great deal of discussion [28]. Booking confirmations, itinerary management, and fraud detection are just some of the repetitive processes that may be automated by artificial intelligence, which saves tourist organizations both time and resources. Their ability to concentrate on improving the travel experience is facilitated by this. If artificial intelligence were to streamline the check-in process at your hotel, it would free up staff members to provide personalized greetings and recommendations for nearby attractions. Personalized tourist suggestions are improved using the collaborative mining and filtering process (CMFP), which decreases the overhead costs associated with data processing and increases the recommendation ratio [22]. The use of artificial intelligence allows for the prediction of demand and the suggestion of appropriate pricing strategies for travel, including flights, hotels, and tours. By doing so, firms are able to optimize their revenue while simultaneously providing travelers with competitive costs.

Take, for example, an artificial intelligence system that, in response to a sudden reduction in demand, offers you a personalized package that is tailored to your budget or suggests a last-minute airfare deal on your preferred vacation. An artificial intelligence chatbot that narrates stories and provides historical insights may be used to lead you through the exploration of ancient ruins. Alternatively, a personalized travel companion could propose hidden jewels depending on your current location and preferences, whether it be self-driving vehicles that whisk you away to stunning perspectives depending on your preferences or traffic management algorithms backed by artificial intelligence that optimize commutes within destinations. In hotels, artificial intelligence improves both the customer experience and the safety of guests, while also posing a challenge to conventional hotel models. The advent of 5G technology has accelerated the development of AI and enhanced its applicability in the post-epidemic situation [23]. An artificial intelligence system that makes recommendations for environmentally sustainable travel options, analyzes tourist behavior to encourage responsible actions, and optimizes resource management in places. Although artificial intelligence has enormous potential, it is essential to handle its problems in a responsible manner.

It is necessary to give serious thought to concerns regarding data privacy, and it is also necessary to remove algorithmic biases in order to guarantee that all travelers have positive experiences. Hotels that are owned and operated by families are synonymous with tourism in Europe. They are the industry's backbone, accounting for an astounding 77% of the market share. These hotels are more than just places to stay; they are cultural ambassadors, providing one-of-a-kind experiences that are braided with tradition, warmth, and a profound connection to the spirit of the local community. Individuality is embraced by family-owned hotels, in contrast to the standardization that is prevalent in chain hotels. Each enterprise reflects the family's heritage and personality, and it provides experiences that are as varied as the terrain of Europe itself. While they are preserving their high-quality services, luxury hotels are implementing measures that promote environmental and social sustainability, lowering their operational costs, and fostering natural environments that are one of a kind [24]. For example, the rustic allure of a Tuscan farmhouse hotel that has been handed down from generation to generation, or the refined grandeur of a converted palace in Venice, where the walls whisper stories of bygone periods. These hotels, which are deeply ingrained in their towns, serve as doorways to the culture of the surrounding area. They obtain their supplies from farms in the immediate vicinity, collaborate with local artists to provide opportunities for handmade experiences, and hire employees that have a similar enthusiasm for the area.

Enjoying homemade pasta dishes that have been lovingly prepared by the matriarch of the family, or going on a nature trip that is led by a local guide who reveals hidden pathways and local folklore will be a memorable experience. The preservation of local tradition, care for the environment, and sustainable practices are all priorities for many hotels that are owned and operated by families. There is a negative correlation between family ownership and the adoption of sustainable practices; however, family owners that have a strong focus on the long term are more likely to adopt these practices [25]. The majority of hotels around the world are owned by family businesses, and in the majority of cases, the owners are unaware of the amount of natural resources that are being consumed. Furthermore, they are unaware of how, through the implementation of green initiatives, they can reduce the emission of carbon dioxide, excess usage of water and electricity, waste control, and participate in the sustainability of their environment [26]. Global chains provide a huge problem since they provide economies of scale and experiences that are standardized over the world.

The only way for family-owned hotels to keep their distinctive competitive advantage is to continually adapt and innovate. It is necessary to engage in thorough preparation and to cultivate a passion for hospitality within the family in order to guarantee a seamless transition of ownership and operation to subsequent generations. The adoption of digital marketing strategies, online booking platforms, and guest management systems is very necessary in order to ensure success in the contemporary travel industry. In Western Australia, sustainable management methods were used by 50% of rural family tourist firms; however, additional study and management concepts are required to encourage the adoption of these practices [26]. Despite the difficulties, there is still a bright future ahead for hotels that are owned by families. There is a growing demand among travelers for authentic experiences, and these establishments are the perfect places to fulfill that want. They are able to incorporate solutions powered by artificial intelligence for the purpose of providing personalized suggestions, virtual tours, and efficient operations, all while protecting the privacy of guests and adhering to ethical data standards. They can work together with local communities, businesses, and artisans to provide one-of-a-kind experiences and to highlight the genuine allure of the area.

Using storytelling, they are able to capitalize on their extensive history and the legacy of their family, thereby encouraging cultural interaction and emotional ties with tourists. AI has a tremendous impact on organizations, particularly the hotel industry, by enhancing ways to save costs, increase customer happiness, and modernize services. Hotels that are owned and operated by families are not merely a modern phenomenon; rather, they are a time-honored custom that is firmly ingrained in the fabric of hospitality all over the world, particularly in Europe. A fascinating look into the social, cultural, and economic fabric of travel may be gained via the examination of their historical relevance and historical development. Around the same time as inns and caravanserais provided travelers with food, shelter, and rest along trade routes, the origins of hotels that are owned and operated by families may be traced back to ancient times. These institutions, which were frequently run by families, were the ones that laid the groundwork for the concept of hospitality that has been handed down from generation to generation. Monasteries and castles were frequently used as places of stay for pilgrims and dignitaries during the Middle Ages. This helped to promote a more organized kind of hospitality within family lineages. Imagine huge estates that can provide travelers with an insight into the life of aristocrats while also providing lodging. The 19th century witnessed a spike in leisure travel, which resulted in the blossoming of both large hotels and smaller guesthouses that were maintained by families.

Family-owned hotels continued to be distinctive in the tourism business throughout the 20th century, despite the proliferation of hotel chains and the standardization of experiences. Authenticity, individualized encounters, and cultural immersion enable them to thrive despite the fact that they are up against competition. They are open to sustainable practices, artificial intelligence, and technology, but they are also confronted with issues such as succession planning and digital transformation. In addition to providing individualized vacation experiences, hotels that are owned and operated by families also help to the preservation of cultural traditions. It is essential for history, cultural legacy, and hospitality that hotels be owned and operated by families. Challenges such as competition from global chains, succession planning, financial viability, and digital transformation are among the obstacles they must work through. On the other hand, they provide genuine and individualized experiences, are appealing to contemporary tourists, and may specialize in niches such as cultural immersion or ecotourism. Partnerships with local communities and businesses encourage a more profound engagement with the culture of the area, so ensuring that these landmarks will continue to be revered in the future. In order for them to be successful, digital tools, specialization, and community collaboration are all necessary components. In the hospitality business, the introduction of chatbots, tailored recommendations, and virtual concierges powered by artificial intelligence is changing client experience. In addition to providing smooth check-in, rapid support, assistance in many languages, personalized recommendations, and cost savings, these technologies also eliminate friction. Among the chatbots that are powered by artificial intelligence are the following: Connie from Hilton Hotels, Chatbot from Marriott Hotels, WeChat Assistant from Shangri-La Hotels, MagicBand from Disney, Huazhu's AI Assistant, and Meliá Hotels International.

The optimization of housekeeping, maintenance, inventory management, and resource allocation are all areas in which artificial intelligence is helping to improve operational efficiency. The housekeeping team is automatically notified by smart sensors whenever a room is vacant, which optimizes cleaning schedules and reduces wait times. Costs may be reduced, visitor pleasure can be improved, and equipment problems can be avoided with the use of predictive maintenance, smart room sensors, robotic cleaners, and automated reporting. Insights that are driven by data optimize processes by considering trends and data in real time. Other applications of artificial intelligence include optimizing inventory and resource distribution across hotels, anticipating demand, replenishing inventory, managing energy, reducing waste, and promoting sustainability.

This ultimately results in decreased costs, better efficiency, and decisions that are driven by data. A few examples of AI-powered systems include the Connected Room offered by Hilton, Yobot offered by Marriott, and Maxims offered by AccorHotels. The use of artificial intelligence provides significant tools for targeted marketing, dynamic pricing, and revenue management in a market that is highly competitive. To provide recommendations for appropriate pricing strategies in real time, dynamic pricing methods require conducting an analysis of market trends, the pricing of competitors, and the preferences of guests.

Maximizing income and attracting a wide variety of guest groups can be accomplished using personalized offers, seasonality, and demand modifications, last-minute discounts, and tracking of competitors. In the hospitality business, artificial intelligence is ushering in a new era of operational efficiency, which is enabling hotels to streamline procedures, conserve resources, and create a more sustainable future. It is essential to implement AI in a responsible manner, ensuring that data is protected and maintaining open communication with employees regarding the integration of data. Through the enhancement of guest experiences, the optimization of operations, and the acceleration of expansion, artificial intelligence has the potential to change family-owned hotels. It has the ability to offer individualized advice, support around the clock, streamlined services, better accessibility, cost savings, dynamic pricing, targeted marketing, predictive maintenance, and sustainability. However, responsible implementation is essential, which includes ensuring data security, adhering to regulations such as the General Data Protection Regulation (GDPR) and the California Consumer Privacy Act (CCPA), adapting and training staff, addressing job displacement, and alleviating resistance to change. Furthermore, the expense of implementation and the availability of technical competence may present difficulties for hotels that are owned and operated by families. Despite these obstacles, artificial intelligence presents family-owned hotels with a tremendous opportunity to flourish in the digital age, which can provide them with a competitive advantage in the hospitality business. To ensure a successful implementation, it is necessary to take a well-rounded strategy that acknowledges the importance of innovation while also preserving human values and ethical standards.

In the future of artificial intelligence in tourism, it is anticipated that significant investments will be made in the fields of data science, deep learning algorithms, biometric identification, natural language processing, applications of artificial intelligence technologies, artificial intelligence of things, and hyper-personalization. An international survey of travel companies was conducted by STATISTA, which revealed that AI influenced 21% of revenue in 2021, which is an increase from 9% in 2018. It is anticipated that this percentage will reach 32% by 2024, indicating a significant growth in sales that are influenced by AI. As a result of the proliferation of artificial intelligence, the tourism sector, which was long dominated by paper maps and helpful local guides, is currently undergoing a momentous transition (AI). Personalized recommendations and automated tasks are just two examples of how artificial intelligence is becoming increasingly integrated into the traveler experience. This integration presents travelers with both exciting prospects and concerns. Personalized tourism suggestions are improved by 64.2% when using a classification system that is based on deep learning. This method in comparison to standard methods offers services that are both more accurate and more convenient [27]. To provide travelers with recommendations for flights, locations, activities, and lodgings that are tailored to their specific preferences, artificial intelligence algorithms analyze huge volumes of traveler data.

Imagine a situation in which artificial intelligence makes a recommendation for a hidden gem vineyard tour based on your affinity for local wines, or a recommendation for a charming homestay set in the countryside if you are looking for tranquility, support in several languages is provided via chatbots that are driven by artificial intelligence. These chatbots answer queries, resolve problems, and provide recommendations. This frees up human staff to focus on more complex jobs while simultaneously ensuring that travelers have access to immediate support whenever and wherever they need it. The hospitality sector has already been significantly impacted by the introduction of machines that are powered by AI and robotics technologies. The extent to which these machines will replace human workers is an issue that has been the subject of intense debate [28]. Using artificial intelligence, tourism organizations may save time and costs by automating repetitive operations such as booking confirmations, itinerary management, and fraud detection. Because of this, they can concentrate on improving the travel experience more.

Artificial intelligence could streamline the check-in process at your hotel, freeing up staff members to offer personalized greetings and recommendations for local dining and activities. Through the reduction of data processing overheads and the enhancement of recommendation ratios, the

CMFP enhances the quality of personalized tourist recommendations [29]. To forecast demand and make recommendations for the most effective pricing methods for flights, hotels, and tours, artificial intelligence analyzes trends and market data. Consequently, this enables enterprises to maximize revenue while simultaneously providing travelers with competitive costs. Imagine a situation in which artificial intelligence makes a recommendation for a last-minute flight deal on your chosen vacation based on a sudden reduction in demand or offers a bespoke package that is matched to your budget preferences. Imagine being led through the exploration of ancient ruins by an artificial intelligence chatbot that narrates stories and provides historical insights, or a personalized travel assistant that suggests hidden jewels depending on your current location and the things that you are interested in: autonomous vehicles that take you to stunning perspectives depending on your preferences, or traffic management that is powered by artificial intelligence and optimizes commuting within destinations. The implementation of artificial intelligence in hotels brings about improvements in customer experience and safety, while also posing a challenge to conventional hotel models. The advent of 5G technology has accelerated the development of AI and enhanced its applicability in the post-epidemic period [30].

The use of artificial intelligence to enhance resource management in locations, offer environmentally friendly travel options, and analyze tourist behavior in order to encourage responsible activities. The issues that artificial intelligence presents must be navigated appropriately if it is to realize its enormous potential. When it comes to ensuring that all travelers have an equal experience, it is necessary to overcome algorithmic biases and give serious thought to concerns around data privacy. With a stunning 77% share of the market, family-owned hotels are the unsung heroes of the European tourism sector. They are the backbone of the industry. By providing one-of-a-kind experiences that are braided with tradition, kindness, and a profound connection to the spirit of the local community, these hotels are more than just suppliers of lodging; they are cultural ambassadors. Family-owned hotels, in contrast to their peers on the market that are part of standardized chains, value originality. Providing experiences that are as varied as the terrain of Europe itself, each business is a reflection of the family's heritage and personality. Even though they are maintaining high-quality services, luxury hotels are implementing measures that promote environmental and social sustainability, lowering their operational costs, and fostering natural environments that are one of a kind [31].

The rustic allure of a Tuscan farmhouse hotel that has been handed down from generation to generation, or the refined grandeur of a converted palace in Venice, where the walls whisper stories of bygone periods, are such examples. In addition to being deeply anchored in their towns, these hotels serve as entrances to the culture of the surrounding area. The company obtains its supplies from farms located in proximity, collaborates with local artists to provide hands-on craft experiences, and employs staff members who have a similar enthusiasm for the region. The matriarch of the family prepares homemade pasta dishes with affection, or going on a nature trek accompanied by a local guide who reveals hidden pathways and local legends. Both activities are enjoyable. A great number of hotels that are owned by families place an emphasis on environmentally responsible operations, respect for the environment, and the preservation of local heritage. These practices are more likely to be adopted by family owners who have a high long-term perspective, but family ownership has a detrimental influence on the adoption of sustainable practices [32].

A significant number of hotels around the world are owned by family businesses. Usually, the owners are unaware of the quantity of natural resources that are being utilized, as well as the ways in which they can reduce the emission of carbon dioxide, excess usage of water and electricity, waste control, and participate in the sustainability of their environment through the implementation of green initiatives [33]. Companies that operate on a global scale provide a big challenge since they provide economies of scale and consistent experiences. Family-owned hotels are required to continuously adapt and develop to maintain their distinctive competitive advantage. Through careful preparation and the cultivation of a family's passion for hospitality, it is possible to ensure a seamless succession of ownership and management to subsequent generations. To be successful in the competitive modern travel industry, it is essential to embrace digital marketing, online booking platforms, and guest management systems. However, additional study and management concepts are required to encourage the adoption of these methods, as just 50% of rural family tourist enterprises in Western Australia have embraced sustainable management techniques [34].

Hotel chains that are owned by families continue to have a promising future, despite the difficulties they face. As the number of travelers who are looking for authentic experiences continues to rise, these venues are performing exceptionally well. In addition to protecting the privacy of their guests and adhering to ethical data practices, they can integrate AI-powered solutions that allow for personalized suggestions, virtual tours, and efficient operations. Providing one-of-a-kind experiences and showcasing the genuine allure of the place can be accomplished through the collaboration of local businesses, artists, and communities. Guests can be encouraged to engage in cultural exchange and emotional ties with them using storytelling, which allows them to capitalize on their extensive history and family tradition. Artificial intelligence has a tremendous impact on organizations, particularly the hospitality industry, by enhancing the reduction of costs, the satisfaction of customers, and the modernization of services.

Hotels that are owned and operated by families are not merely a modern phenomenon; rather, they are a time-honored custom that is firmly ingrained in the fabric of hospitality. A fascinating look into the social, cultural, and economic fabric of travel can be gained via the use of their historical relevance and evolution. Family-owned hotels can trace their origins back to ancient times, when inns and caravanserais were established along trade routes to provide travelers with food, shelter, and a place to rest when they were traveling. This concept of hospitality, which has been passed down from generation to generation, was established by these institutions, which were frequently operated by families. A more organized kind of hospitality was fostered within family lines during the Middle Ages by the fact that monasteries and castles frequently provided accommodation for pilgrims and nobles. Imagine huge estates that provide travelers with a glimpse into the life of aristocrats so that they can stay there. As a result of the rise in leisure travel that occurred throughout the 19th century, both large hotels and smaller guesthouses that were owned by families flourished. The 20th century witnessed the establishment of hotel chains and the standardization of experiences; nonetheless, family-owned hotels continued to be distinctive within the tourism industry.

However, they profit from authenticity, individualized encounters, and cultural immersion, even though they confront significant competition. Despite their embrace of technology, artificial intelligence, and environmentally responsible practices, they are confronted with issues such as succession planning and digital transformation. Personalized travel experiences, cultural preservation, and community engagement are all benefits that come from staying at a hotel that is owned and operated by a family. Hotels that are owned and operated by families are essential for preserving history, cultural heritage, and hospitality. Their challenges include competition from global chains, succession planning, financial viability, and digital transformation. They also confront challenges related to digital transformation. On the other hand, they provide genuine and individualized experiences, are particularly appealing to contemporary tourists, and may specialize in niches such as cultural immersion or ecotourism. Through partnerships with local companies and communities, a more profound engagement with the culture of the area is fostered, ensuring that the landmarks will continue to be treasured in the future. Their success is dependent on the utilization of digital tools, the development of specialized skills, and the participation of the community.

Guest services in the hospitality business are undergoing a revolution because of the introduction of chatbots, virtual concierges, and tailored suggestions powered by artificial intelligence. Automated check-in, quick help, assistance in several languages, individualized advice, and cost reductions are among the features that these technologies provide. Several examples of chatbots that are powered by artificial intelligence include the Connie chatbot from Hilton, the Chatbot from Marriott, the WeChat Assistant from Shangri-La, the MagicBand from Disney, the AI Assistant from Huazhu, and Meliá Hotels International. Optimization of housekeeping, maintenance, inventory management, and resource allocation are all areas in which artificial intelligence is helping to improve operational efficiency. To optimize cleaning schedules and reduce wait times, smart sensors are able to instantly notify housekeeping personnel when a room is vacant.

To cut expenses, improve guest happiness, and prevent equipment failures, predictive maintenance, smart room sensors, robotic cleaners, and automated reporting are essential. For optimizing operations based on real-time data and trends, data-driven insights are utilized. By forecasting demand, refilling inventory, managing energy, reducing waste, and promoting sustainability, artificial intelligence also improves inventory and resource allocation among hotels. This results in decreased expenses, better efficiency, and decisions that are driven by data that is collected. The Connected Room at Hilton, the Yobot at Marriott, and the Maxims at AccorHotels are all examples of systems that are powered by artificial intelligence. When applied in a market that is highly competitive, artificial intelligence provides powerful capabilities for targeted marketing, dynamic pricing, and revenue management. Dynamic pricing strategies involve conducting an analysis of market trends, the pricing tactics of competitors, and the preferences of guests in order to provide recommendations for appropriate pricing strategies in real time. It is possible to maximize revenue and attract a varied range of guest segments by utilizing personalized offers, seasonality, and demand modifications, last-minute discounts, and tracking of competitors. By enabling hotels to streamline procedures, conserve resources, and build a more sustainable future, artificial intelligence is ushering in a new era of operational efficiency in the hospitality industry. Maintaining data protection and maintaining open lines of communication with employees regarding the incorporation of AI is essential for responsible implementation.

The use of artificial intelligence has the potential to revolutionize family-owned hotels by improving the experiences of guests, optimizing operations, and driving expansion, respectively. Personalized advice, support around the clock, streamlined services, increased accessibility, cost savings, dynamic pricing, targeted marketing, predictive maintenance, and sustainability are all capabilities that it can offer the user. However, responsible implementation is essential, which includes ensuring data security, adhering to regulations such as the GDPR and the CCPA, adapting, and training staff, addressing job displacement, and reducing resistance to reform. Further complicating matters for smaller family-owned hotels is the possibility that the cost of installation and technical skills will be prohibitive. Even with these obstacles, artificial intelligence presents family-owned hotels with a tremendous opportunity to flourish in the digital age, which can provide them an advantage over their competitors in the hospitality business. For an implementation to be effective, it is necessary to have a well-rounded strategy that, while embracing innovation, also upholds human values and ethical norms.

5.3.2 RESHAPING TOURISM'S CANVAS WITH INNOVATION

In the future of artificial intelligence in tourism, it is anticipated that significant investments will be made in the fields of data science, deep learning algorithms, biometric identification, natural language processing, artificial intelligence technologies, artificial intelligence of things, and hyper-personalization. These are all areas that are expected to receive significant investments. STATISTA conducted a global survey of travel companies, which revealed that AI influenced 21% of revenue in 2021, which is an increase from 9% in 2018. It is anticipated that AI-influenced sales will reach 32% by 2024, indicating a significant growth in AI-influenced sales. Paper maps and pleasant local guides were once the norm in the tourism sector, but now, thanks to the emergence of artificial intelligence, the industry is undergoing a drastic transition (AI). The incorporation of artificial intelligence into traveler experiences is bringing forth a plethora of intriguing prospects as well as challenges. This includes tailored recommendations and automated duties. Personalized tourism suggestions are improved by 64.2% when using a classification method that is based on deep learning. This method also provides services that are more accurate and hassle-free than standard methods [27]. A tremendous quantity of traveler data is analyzed by AI algorithms, which then create individualized suggestions for flights, destinations, activities, and accommodations that are tailored to the tastes of each personal traveler.

Consider the possibility of artificial intelligence advising a wonderful homestay in the countryside if you are looking for peace and quiet, or a hidden gem vineyard tour based on your affinity for the wines of the region. Using artificial intelligence, chatbots offer service in multiple languages around the clock, answering questions, fixing problems, and providing recommendations. As a result, human staff are freed up to focus on more difficult responsibilities, and travelers are guaranteed to receive prompt support whenever and wherever they need it. The hospitality industry has already been significantly impacted by the introduction of machines that are powered by AI and robotics technologies. The topic of how the replacement of these machines will impact the human workforce has been the subject of a great deal of ongoing debate [28]. Businesses in the tourist industry can save time and costs by utilizing artificial intelligence to automate repetitive operations such as booking confirmations, itinerary management, and fraud detection. As a result, they are able to concentrate on improving the trip experience as a group. What if artificial intelligence were to streamline the check-in procedure at your hotel, freeing up staff members to deliver personalized greetings and recommendations for nearby attractions?

By decreasing the amount of data processing overheads and raising the recommendation ratio, the CMFP makes it possible to improve tailored tourism recommendations [29]. The use of artificial intelligence allows for the prediction of demand and the suggestion of ideal pricing methods for trips, hotels, and flights. The ability to maximize revenue while also providing travelers with competitive prices is facilitated by this. An artificial intelligence system may, for example, offer you a bespoke package that is tailored to your budget or propose a last-minute airfare price on your chosen location based on a sudden reduction in demand. Imagine being led through the exploration of ancient ruins by an artificial intelligence chatbot that narrates stories and provides historical insights, or a personalized travel assistant that suggests hidden jewels based on your current location and the passions you have. The use of artificial intelligence to control traffic and optimize commutes inside locations, or the use of self-driving vehicles to transport you to stunning perspectives depending on your preferences. By boosting customer experience and safety, AI in hotels poses a challenge to existing hotel models. The development of AI applications in the post-epidemic age is accelerated by 5G technology, which also boosts AI applications [30]. Artificial intelligence that analyzes tourist behavior to promote ethical habits, recommends environmentally friendly travel options, and optimizes resource management in destinations. It is essential to negotiate the issues that artificial intelligence presents in a responsible manner. Careful consideration is required for concerns around data privacy, and algorithmic biases need to be addressed in order to guarantee that all travelers have an equal experience.

With a stunning 77% share of the market, family-owned hotels are the backbone of the European tourism sector. They are synonymous with the entire continent. Not only do these hotels provide lodging, but they also serve as cultural ambassadors, providing guests with one-of-a-kind experiences that are woven with tradition, warmth, and a profound connection to the spirit of the neighborhood. Individuality is embraced by family-owned hotels, in contrast to the standardization that their chain rivals exhibit. Experiences that are as varied as the terrain of Europe itself are provided by each establishment, which embodies the family's heritage and personality. Luxury hotels are implementing methods that are environmentally and socially sustainable, lowering their operational expenses, and supporting natural environments that are one of a kind, all while retaining their focus on providing high-quality services [31]. Similar to the rustic allure of a Tuscan farmhouse hotel that has been handed down from generation to generation, or the tasteful grandeur of a restored palazzo in Venice, where the walls whisper stories of bygone periods.

Such hotels, which are deeply ingrained in their towns, serve as doorways to the culture of the surrounding area. They hire staff members that have a similar enthusiasm for the area, they obtain their supplies from nearby farmers, and they collaborate with local craftsmen to provide crafts experiences. Indulging in homemade pasta dishes that have been lovingly prepared by the matriarch of the family, or going on a nature trip that is led by a local guide who introduces you to hidden pathways and local mythology. There are a lot of hotels that are owned by families that put an emphasis on sustainability, respecting the environment, and conserving the local tradition. A detrimental influence on the adoption of sustainability practices is exerted by family ownership; however, family owners that have a strong focus on the long term are more likely to embrace sustainable behaviors [22]. The majority of hotels around the world are owned by family businesses, and in the majority of cases, the owners are unaware of the enormous amount of natural resources that are being used up. Furthermore, they are unaware of the ways in which they can reduce the emission of carbon dioxide, excess usage of water and electricity, waste control, and participate in the sustainability of their environment by adopting green initiatives [33].

By providing economies of scale and consistent experiences, global chains provide a big challenge to businesses. In order to preserve their distinctive competitive advantage, hotels that are owned and operated by families must continually adapt and develop. Taking the time to carefully prepare and cultivate a passion for hospitality within the family is necessary in order to guarantee a seamless transfer of ownership and management to subsequent generations. If you want to be competitive in the modern travel industry, it is absolutely necessary to embrace digital marketing, online booking platforms, and guest management systems. There is a need for additional research and management concepts to support the adoption of sustainable management techniques; however, 50% of rural family tourist firms in Western Australia have already embraced these principles [34].

Family-owned hotels continue to have a promising future, despite the difficulties they face. Genuine experiences are being increasingly sought after by travelers, and these places are shining examples of this trend. Personalized recommendations, virtual tours, and efficient operations may all be accomplished with the integration of AI-powered solutions, all while maintaining the confidentiality of guests and adhering to ethical data policies. When they work together with local communities, businesses, and artisans, they are able to provide one-of-a-kind experiences and highlight the genuine allure of the area. Through the use of storytelling, they are able to facilitate cultural exchange and emotional ties with guests, thereby capitalizing on their extensive past and the legacy of their family. Artificial intelligence has a huge impact on organizations, particularly the hotel industry, by enhancing the experience of customers, lowering costs, and upgrading services. When it comes to hospitality, family-owned hotels are not just a modern phenomenon; rather, they are a time-honored tradition that is firmly ingrained in the fabric of hospitality all over the world, particularly in Europe. There is a fascinating view into the social, cultural, and economic fabric of travel that can be gained from their historical significance and history. Inns and caravanserais, which were located along trade routes and provided travelers with food, shelter, and rest, are the origins of hotels that are owned and operated by families. As a result of these institutions, which were frequently run by families, the concept of hospitality was established and has been passed down from generation to generation. It was common practice during the Middle Ages for monasteries and castles to provide lodging for pilgrims and nobles. This practice helped to cultivate a more structured style of hospitality among royal families. Imagine opulent estates that provided lodging for tourists and provided peeks into the lives of aristocrats. A spike in leisure travel occurred during the 19th century, which resulted in the proliferation of both large hotels and smaller guesthouses owned by families.

Hotel chains and homogenized experiences were prevalent in the 20th century; nonetheless, family-owned hotels continued to be distinctive in the tourism business. The fact that they are authentic, have individualized experiences, and are immersed in culture helps them stand out from the competitors. There are obstacles that they confront, such as succession planning and digital transformation, but they embrace technology, artificial intelligence, and sustainable practices. Cultural preservation, community engagement, and the creation of individualized travel experiences are all benefits that come from staying at family-owned hotels. Hotels that are owned and operated by families are the backbone of hospitality, history, and cultural heritage. They are confronted with issues such as preparation for succession, financial viability, digital transformation, and competition from global chains. However, they provide genuine and individualized experiences, appealing to contemporary travelers, and have the potential to specialize in niches such as cultural immersion or ecotourism. In order to ensure that these landmarks continue to be treasured in the future, partnerships with local companies and communities encourage a more profound engagement with the culture of the area. It is crucial for their success that they utilize digital technologies, specialize, and collaborate with the community. Personalization of recommendations, chatbots, and virtual concierges powered by artificial intelligence are bringing about a transformation in the hospitality industry's client service. A flawless check-in process, instantaneous help, assistance in several languages, personalized advice, and cost savings are all provided by these technologies.

The chatbots Connie from Hilton, Chatbot from Marriott, WeChat Assistant from Shangri-La, MagicBand from Disney, Huazhu's AI Assistant, and Meliá Hotels International are all examples of technologies that are powered by artificial intelligence. Additionally, artificial intelligence is improving operational efficiency by optimizing aspects such as housekeeping, maintenance, inventory management, and resource allocation. It is possible to optimize cleaning schedules and reduce wait times by utilizing smart sensors that immediately notify housekeeping staff when a room is vacant. It is possible to cut costs, improve visitor happiness, and prevent equipment breakdowns with the use of predictive maintenance, smart room sensors, robotic cleaners, and automated reporting. On the basis of real-time data and trends, data-driven insights ensure that processes are optimized. In addition, artificial intelligence helps hotels improve their inventory and resource allocation, as well as estimate demand, replenish inventory, manage energy, reduce waste, and promote sustainability. The result is decisions that are driven by data, which leads to decreased costs and better efficiency. Hilton's Connected Room, Marriott's Yobot, and AccorHotels' Maxims are all examples of systems that are powered by artificial intelligence.

Artificial intelligence provides significant capabilities for effective revenue management, dynamic pricing, and tailored marketing in a market that is highly competitive. Real-time pricing methods that are optimal are suggested by dynamic pricing techniques, which involve analyzing market trends, the price of competitors, and the preferences of guests. In order to maximize income and attract a wide variety of guest categories, it is helpful to have personalized offers, seasonality, and demand modifications, last-minute discounts, and tracking of competitors. With the help of AI, the hospitality sector is entering a new era of operational efficiency. This will enable hotels to optimize procedures, save resources, and build a more sustainable future. Assuring data protection and maintaining open communication with staff members regarding the incorporation of AI is an essential component of responsible implementation. There is a possibility that artificial intelligence will revolutionize family-owned hotels by improving the experiences of guests, managing operations, and driving growth. It is able to offer individualized advice, support around the clock, streamlined services, better accessibility, cost savings, dynamic pricing, targeted marketing, predictive maintenance, and maintenance that is sustainable. Nevertheless, responsible implementation is of the utmost importance. This includes maintaining data security, adhering to legislation such as GDPR and CCPA, adapting, and training people, resolving job displacement, and developing strategies to reduce resistance to change. Smaller hotels that are owned by families may also face difficulties due to the high cost of implementation and the shortage of technical competence. Artificial intelligence presents family-owned hotels with a significant opportunity to thrive in the digital age, so providing them with a competitive advantage in the hospitality business. To ensure a successful implementation, it is necessary to take a well-rounded approach that, while embracing innovation, also upholds human values and ethical norms.

5.3.3 FAMILY-OWNED HOTELS OF EUROPE

There is a dynamic tapestry at the center of the hospitality industry in Europe, which has been produced by generations of families who have been committed to providing exceptional experiences for their visitors. This tradition has been passed down from generation to generation. This industry is well-known for the unique allure that it possesses. The cornerstone of this industry is made up of hotels that are owned by families, who account for an incredible 77% of all enterprises on the continent. Infusing the hospitality business with a sense of warmth, heritage, and a strong connection to the culture of the region, these hotels are a significant contributor.

The hospitality heritage is carried on by these hotels, which are typically passed down from one family to the next. As a result, each stay is imbued with a sense of its own distinctive personality. If you were to inherit a charming inn that has been there for hundreds of years and is located in the middle of rolling vineyards, how would you feel about accepting the inheritance? There are tales of generations of people welcoming guests with open arms that are written on the walls of the inn. In contrast to their chain competitors, hotels that are owned and operated by families place a significant focus on individuality. Each business is a manifestation of the family's character and the traditions that have been passed down through the generations, and it offers experiences that are as diverse as the landscape of Europe itself. Imagine the rustic allure of a Tyrolean farmhouse hotel, complete with hand-carved furniture and hearty local cuisine, or the elegant grandeur of a Venetian palazzo-turned-hotel, with its frescoed ceilings adorned with stories of bygone eras.

Both of these hotels are perfect examples of the elegance and romance that can be found in Italy. While staying at either of these hotels, you will have the chance to experience the splendor and sophistication of the surrounding area. As a result of their deep roots in the communities in which they are located, hotels that are owned and operated by families act as cultural ambassadors for the local area. Obtaining its fresh commodities from farms in the surrounding area, working together with local artists to produce one-of-a-kind experiences, and employing staff members who share their excitement for the region are all things that the company does. Imagine yourself indulging in regional specialties that have been painstakingly cooked by the matriarch of the family or having the option to go on a guided stroll through hidden routes that is led by a local environment enthusiast. Both of these experiences are available to you. Businesses in the tourism industry that cater to families have been expanding despite the pandemic that has been going on this year. This is because they have cancellation rules that are considerate, and they approach the market in a friendly manner. Both of these factors contribute to their success [6].

Family-owned hotels, which are already facing tremendous competition, face a formidable obstacle in the form of international hotel chains that offer standardized hotel experiences and economies of scale. In order to maintain their distinguishing advantage over other hotels in the industry, hotels that are owned and operated by families are obliged to consistently adapt and improve. The family must engage in extensive planning and build a passion for hospitality in order to ensure a smooth transition of ownership and operation to succeeding generations. This is important in order to guarantee a smooth transition. When it comes to ensuring success in the modern travel sector, the implementation of digital marketing techniques, online booking platforms, and guest management systems is vital. Even though family-owned businesses constitute the backbone of the European tourism industry, thriving in this fast-paced and dynamic sector comes with its fair share of problems. The following is a list of significant challenges that these companies must overcome: It can be challenging to ensure a smooth transition of ownership and management to the next generation, which is why it is necessary to engage in rigorous planning and communication within the family. The presence of conflict can be caused by different leadership styles and visions.

Additionally, it can be challenging to keep a healthy separation between the dynamics of the family and the decisions that are made in the workplace. Incorporating personal relationships into company processes might result in feelings of resentment and unjust treatment of employees. Family businesses typically have lesser expenditures for marketing, technology, and renovations when compared to larger chains. This makes it more difficult for family businesses to compete and keep up with the latest trendy trends. Family enterprises that are smaller in size may rely on members of the family to fill numerous tasks, often without official training or competence, which can have a negative influence on both efficiency and professionalism. Global hotel chains and internet booking platforms provide a big challenge since they provide standardized experiences and economies of scale that are tough to compete with. The travel and tourism sector is particularly vulnerable to economic downturns, which can have a disproportionately negative impact on smaller enterprises that have less financial cushion.

It may be a laborious and expensive endeavor, particularly for smaller businesses, to navigate the complicated rules and labor laws that are in place. Adapting to modern technologies such as online booking platforms, digital marketing, and guest management systems takes financial investment and specialized knowledge, which can be difficult for establishments that are on the smaller side. It is not always easy to find and keep skilled people, particularly in tourist destinations that are highly competitive. This can have a negative influence on both the quality of service and the efficiency of operations. Smaller firms may face challenges and additional expenses when it comes to implementing environmentally friendly practices and achieving sustainability regulations. It might be difficult to deal with seasonal variations in demand, which necessitates employing flexible employment tactics and innovative marketing approaches. When negative reviews are posted on the internet, they can quickly spread and do damage to the reputation of a family-owned business, which is essential for attracting customers.

5.3.4 ARTIFICIAL INTELLIGENCE (AI)'S ROLE IN SUSTAINABLE TOURISM PRACTICES

AI is being utilized by the tourist industry to encourage environmentally responsible travel practices and lessen the impact on the environment. Personalized recommendations, dynamic pricing, and resource efficiency are some of the ways that artificial intelligence might help promote environmentally responsible tourism. Additionally, it monitors the flow of tourists, the reduction of waste, and the conservation of wildlife. AI also delivers insights that are driven by data, identifying areas that require efforts to be made in the fields of conservation and sustainable development. Additionally, it forecasts the destruction of the environment and the depletion of resources, which encourages ongoing improvement. Artificial intelligence platforms have the potential to improve knowledge about ethical travel habits and connect tourists with local businesses. Nevertheless, ethical issues are of the utmost importance, and they include aspects such as data transparency, fair algorithms, and job displacement. AI may also have an effect on the hospitality business, which will require the development of initiatives to retrain and educate the staff. As well as being vital, human-AI collaboration and societal responsibility are also essential. It is possible for the industry to build a future in which travel is beneficial to both people and the world if it adopts AI in a responsible manner.

Artificial intelligence is bringing about a change in the hotel business by providing new technologies such as hyper-personalization, immersive experiences, emotion detection, predictive maintenance, and conversational AI. Through the provision of highly tailored travel, dynamic pricing and revenue management, seamless travel experiences, sustainability, and niche tourism, it will bring about a transformation in the tourism business in Europe. On the other hand, artificial intelligence presents family-owned hotels with both obstacles and opportunities. The competition from platforms powered by artificial intelligence, concerns about data protection, and job displacement are all examples of disruptions. A number of opportunities exist, such as the benefit of early adopters, improved guest experiences, increased operational efficiency, and decision-making that is driven by data. Family-owned hotels have the potential to leverage AI to create experiences that are unforgettable and to secure a competitive edge in the future of European tourism. This can be accomplished by putting an emphasis on personalization, sustainability, and the unique human touch.

Family-owned hotels have the potential to prosper in this new era and offer experiences that will be unforgettable while also ensuring a competitive edge in the future of European tourism if they adopt artificial intelligence in a responsible and planned manner. In the hospitality industry, artificial intelligence presents opportunities for family-owned hotels to improve the experiences of their guests, streamline their operations, and achieve sustainable growth. The benefits include the creation of individualized experiences, reductions in costs, and increases in revenue through the use of automation and dynamic pricing. Practices that are environmentally sustainable and responsible travel behavior are encouraged by AI. Among the challenges are the incorporation of emerging technologies and the consideration of ethical issues.

Machine learning has the potential to tailor travel, optimize price, and offer unique tourism experiences. The operations can also be transformed, which will free up staff members to engage in meaningful relationships. Hotels have the opportunity to differentiate themselves, engage with younger generations, save expenses, and promote sustainability if they adopt AI in a responsible manner. AI could appear to be intimidating, but keep in mind that it is a technology that will strengthen your family business rather than replace it. Begin with a modest objective in mind and work your way up. Enhance the skills of your employees and collaborate with reputable AI solution providers. Additionally, it is essential to keep in mind that the human touch is still priceless.

Utilize artificial intelligence to augment your one-of-a-kind family hospitality and to build a more promising and environmentally responsible future for your hotel. The landscape of tourism in Europe is undergoing fast change, and artificial intelligence is at the forefront of this transformation. Your family-owned hotel has the potential to not only endure but also flourish in the years to come if it adopts this technology in a responsible and strategic manner. This will ensure that the hotel's legacy is preserved and that it is able to provide extraordinary experiences for future generations of travelers. Take into consideration that the trip begins with a single step. Today is the day to take the first step toward a future powered by artificial intelligence.

5.4 CONCLUSION

AI is revolutionizing the hospitality and tourism sector by enhancing customer experience and providing personalized services. AI-enabled smart tourism boosts customer happiness by providing individualized experiences and activities, leading to automated and cost-efficient services. AI algorithms automate repetitive processes like booking confirmations, itinerary management, and fraud detection, saving time and resources. Chatbots with human-like empathy are becoming indispensable travel companions, providing answers, resolving concerns, and making recommendations in various languages. The hospitality sector in Europe, which accounts for about half of the worldwide hospitality market, has been significantly transformed by AI adoption in family-run hotels. AI technology has improved client experiences, increased efficiency, and improved performance. However, challenges such as data privacy and cyberattacks persist.

The COVID-19 pandemic has changed the industry, with AI being used in various applications, such as travel agents, operations optimization, sentiment analysis, customer segmentation, personalization, and luggage handling. The proliferation of Internet of Things devices and blockchain technology are allowing AI and travel to successfully combine, with applications like Flight Beat monitoring heart rate and British Airways tracking emotions. AI is poised to transform the tourism sector, particularly for Generation Z and Millennials, by upgrading travel experiences and providing better services. The advent of 5G technology has accelerated AI development and enhanced its applicability in post-epidemic situations. Family-owned hotels, accounting for 77% of the European tourism industry, offer unique experiences and promote environmental and social sustainability. They are deeply rooted in their towns, sourcing supplies from nearby farms and collaborating with local artists for handmade experiences. Despite challenges such as competition from global chains, succession planning, financial viability, and digital transformation, family-owned hotels continue to thrive.

AI is transforming the hospitality industry by providing chatbots, tailored recommendations, and virtual concierges, improving operational efficiency and customer experience. AI-powered systems like Connected Room, Yobot, and Maxims offer targeted marketing, dynamic pricing, and revenue management. However, responsible implementation of AI is crucial, including data security, adhering to regulations, adapting staff, addressing job displacement, and overcoming resistance to change. AI can save time and costs by automating repetitive operations, forecast demand, and make recommendations for effective pricing methods. The advent of 5G technology has accelerated AI development, but challenges such as algorithmic biases and concerns around data privacy must be navigated. Family-owned hotels hold a significant market share in the European tourism sector, providing unique and culturally authentic experiences. To succeed in the modern travel industry, family-owned hotels need to embrace digital marketing, online booking platforms, and guest management systems. Family-owned hotels, with a rich history dating back to ancient times, play a crucial role in the European hospitality industry. Despite facing challenges such as competition, succession planning, financial viability, and digital transformation, they continue to be distinctive. AI-powered guest services, chatbots, and virtual concierges are revolutionizing the hospitality industry, offering automated check-in, quick help, and cost reductions. AI is also improving operational efficiency by optimizing housekeeping, maintenance, inventory management, and resource allocation. To maintain their competitive advantage, family-owned hotels must embrace digital marketing, online booking platforms, and guest management systems. AI-powered solutions can enhance customer experiences, lower costs, and upgrade services while maintaining guest confidentiality and adhering to ethical data policies.

Despite the pandemic, family-owned hotels have expanded due to their considerate cancellation rules and friendly approach to the market. To maintain their distinguishing advantage, they must consistently adapt and improve, engaging in extensive planning and building a passion for hospitality. AI is playing a crucial role in sustainable tourism practices, promoting environmentally responsible practices and reducing environmental impact. It offers personalized recommendations, dynamic pricing, and resource efficiency, while monitoring tourist flow, waste reduction, and wildlife conservation. However, ethical issues like data transparency, fair algorithms, and job displacement remain important. AI also impacts the hospitality industry, necessitating staff retraining and education. Family-owned hotels can leverage AI to create unforgettable experiences and secure a competitive edge in the future of European tourism. AI is revolutionizing the tourism industry by offering personalized services, automating repetitive tasks, and analyzing market data to predict demand and suggest optimal pricing strategies.

AI-powered chatbots provide 24/7 multilingual support, analyze tourist behavior, and improve accessibility for disabled travelers. The future of AI in tourism is predicted to see significant investments in data science, deep learning algorithms, biometric identification, NLP, AI technologies, AIoT, and hyper-personalization. AI can enhance customer experiences, promote sustainability, and ensure equitable access to technology. Family-owned hotels, which play a significant role in European tourism, can benefit from AI-powered virtual concierges and chatbots, enhancing operational efficiency and driving growth. However, responsible implementation is crucial, including data security, adhering to regulations, staff adaptation, and addressing job displacement.

5.5 IMPLICATIONS

AI is revolutionizing hospitality and tourism by personalizing experiences and reducing costs. It automates booking confirmations, itinerary management, and fraud detection, saving time and resources. AI is becoming essential in family-run hotels in Europe and improves customer service, efficiency, and performance, while addressing data privacy and cyberattacks. This is a qualitative study which has been conducted on the family business hotels of Europe, and it will help industry professionals and family business owners understand the trends of transformation. Further, it can enhance the experience of currently AI-implemented family business hotels in Europe, who can check which ways are opted for by different hotels. They can learn that AI can forecast demand, automate operations, and offer pricing solutions, but data protection, rule compliance, staff adaptation, and change resistance are necessary, and it can help family-owned hotels compete in European tourism and offer great experiences.

5.6 LIMITATIONS AND FUTURE RESEARCH

This chapter has focused on only European hotels and their transformation, while the transformation and adoption of AI varies from country to country, and how this adoption can help those family business hotels. This study is based on secondary data, case studies, and the literature; therefore, a deep analysis or quantitative study may have different results. Future studies should consist of a longitudinal study to learn the long-term impact of the adoption of AI and transforming their businesses, as most family businesses do not go for change or transformation to keep their legacy.

KEYWORDS

- **artificial intelligence**
- **canvas**
- **chatbots**
- **data analysis**
- **family businesses**
- **innovation**
- **tourist industry**

REFERENCES

1. Kong, H., Wang, K., Qiu, X., Cheung, C., & Bu, N. (2023). 30 years of artificial intelligence (AI) research relating to the hospitality and tourism industry. *International Journal of Contemporary Hospitality Management, 35*(6), 2157–2177.
2. Grundner, L., & Neuhofer, B. (2021). The bright and dark sides of artificial intelligence: A futures perspective on tourist destination experiences. *Journal of Destination Marketing and Management, 19*, 100511. https://doi.org/10.1016/j.jdmm.2020.100511 (accessed on 29 August 2025).
3. Tussyadiah, I. (2020). A review of research into automation in tourism: Launching the Annals of Tourism Research Curated Collection on Artificial Intelligence and Robotics in Tourism. *Annals of Tourism Research, 81*, 102883.
4. Kazak, A. N., Chetyrbok, P. V., & Oleinikov, N. N. (2020). Artificial intelligence in the tourism sphere. In *IOP Conference Series: Earth and Environmental Science, 421*(4), 042020.
5. Samala, N., Katkam, B. S., Bellamkonda, R. S., & Rodriguez, R. V. (2020). Impact of AI and robotics in the tourism sector: A critical insight. *Journal of Tourism Futures, 8*(1), 73–87.
6. Jamshed, K. A., Shah, S. H. A., & Al-Ghazali, B. M. (2023b). Family tourism businesses and post pandemic: An overview of the hospitality industry of Europe. In *Women's Empowerment Within the Tourism Industry* (pp. 102–115).
7. Stănciulescu, G. D. (2023). A critical view on defining the concept of family business in Romanian, European and international context. In *International Conference of Management and Industrial Engineering, 11*, 92–99.

8. Joshi, M. (2019). Burnout and stressors as influencers on work engagement among law enforcement agents in selected cities. In *Management Techniques for Employee Engagement in Contemporary Organizations* (pp. 268–283). IGI Global.
9. Joshi, M., & Brahmi, M. S. (2023). A mediation-based analysis of emotional intelligence effect on cognition and consumer decision-making. *International Journal of Public Sector Performance Management, 12*(1, 2), 223–251.
10. Joshi, M. (2023). A qualitative assessment of inter-organizational networks, organizational ecosystems, and joint venture associations. In *Exploring Business Ecosystems and Innovation Capacity Building in Global Economics* (pp. 1–25). IGI Global.
11. Joshi, M., Joshi, G., & Pathak, S. (2020). Awareness, entrepreneurial event theory and theory of planned behaviour as antecedents of student entrepreneurial intentions: An Indian perspective. *International Journal of Business and Globalization, 25*(2), 170–184.
12. Joshi, M. (2018). Workforce trends and challenges: A peek into the future. In *Management Techniques for a Diverse and Cross-Cultural Workforce* (pp. 39–53).
13. Dawar, G., Singh, S., Joshi, M., & Kumar, P. (2021). Effective corporate social responsibility in small and medium enterprises. In *Organizing Entrepreneurship and MSMEs Across India* (pp. 231–246).
14. Esposito, L., Brahmi, M., & Joshi, M. (2023). The importance of innovation diffusion in the renewable energy sector. In *Exploring Business Ecosystems and Innovation Capacity Building in Global Economics* (pp. 283–302). IGI Global.
15. Forés, B., Breithaupt Janssen, Z., & Takashi Kato, H. (2021). A bibliometric overview of tourism family business. *Sustainability, 13*(22), 12822.
16. Doe, J. K., & Hinson, R. E. (2023). AI-driven sustainability brand activism for family businesses: A future-proofing perspective article. *Journal of Family Business Management*.
17. Sharma, M., Bathla, G., Kaushik, A., & Rana, S. (2023). A study on impact of adaptation of AI-artificial intelligence services on business performance of hotels. In *2023 2nd International Conference on Computational Modelling, Simulation and Optimization (ICCMSO)* (pp. 28–32). IEEE.
18. Thakar, M. (2018). Award-winning AI technology helps IHG hotels track, measure and reduce food waste. https://www.ihgplc.com/en/news-and-media/news-releases/2019/award-winning-ai-technology-helps-ihg-hotels-track-measure-and-reduce-food-waste (accessed on 29 August 2025).
19. Hoteles, I. (2022). Hotel Group Iberostar uses artificial intelligence to become zero waste and save 1,600 tons of food per year. *Hospitality Net*. https://www.hospitalitynet.org/news/4112837.html (accessed on 29 August 2025).
20. Ruel, H., & Njoku, E. (2020). AI redefining the hospitality industry. *Journal of Tourism Futures, 7*(1), 53–66.
21. Bulchand-Gidumal, J., Secin, E. W., O'Connor, P., & Buhalis, D. (2023). Artificial intelligence's impact on hospitality and tourism marketing: Exploring key themes and addressing challenges. *Current Issues in Tourism*, 1–18.
22. Blöcher, K., & Alt, R. (2021). AI and robotics in the European restaurant sector: Assessing potentials for process innovation in a high-contact service industry. *Electronic Markets, 31*, 529–551.

23. Shah, S. H. A., Jamshed, K., Saleem, S., Al-Ghazali, B. M., & Kiani, O. I. (2023). Rebuilding tourism in Asia for future (post-COVID-19). In *Resilient and Sustainable Destinations After Disaster* (pp. 109–119). Emerald Publishing Limited.
24. Jamshed, K. A., Afzal, M. I., Al-Ghazali, B. M., Jamshaid, S., Eman, N. E., & Shamsi, A. I. (2023a). Tourism as an empowerment tool in sustainable development: Evidence from the hospitality industry of China. In *Women's Empowerment Within the Tourism Industry* (pp. 132–146). IGI Global.
25. Harb, G., & Bassil, C. (2021). Harnessing cross-region disparities to assess the impact of tourism on regional growth in Europe. *Current Issues in Tourism, 24*(11), 1491–1504.
26. Raza, G., Asif, A., Yousaf, R., Rahman, E. Z., & Jamshed, K. (2023). Green human resource practices on pro-environmental behaviour: Role of talent engagement in hotel industry of Pakistan. *International Journal of Business and Management Sciences, 4*(2), 48–67.
27. Wang, M. (2020). Applying internet information technology combined with deep learning to tourism collaborative recommendation system. *PLoS One, 15*(12), e0240656.
28. Li, J. J., Bonn, M. A., & Ye, B. H. (2019). Hotel employee's artificial intelligence and robotics awareness and its impact on turnover intention: The moderating roles of perceived organizational support and competitive psychological climate. *Tourism Management, 73*, 172–181.
29. Nan, X., & Wang, X. (2022). Design and implementation of a personalized tourism recommendation system based on the data mining and collaborative filtering algorithm. *Computational Intelligence and Neuroscience, 2022*, Article ID 1234567.
30. Liu, Y., & Zhang, N. (2021). Study of hotel AI application and development trends in 5G era. In *2021 4th International Conference on Advanced Electronic Materials, Computers and Software Engineering (AEMCSE)* (pp. 1051–1054). IEEE.
31. Pereira, V., Silva, G. M., & Dias, Á. (2021). Sustainability practices in hospitality: Case study of a luxury hotel in Arrábida Natural Park. *Sustainability, 13*(6), 3164.
32. Memili, E., Fang, H. C., Koc, B., Yildirim-Öktem, Ö., & Sonmez, S. (2018). Sustainability practices of family firms: The interplay between family ownership and long-term orientation. *Journal of Sustainable Tourism, 26*(1), 9–28.
33. Shah, S. H. A., Jamshed, K. A., Saleem, S., Bashir, M., & Kiani, O. I. (2022). Sustainable development in the hospitality industry of Europe: Role of green HRM practices. In *Sustainable Development of Human Resources in a Globalization Period* (pp. 49–67). IGI Global.
34. Carlsen, J., Getz, D., & Ali-Knight, J. (2001). The environmental attitudes and practices of family businesses in the rural tourism and hospitality sectors. *Journal of Sustainable Tourism, 9*(4), 281–297.
35. Ferràs, X., Hitchen, E. L., Tarrats-Pons, E., & Arimany-Serrat, N. (2020). Smart tourism empowered by artificial intelligence: The case of Lanzarote. *Journal of Cases on information Technology (JCIT), 22*(1), 1–13.

CHAPTER 6

Impact of Artificial Intelligence on E-Learning and Technology Education: Nexus of Technostress and Perceived Danger in E-Learning

FIZZA ASIF,[1] KAMRAN JAMSHED,[1,*] RABIA KISHWER,[2] MUHAMMAD NOUMAN,[3] and FAIZA LIAQAT[3]

[1]*University of Chieti-Pescara, Chieti, Italy*

[2]*Ulster University, London, United Kingdom*

[3]*LUISS Guido Carli University, Rome, Italy*

*Corresponding author

ABSTRACT

Artificial Intelligence (AI) has significantly impacted various sectors, including education, particularly e-learning. AI technologies, such as machine learning, natural language processing models, and data analytics, enhance the educational experience through personalized learning, adaptive assessment, automation of administrative tasks, chatbots, and predictive analytics. However, the integration of AI introduces technostress, a psychological discomfort caused by technology use. Technostress can arise from rapid technological changes, increased screen time, privacy concerns, and fear of job displacement. Ethical considerations are crucial for responsible use of AI in learning environments. Understanding the challenges faced by educators and students can help develop support systems and resources. This chapter will add more knowledge in literature on balancing technological progress and technostress which are essential

Embracing the AI Frontier: Perspectives on Business and Organizational Development. Mihir Joshiand and Mohsen Brahmi (Eds.)

DOI: 10.1201/9781779641311-6

for devising strategies to mitigate its impact and enhance the learning experience. The study examines the impact of AI on e-learning and technology education, highlighting its potential for enhancing accessibility and personalization but also raising ethical concerns about data privacy and application. It suggests that AI integration can lead to skewed data, biased learning paths, and misuse of student information, necessitating collaboration among educators, technologists, policymakers, and students.

6.1 INTRODUCTION

The rapidly expanding field of study that is emerging at the convergence of e-learning and artificial intelligence (AI) in the field of technology education is marked by its rapid growth and significant implications for instructional tactics, student engagement, and academic outcomes. With a particular emphasis on the nuances of technostress and the perceived dangers associated with the incorporation of AI technologies into educational settings, the purpose of this qualitative study is to investigate the myriad of implications that AI has on online learning and technology education. The growing use of AI in educational settings presents both unprecedented opportunities for individualized learning and challenges regarding the digital welfare of children. It is difficult to overstate the significance of this topic because of the interplay between these two factors. Within the context of artificial intelligence-enhanced e-learning, the concept of technostress, which is a word used to characterize the stress that individuals experience when utilizing technology, emerges as a crucial topic of concern. There is a possibility that instructors and students will experience increasing levels of worry and tension because of the demand to adapt to sophisticated platforms driven by AI and the quick speed of technological breakthroughs.

The purpose of this study is to examine the existing literature to determine the degree to which AI in online learning settings contributes to the phenomenon of technostress. In addition to this, it will investigate the elements that contribute to the severity of this problem as well as the potential solutions that can lessen the impact of its negative consequences. This study also includes a large component that focuses on the perceived dangers of e-learning, which includes concerns over the privacy of data, the ethical application of artificial intelligence, and related issues.

A growing number of people are expressing concerns regarding the security of personal information and the possibility of technology being abused, as artificial intelligence systems are getting more and more adept at personalizing learning experiences through data analysis. By conducting an analysis of the trade-off between the advantages of AI in education and the necessity of safeguarding people's rights and welfare in digital learning environments, the purpose of this qualitative study is to shed light on these concerns and provide some insight into the situation. The purpose of this study is to provide an in-depth discussion of the impact that AI has had on e-learning and technology education by utilizing a comprehensive analysis of the literature. The importance of technostress and perceived threat will be highlighted throughout the course of this discussion. The purpose of this research is to provide valuable insights into the ways in which AI technologies can be effectively integrated into educational settings. This will ensure that the development of e-learning environments is both innovative and inclusive, while also addressing the challenges that are posed by the digital age.

6.2 NATURAL LANGUAGE PROCESSING (NLP) MODELS AND EDUCATION

The incorporation of NLP models into the educational ecosystem has been met with a selection of responses from various individuals. Others raise concerns about the ethical implications and the issues that could arise from the situation, even though many people see immense promise for life-changing educational opportunities. NLP is a subfield of artificial intelligence that comprises a wide variety of language-related activities that are difficult, advanced, and demanding. Some examples of these tasks include summarization, machine translation, and answering inquiries. Creating computers that can interpret and comprehend human languages is the objective of this subfield of AI. The beginnings of natural language processing may be traced back to the 1950s, when the first investigations involved the use of rule-based processes. In the 1990s, extensive data sets made statistical learning approaches suitable for natural language processing applications [1]. To handle problems that occur in the real world with language understanding, it is necessary to develop models, methodologies, and algorithms and then put them into utilization. It has been possible for natural language processing to make quick progress in fields such as machine translation, question answering, and machine reading comprehension over the course of the previous five years thanks to deep learning and a large amount of data that is both annotated and unannotated. Through the analysis of student writing and voice, natural language processing models can tailor feedback and instruction to the specific needs and preferences of each individual student [2].

Learners can immerse themselves in natural discussions and receive feedback with the use of NLP techniques. To provide teachers with automated grading and feedback that is more targeted, natural language processing models may be employed to evaluate written responses and essays. Because of this, teachers can spend more time with each kid on an individual basis [2, 3]. Techniques from the field of deep learning, including transformer models, recurrent neural networks, and convolutional neural networks, are utilized by the most advanced natural language processing models. Using these techniques, the capacity of machines to interpret and synthesize human language from enormous amounts of textual input is significantly improved. In order to enhance accessibility, personalize training, and enhance learning experiences, NLP models are utilized in the field of technology education and e-learning. Personalized learning, automatic grading, content summarization, language translation, voice-activated learning, intelligent tutoring systems, accessibility enhancements, sentiment analysis for feedback, chatbots, and virtual assistants are some of the most important applications of this technology.

These models contribute to more successful training because they take into consideration the preferences, styles, and speeds of individual students at the time of instruction. In addition, NLP assists with real-time language translation, which makes educational content accessible to a larger audience. The introduction of NLP models into e-learning and technology education results in the creation of learning environments that are more inviting, productive, and interesting to students. NLP models significantly enhance educational experiences while simultaneously enhancing the efficiency and effectiveness of learning. This is accomplished through the customization of learning systems, which adapt both content and evaluations to meet the specific requirements of each individual learner [4]. It has been demonstrated to be beneficial in increasing students' reading and writing proficiency, encouraging students to revise their essays, and improving the style of general writers. There is still some disagreement on whether it can be applied to other fields, such as reading, writing, and motivation. Writing NLP solutions can provide useful advice on grammar, prose, and other aspects of writing mechanics. NLP is a helpful tool for educators to employ to monitor the cognitive growth of their students and provide recommendations for further development. NLP can also be used to assist in the process of providing challenging reading to students, which will result in increased productivity. With the help of NLP technologies, businesses can grade the reading scores of students with greater precision than they can with traditional formulas. In addition, NLP can be utilized in the field of behavior modification and motivation.

The language that is used by both students and teachers in the classroom can be evaluated using machine learning technology to gain an understanding of the mental states that are being experienced by both parties. This provides educators with a better understanding of how their students react to various pedagogical approaches and methodologies for enhancing student engagement. Monitoring tools for NLP can be utilized in the classroom to keep an eye on the behavior and attention spans of pupils. The use of stealth testing can be required in order to obtain reliable results. When providing services to businesses, it is possible that it will be essential to take rules into consideration. When everything is taken into consideration, natural language processing technology offers a multitude of opportunities to improve learning. These opportunities include evaluating complex student behavior, providing professors and students with immediate feedback on the quality of their work, and improving learning environments as a whole. By providing instant feedback on pronunciation, grammar, and vocabulary, NLP quickens the process of language acquisition in the field of language education. This is accomplished using technologies that simulate real-life conversations [5].

In addition, automatic essay scoring systems that are powered by NLP offer fast feedback on writing, which enables learners to make improvements more quickly and assists teachers in managing their workload [6]. In the process of education, NLP aids both instructors and students by assisting with the efficient organization and analysis of educational content, reorganizing the production of study materials, and enabling the generation of quizzes from textual content [7]. By making educational resources more accessible to students with disabilities, NLP technologies, such as text-to-speech and speech-to-text, ensure that students with disabilities are included in learning opportunities [8]. Teachers can also benefit from NLP since it helps them detect areas of misunderstanding in student interactions and assignments. This allows for the implementation of individualized instructional strategies that are tailored to match the specific educational requirements of each student [9]. When managing student data for NLP model training, it is important to exercise caution and take ethical considerations into account to preserve the privacy and security of students. Although neuro-linguistic programming (NLP) has the potential to improve language fluency, there are concerns that it may not be able to sufficiently foster creative thinking and improve critical thinking skills [10].

Even though tools powered by NLP can enhance and supplement instructional methods, some education professionals are concerned that these technologies could eventually replace their professions. The educational sector has reaped significant benefits from the unique approaches to teaching, learning, and evaluation that have been brought about by the implementation of NLP principles. With neuro-linguistic programming, educators are exposed to novel ways that enhance both communication and personal development. This approach not only enhances the outcomes of education but also introduces new ideas and streamlines the academic process. It also gives educators the opportunity to employ "modeling" as a distinctive way of instruction [11]. Furthermore, NLP tools play a significant role in the assessment and evaluation of students' competencies, particularly in the field of STEM education [12]. This is because these tools provide more individualized feedback on communication skills and insights into the effectiveness of learning processes. In addition to assisting in the reduction of evaluation biases and boosting the sense of assessment validity and reliability, these technologies also assist students in becoming more proficient in digital literacy [13].

NLP is utilized in a wide range of educational settings to help in the process of developing, analyzing, and evaluating educational content. This versatility makes NLP an adaptable tool for enhancing both teaching and learning [14]. Consequently, the implementation of NLP models in educational settings constitutes a significant step forward in the modernization of educational procedures, the development of practical evaluation strategies, and the promotion of the development of critical skills that are applicable to the digital age. The educational environment's reaction to NLP models is dynamic and constantly shifting, and it is constantly evolving. There are several practical and ethical concerns that need to be carefully explored, even though the idea of automating activities, boosting accessibility, and personalizing learning is appealing [15]. To successfully traverse this complex environment, it is necessary to have open communication, to collaborate between educators and technologists, and to use strategies that are responsible and place the welfare of students and learning objectives at the forefront. It is possible for a variety of answers and difficulties to emerge, depending on the type of NLP model, the implementation approach, and the educational environment [16]. It is vital to engage in continuous research and development to resolve ethical difficulties and ensure that NLP models are applied in an appropriate manner and with effectiveness in the educational setting. It is of the utmost importance that teachers participate in continual professional development to guarantee that they have the knowledge and skills necessary to effectively implement NLP models in their classrooms.

6.3 NATURAL LANGUAGE PROCESSING (NLP) AND CHATBOTS

NLP is an effective teaching strategy that improves learning through natural acquisition, tackles a variety of problems in a range of contexts, including social and cultural ones, and is widely incorporated into educational settings to support successful learning in colleges, universities, and higher education [17]. Chatbots, also known as conversational agents, are computer programs that are designed to simulate human-user dialogue. This is accomplished through the utilization of NLP, which allows them to grasp human speech and reply appropriately. These virtual assistants are accessible through a range of channels, including social media and online applications, and they provide services using conversational user interfaces [18]. Other outlets include the internet. Significant progress has been made in the field of chatbots ever since they were first introduced in the 1960s. The deployment of open-source code, development platforms, and Software as a Service (SaaS) has made them more accessible to a wider audience and easier to use. Even though their ability to spread false information or carry out cyber-attacks creates ethical concerns, their applications range from enhancing the experiences of consumers to aiding with educational endeavors [19].

Chatbots that are powered by natural language processing can help around the clock, answering questions, clearing up misunderstandings, and guiding students through academic courses [20]. To replicate human conversation with customers, these chatbots make use of sophisticated AI algorithms. They can interpret both spoken and written language [21]. As a result of natural language processing, these chatbots can absorb user inputs, comprehend context and intent, and generate responses that are comprehensible (NLP). It is vital to have this technology to create chatbots that can interact with various applications in an effective manner. Some examples of these applications are instructional help and customer service. Increasing accessibility and encouraging inclusion for students with impairments can be accomplished using text-to-speech and speech-to-text technologies. Developing critical thinking and interpersonal skills may be hampered by an excessive dependence on technologies powered by NLP. Due to the lack of transparency in the decision-making process of NLP models, concerns have been raised regarding the unfairness and bias of automated evaluations and feedback [22]. NLP models have shown a great deal of reliability in a variety of applications; however, the level of reliability of the models can be affected by several factors, including the specific task at hand, the quality and quantity of the training data, and the algorithms that are used.

Activities such as information extraction, sentiment analysis, and language translation are all areas in which natural language processing models do exceedingly well. It is remarkable that they have achieved such a high level of accuracy, frequently approaching, or even surpassing human performance in certain categories [23]. A considerable influence on the reliability of natural language processing models is exerted by the quality and variety of the datasets that are used for training. To train models that are more reliable and less biased, it is common practice to employ datasets that are both large-scale and diverse. Despite the progress that has been made in the field, natural language processing models occasionally struggle to understand sarcasm, context, and sophisticated language. Because of this, there is a possibility that reliability will be affected, particularly in situations that need a comprehensive knowledge or interpretation of material [24]. NLP models have been the subject of worries regarding bias for a considerable amount of time since they have the potential to unintentionally reinforce or exaggerate biases that are present in their training set. To find solutions to these issues, more ethical developments in artificial intelligence are being implemented [25]. The field of NLP is undergoing rapid development, and new models and methods are being developed on a regular basis to improve its application, efficiency, and reliability across a wide range of languages and topics.

6.4 ARTIFICIAL INTELLIGENCE (AI) AND E-LEARNING

The field of education, particularly online learning, has been profoundly impacted by AI, which has had a significant impact on a variety of businesses. Machine learning, natural language processing models, and data analytics are examples of AI technologies that can improve the educational experience. These technologies automate administrative processes, provide personalized learning, adaptive assessment, chatbots for assistance, and predictive analytics. Traditional classroom instruction has the potential to be revolutionized by technologies such as artificial intelligence, data science, multimodal learning analytics, eye tracking, and others. These technologies could enhance student accomplishment, engagement, and collaboration [26]. Streamlining classes, encouraging collaboration, and boosting creative capacity in online learning are all ways in which artificial intelligence has the potential to affect computer thinking and abilities in higher vocational education [27]. Through the implementation of artificial intelligence in online education, it is possible to realize the goal of creating a society that is both egalitarian and inclusive, in which intelligent technologies coexist under control and for the benefit of individuals.

By influencing assessment, learning analytics, and student support, artificial intelligence has the potential to compromise students' right to privacy and to enhance the amount of surveillance that occurs in online learning environments. The incorporation of artificial intelligence, on the other hand, is accompanied by a psychological problem known as technostress, which is a result of the utilization of technology. There are several factors that could lead to technostress, including rapid technological breakthroughs, more screen time, concerns around privacy, and the fear of losing one's existing work. On the other hand, the perceived risks that relate to e-learning include a dependence on technology, a loss of personal connection, ethical concerns, and algorithms that are biased. It is vital to understand how artificial intelligence is influencing e-learning and technological education to comprehend the changes that are occurring in the educational landscape. The chapter provides information regarding the challenges that are posed by technostress, the way the educational system is tackling artificial intelligence, and the potential risks that are associated with e-learning. Developing strategies that strike a balance between the effects of technology innovation and the stress caused by it is necessary to lessen its impact and enhance the educational process. Ethical concerns need to be carefully considered to guarantee that artificial intelligence is employed in educational settings in a responsible manner.

Artificial intelligence has the potential to totally revolutionize educational practices and generate innovative solutions that will lead to enhanced learning results. If both teachers and students are aware of the challenges they face, it may be advantageous to make available resources and support networks. Long-term effects have the potential to impact decisions regarding the incorporation of AI into practices and curriculum. Furthermore, a nation's capacity to compete on an international level in the field of education can be improved by improving its awareness of potential risks, obstacles, and solutions [28]. To mitigate the impact of these challenges, a well-rounded approach is required. The following are essential components: continuous evaluation, stated ethical norms, hybrid models, and educator training. To add insult to injury, problems of prejudice, privacy, and data security can be addressed by defining explicit ethical norms for the application of artificial intelligence. Through the combination of AI-enhanced e-learning with more conventional instructional strategies, it is possible to preserve the benefits of technology while preserving the human connection [29]. Keeping a healthy learning environment needs routinely evaluating how artificial intelligence is affecting online education and finding solutions to emerging problems [30]. An enormous amount of disruption is being brought about in the field of technological education and online learning because of the increasing incorporation of AI [28].

Concerns concerning unintended repercussions, such as technical stress and even perceived risk, have surfaced in relation to AI, even though it promises to provide individualized training, flexible course design, and automated evaluation. To gain a deeper understanding of the complex link between the two, this qualitative study investigates the lived experiences of individuals who are participating in AI-augmented e-learning environments. Through the documentation of their diverse narratives and individual experiences, we seek to achieve a deeper comprehension of the multifaceted implications that artificial intelligence is having on the educational landscape that is undergoing transformation. This research is significant because it has the potential to provide light on the human aspect of online education that is driven by artificial intelligence. We can identify the potential benefits and challenges associated with this technology revolution by doing a study of the experiences that learners have had in their own lives. When all is said and done, our research has the potential to contribute to the development of more human-centered and effective strategies for integrating artificial intelligence into educational environments. This will ensure that technological advancements provide support for the learning process rather than hindering it. Concerns have been expressed over the potential risks associated with the incorporation of AI into e-learning systems. This is even though AI offers a significant potential to personalize learning and improve educational experiences [31]. It is possible for skewed data to reinforce and intensify inequity in the educational system.

AI systems can acquire knowledge from data. It is possible that this will lead to biased learning paths that reinforce preexisting views, unfair judgments, and unequal access to resources. When it comes to student information, e-learning systems collect massive amounts of data, and if they are not well safeguarded, this data could be compromised and used inappropriately [32]. Concerns have been raised regarding unauthorized access, the profiling of students, and the possibility of surveillance. When it comes to educating and evaluating students, placing an excessive amount of dependence on AI tools could potentially hinder the development of problem-solving, critical thinking, and independent learning skills. Students may develop an unhealthy dependence on technology and struggle to adapt to new learning environments if they are not properly prepared [33]. It is possible that AI will not be able to replace the social contact and emotional connection that are so essential to the development of a student, even though AI can provide fast feedback and customized learning.

6.5 OVERRELIANCE ON TECHNOLOGY

It has been suggested by Romero-López et al. [34] that an excessive reliance on technology can hinder the development of interpersonal skills and lead to feelings of isolation. Educators might be concerned that artificial intelligence would eventually take over their employment, particularly in terms of automated grading and personalized feedback. Even if artificial intelligence has the potential to enhance instructional strategies, it is essential to keep human-centered approaches at the forefront [35]. Several of the algorithms used in artificial intelligence are "black boxes," which may make it difficult to understand how they arrive at their conclusions. Because of this lack of transparency, there is a possibility that concerns over accountability and fairness in assessments and suggestions for personalized learning will emerge [36, 37]. There is a possibility that malevolent actors would utilize e-learning platforms that are driven by artificial intelligence to spread misleading information or influence students. To reduce the impact of such dangers, it is necessary to implement stringent safety precautions and ethical principles. There are certain people who do not have access to technology and internet connections that are reliable. It is possible that an excessive dependence on AI to power online education could exacerbate existing inequalities and prevent persons from disadvantaged backgrounds from gaining access to education of a high standard [38]. Concerns have been raised regarding the potential for certain AI-powered applications to cause "addiction" or to have a negative impact on the mental health of students, particularly in relation to gamification and the excessive use of data-based comparisons. It is imperative that the ethical implications of AI in the field of education be properly studied, with consideration given to problems of data ownership, responsible development, and the possibility of unanticipated consequences or outcomes [39, 40].

6.6 TECHNOSTRESS: THE NEW NORMAL FOR EDUCATORS AND LEARNERS?

Craig Brod, a clinical psychologist, identified technostress as a contemporary condition that is induced by information and communication technology in those who have difficulty overcoming problems in the year 1984 [41]. There is a correlation between negative emotions including scepticism, inefficiency, mental tiredness, stress, and technostress, according to studies that have indicated this connection [42]. Anxiety over using computers appears to have a significant influence on job overload due to the perceived importance of computers and the ease with which they may be used [43]. One of the negative cognitive, emotional, and physical reactions that can occur because of the usage of technology in the classroom is known as technostress. Inability to create limits, anxiety over data security, inability to manage assignments, heavy workload, and dissatisfaction with faulty technology and minimal technical help are all manifestations of this condition. They can also manifest themselves as an inability to manage tasks [44, 45]. The way in which people are affected by technostress is influenced by a variety of factors, including individual experiences, personality types, and the availability of resources; therefore, additional research is required to develop effective treatments.

A decrease in creative and critical thinking abilities, as well as job dissatisfaction and burnout, are all potential outcomes of technostress, which has an impact on psychological well-being [46, 47]. Some of the measures that can be taken to lessen its influence include the establishment of tech-free zones, the promotion of mindfulness and stress management, the utilization of technology that is user-friendly, the provision of professional development opportunities to educators, the instruction of digital literacy to students, and the encouragement of open communication [48, 49]. As technology continues to improve, it is very important to prioritize the well-being of people and to take precautionary steps.

6.7 ADAPTIVE LEARNING SYSTEMS (ALS)

ALS, which are a potentially beneficial educational tool, offer personalized learning experiences that are adjusted to the specific requirements and preferences of each individual student [50]. In addition, they have the potential to put education in jeopardy due to issues such as algorithmic bias, an excessive reliance on technology, concerns about teachers being replaced, a lack of social connection, black box issues, and concerns over data privacy. As an adjunct to teachers, ALS should be given top priority to achieve a compromise. It should also guarantee openness and explainability, protect student data, encourage social engagement and critical thinking, and consider the specific requirements and circumstances of everyone [38]. ALS has the potential to be a beneficial tool in the establishment of learning experiences that are both fair and attractive for all individuals, provided that due attention is given to both the benefits and the potential negatives [51]. It is necessary to conduct additional study and work together to improve ALS, address ethical concerns, and ensure that they are successfully integrated into a variety of educational settings.

Education professionals absolutely need to participate in continual professional development to acquire the skills and knowledge necessary to make effective use of ALS. Through the implementation of AI in educational settings, the learning process is undergoing a revolutionary transformation [52]. The paradigm of teaching and learning is shifting from being centered on the teacher to being centered on the learner because of the implementation of personalized learning, active learning, data-driven instruction, engaging experiences, critical thinking, lifelong learning, constant feedback, and an emphasis on mastery over grades [50, 53, 54]. On the other hand, ethical concerns must also be taken into consideration. The creation of policies for the use of artificial intelligence, the provision of the tools that teachers require to successfully incorporate AI, the guarantee that everyone has equal access to AI resources, and the promotion of creativity and human interaction in addition to AI are some of the things that fall under this category. In a world that is constantly evolving, it is necessary for instructional methods to undergo metamorphosis for this transformation to be successful.

6.8 THE ROLE OF TEACHERS IN THE AGE OF ARTIFICIAL INTELLIGENCE (AI)

Teachers are transitioning from being information distributors to informed mentors, advisors, and facilitators of customized learning journeys because of AI, which is transforming the roles that teachers play in the educational system [55]. By allowing AI systems to undertake routine tasks, teachers can devote their attention to addressing the special requirements and interests of individual pupils. By data, they provide insights that indicate areas of learning need and allow for the customization of training. Solutions that are powered by artificial intelligence offer quick feedback, which encourages a growth mindset and self-evaluation [56]. When traditional schooling transitioned to an online system, instructors encountered factors that contributed to technostress. As a result, their workload increased, but their computer self-efficacy allowed them to manage the situation. An emphasis is placed on the mastery of both ideas and skills when instructors transition from summative to formative evaluations. Using artificial intelligence, teachers may be able to facilitate group projects and free-flowing talks, as well as stimulate creative thinking and critical thinking [33].

However, it is vital to include professional development, equitable access to technology, and ethical frameworks for artificial intelligence technologies. The varied range of opportunities and challenges that comprise the student experience are a significant factor in determining both academic achievement and personal growth. The challenges include, but are not limited to, academic pressure, financial strain, social inclusion, mental health, and the ability to navigate technology [57, 58]. Developing one's passions, building connections, maturing both personally and academically, and acquiring a global perspective are all possibilities that can be pursued during this experience [59]. The gap can be closed, and students can be assisted in overcoming these challenges through the implementation of strategies such as providing financial assistance, providing mentorship, encouraging diversity, providing funding for mental health services, providing financial aid, putting in place accessible technology, and actively encouraging open communication. Recognizing the specific challenges and opportunities that children face is of the utmost importance, as is working together with students, teachers, and legislators to create an educational setting that is more empowering and helpful to children. AI is causing changes in education, which creates ethical concerns such as bias, data privacy, excessive reliance on technology, emotional alienation, and transparency.

These concerns are being raised because of the changes [60]. To ensure that artificial intelligence facilitates the empowerment of both instructors and students, it is essential to develop AI solutions that prioritize inclusivity, data security, and a human-centered approach. It is vital to put in place robust data governance structures, clear data gathering practices, and stringent security measures to accomplish this goal. In the development of artificial intelligence, there should be transparency, explicability, and adherence to ethical principles that are unequivocal [61]. Additionally, it is of the utmost importance to continually evaluate and improve the effects that AI has on learning outcomes, educational equity, and students. To encourage the right application of artificial intelligence in the classroom, it is essential that students, educators, engineers, and legislators participate in open communication with one another. It is also vital to conduct continual research and development to eliminate ethical problems and guarantee that developments in artificial intelligence are in accordance with egalitarian principles and educational values. The implementation of AI in several sectors, such as the financial sector, the healthcare industry, and the educational sector, may bring about opportunities for positive change [62]. It is necessary to address certain imagined hazards to ensure the safe and effective integration of AI. Important strategies include addressing issues of discrimination and fairness, ensuring that algorithms are transparent, having human oversight, and conducting audits on a regular basis [63]. Privacy and security are equally important, and they should be considered alongside strong data governance systems, encryption, and anonymization technologies.

The importance of cybersecurity training and awareness cannot be overstated. Using interpretable artificial intelligence models, decision-making processes can be described [64]. The provision of open forums for public discourse and discussion, in addition to the provision of clear information and education, is crucial. The development of human and technical capabilities occurs simultaneously. Collaboration between people and artificial intelligence is encouraged, with an emphasis placed on ethical principles. Having rules and ethical standards that are clear and unambiguous helps to create trust and responsibility. Continuous learning and improvement are essential, especially when there are frequent evaluations, comments, and investments in research and development. Stakeholder involvement is necessary for the development and integration of AI in a responsible manner. People need to be educated and informed of artificial intelligence for them to bring about a future that is both safe and moral.

6.8.1 SHAPING THE INTERSECTION OF ARTIFICIAL INTELLIGENCE (AI) AND EDUCATION

With potential benefits such as individualized instruction, instantaneous feedback, adaptable learning environments, AI-enabled teachers serving as mentors and facilitators, international collaboration, the reduction of the wealth gap, and opportunities for learning that continue throughout one's life, the future of artificial intelligence in education appears to be bright. Technologies based on artificial intelligence will make it feasible to translate languages, will accommodate a variety of learning preferences, and will provide experiences that are both inclusive and accessible [65]. On the other side, there are several ethical concerns regarding bias, privacy, security, mental health, and the preparation of teachers. Future advancements in technology, ethics, and research and development will be particularly important for the application of artificial intelligence in education. For fostering an open and fruitful dialogue and collaboration concerning the future of AI-powered education, educators, technologists, policymakers, and students all need to work together.

Putting human-centered principles such as empathy, creativity, and critical thinking at the forefront of education will be necessary to cultivate well-rounded individuals who are capable of effectively navigating the complexities of the future [66, 67]. Through the customization of learning paths based on the requirements, preferences, and interests of each individual learner, artificial intelligence is revolutionizing lifelong learning. According to Dwivedi et al. [30]; Díaz Redondo et al. [73], the platform offers customized content, adaptive platforms, and microlearning to guarantee continuous skill enhancement. Language translation technology powered by artificial intelligence makes education more inclusive and equitable by reducing barriers related to language [68]. Platforms that are powered by artificial intelligence offer highly interactive learning experiences, solutions that are flexible and economical, and individualized feedback. The artificial intelligence system does data analysis on the work market, provides individualized career coaching, and curates learning resources to support professional development throughout a lifetime [69]. On the other hand, there are difficulties that need to be addressed, such as ensuring equity, paying attention to human-centered design, and ethical concerns. Depending on factors such as human circumstances, technological advancements, and ongoing study, the influence of artificial intelligence on lifelong learning will vary. It is possible for students, educators, politicians, and tech developers to collaborate to ensure that AI-powered lifelong learning continues in a safe manner. A culture of lifelong learning, in which individuals are empowered and encouraged to continuously learn and adapt, is necessary to successfully navigate the problems that will be faced in the future.

6.9 IMPLICATIONS OF THE STUDY

Based on the findings extracted through the review of literature, this chapter can be helpful for educational industry experts who are either working or thinking of implementing AI-based solutions in education. While the introduction of online learning systems was formerly the main cause of technostress owing to increasing workload, the integration of AI in education has prompted several issues [70]. However, the introduction of AI-driven tools into the classroom has led to other issues with academic integrity, like plagiarism and cheating, and these issues raise ethical questions about responsible AI usage and data privacy. They emphasize the necessity for educational institutions to create guidelines and policies for the use of AI tools in the classroom [71]. This chapter highlights that even though the integration of AI in education offers several benefits to pupils (i.e., personalized learning, automatic grading, and enhanced accessibility), it also presents some challenges (i.e., biased learning mechanisms, unequal access to resources, and the possibility of data manipulation). Given these concerns, educators and policymakers should try to maintain a balance between the potential risks and benefits associated with the integration of AI in education. Thus, the need of the hour is the responsible use of AI, considering the ethical aspects while integrating AI in education. This requires collaboration among stakeholders, especially educators, students, and policymakers. Furthermore, the transition of education from traditional teaching methods to personalized teaching requires educators to deploy AI tools to enhance their teaching and learning experience. Educators should also ensure equal and fair distribution of AI resources in order to mitigate the barriers to learning. Continuous development of AI-based technological solutions in education is needed to address these challenges and, finally, the responsible use of AI in education.

6.10 CONCLUSION

Growing AI use in school offers individualized learning but raises digital welfare concerns. Technostress is the stress people experience when utilizing technology. This study examines the literature to evaluate its contribution, severity, and solutions. E-learning risks, including data privacy and ethical application, are addressed. The study seeks to reveal how AI may be integrated into education to create new and inclusive e-learning environments and handle digital age concerns. This research seeks to illuminate the conflict between AI's benefits and the necessity to protect people's rights and welfare in digital learning settings. This qualitative study examines technostress and perceived hazards in e-learning and technology education due to AI. NLP models in the educational ecosystem provide personalized learning, automatic grading, content summary, language translation, voice-activated learning, intelligent tutoring systems, accessibility advancements, sentiment analysis for feedback, chatbots, and virtual assistants [72]. Deep learning methods like transformer models, recurrent neural networks, and convolutional neural networks improve machines' ability to read and synthesize human language from vast textual input [73]. NLP models improve accessibility, personalization, and learning in technology education and e-learning. They promote pupils' reading and writing, revising, and writing style [74]. Its use in reading, writing, and motivation is still debated. By assessing complex student behavior, delivering fast feedback on task quality, and improving learning settings, NLP technology can increase learning. It helps organize and analyze instructional content, makes resources more accessible to students with impairments, and helps teachers spot misunderstandings in student interactions and tasks.

However, protecting student privacy and security requires caution and ethical thought while managing student data for NLP model training. NLP may increase language fluency, but its ability to stimulate creative and critical thinking is uncertain. NLP tools can improve and supplement instruction, but some educators worry they may replace their jobs. The use of NLP in school has enhanced communication, personal growth, and academic performance [75]. NLP techniques help assess students' competencies, especially in STEM education, by delivering individualized feedback on communication skills and learning efficacy. They improve kids' digital literacy. NLP is used to design, analyze, and evaluate educational content, making it a versatile tool for improving teaching and learning. However, educational responses to NLP models change over time. Open communication, educator-technologist collaboration, and responsible solutions are needed to traverse this complex environment. Computer programs called chatbots utilize natural language processing to simulate human-user dialogue (NLP). Virtual assistants can answer questions, resolve conflicts, and help students with academic courses 24/7. However, their ability to propagate misinformation or launch cyberattacks creates ethical considerations. NLP models are reliable in many applications, although task specificity, training data quality and quantity, and techniques might affect dependability [76]. NLP models can extract information, analyze sentiment, and translate language, but they may struggle with sarcasm, context, and complex language. Bias concerns arise because NLP models may unintentionally reinforce or magnify biases in their training set. More ethical AI innovations are being applied to address these challenges.

NLP is rapidly developing new models and ways to increase its application, efficiency, and dependability across languages and themes [77].

AI has greatly changed education, particularly online learning. Automating administrative operations, personalizing learning, adaptive assessment, and predictive analytics with machine learning, natural language processing models, and data analytics can improve education. AI can potentially boost online learning surveillance and threaten students' privacy [78]. Technology-related stress can result from rapid technological advancements, screen usage, privacy issues, and job loss. Responsible AI application in education requires rigorous ethical consideration [79]. Resources and support networks help teachers and students comprehend their issues. Continuous review stated ethical principles, hybrid models, and educator training are needed to address these issues. Training and mentoring in AI use can reduce technological stress and improve AI effectiveness. By defining AI ethics, discrimination, privacy, and data security can be addressed [79]. Combining AI-enhanced e-learning with traditional teaching methodologies preserves technology's benefits while keeping human connection. Maintaining a healthy learning environment requires regular monitoring of AI's impact on online education and problem-solving. E-learning systems using AI may lead to skewed data, biased learning paths, unequal resource access, and student data exploitation [80]. AI overuse can also hamper problem-solving, critical thinking, and autonomous learning. Unprepared students may become tech-dependent and difficult to adjust to new learning contexts. Technology addiction can increase isolation and inequality [81]. Some AI algorithms are "black boxes," making their results hard to grasp, raising questions about assessment accountability and fairness. AI-powered programs may promote "addiction" or harm students' mental health, especially gamification and data-based comparisons. Technostress, caused by information and communication technology, can cause cognitive, emotional, and physical problems include inability to set limits, data security worry, and task management issues. It can reduce creativity, critical thinking, job satisfaction, and burnout [82].

Technostress can be reduced by creating tech-free zones, encouraging mindfulness and stress management, employing user-friendly technology, giving professional development, educating digital literacy, and fostering open communication [17]. As technology advances, people's well-being must be prioritized, and threats mitigated. ALS provide personalized learning experiences, but algorithmic bias, excessive technology use, and instructor substitution raise ethical problems. For balance, ALS should promote openness, explainability, data protection, social participation, critical thinking, and individual situations. AI is reshaping education by moving the focus from instructor to student [83]. Teachers are becoming informed mentors, advisors, and facilitators of individualized learning journeys. AI algorithms identify learning gaps and customize instruction. However, ethical issues must be handled by defining AI policies, offering tools, assuring fair access to AI resources, and encouraging creativity and human connection. In the age of AI, teachers are becoming knowledgeable mentors, advisors, and facilitators of tailored learning journeys. Financial aid, mentorship, diversity, mental health financing, and open communication can help students overcome obstacles. To empower educators and students with AI, bias, data privacy, excessive technology use, emotional estrangement, and transparency must be addressed [84]. Strong data governance, transparent data collection, and strict security are essential. Continuous study and development are needed to eliminate ethical issues and ensure AI breakthroughs are egalitarian and enlightening. AI in finance, healthcare, and education may improve things.

Discrimination and fairness, transparency, human oversight, regular audits, privacy, and security, cybersecurity training, interpretable AI models, open forums for public discourse, collaboration between people and AI, and continuous learning and improvement are strategies for safe and effective AI integration. Responsible AI development and integration require stakeholder input [85]. AI will transform education by providing individualized training, instantaneous feedback, flexible learning environments, AI-enabled teachers, international collaboration, and wealth reduction [86–93]. Bias, privacy, security, mental health, and teacher preparation remain ethical issues. The success of AI-powered education depends on collaboration between educators, technologists, policymakers, and students. Empathy, creativity, and critical thinking are essential for well-rounded people. AI-powered platforms provide tailored information, adaptable platforms, and microlearning to improve skills. Data analysis, career coaching, and professional development resource curation are also offered by AI. However, equity, human-centered design, and ethics must be addressed. A lifelong learning culture is needed for future difficulties.

KEYWORDS

- **artificial intelligence**
- **chatbots**
- **data privacy**
- **digital disruption**
- **e-learning**
- **natural language processing (NLP) models**
- **personalized learning**
- **predictive analytics**
- **technology**
- **technostress**

REFERENCES

1. Zhou, M., Duan, N., Liu, S., & Shum, H. Y. (2020). Progress in neural NLP: Modelling, learning, and reasoning. *Engineering, 6*(3), 275–290.
2. Alqahtani, T., Badreldin, H. A., Alrashed, M., Alshaya, A. I., Alghamdi, S. S., bin Saleh, K., & Albekairy, A. M. (2023). The emergent role of artificial intelligence, natural learning processing, and large language models in higher education and research. *Research in Social and Administrative Pharmacy, 19*(8), 1236–1242.
3. Roche, C., Deinlein, N., Dawkins, D., & Javed, F. (2022). Using natural language processing to increase modularity and interpretability of automated essay evaluation and student feedback. *SMU Data Science Review, 6*(2), 1–22.
4. Otter, D., Medina, J., & Kalita, J. (2018). A survey of the usages of deep learning for natural language processing. *IEEE Transactions on Neural Networks and Learning Systems, 32*, 604–624.
5. Qiu, X., Sun, T., Xu, Y., Shao, Y., Dai, N., & Huang, X. (2020). Pre-trained models for natural language processing: A survey. *Science China Technological Sciences, 63*, 1872–1897.
6. Liu, P., Yuan, W., Fu, J., Jiang, Z., Hayashi, H., & Neubig, G. (2021). Pre-train, prompt, and predict: A systematic survey of prompting methods in natural language processing. *ACM Computing Surveys, 55*, 1–35.
7. Young, T., Hazarika, D., Poria, S., & Cambria, E. (2017). Recent trends in deep learning based natural language processing [Review Article]. *IEEE Computational Intelligence Magazine, 13*, 55–75.

8. Speier, W., Arnold, C., & Pouratian, N. (2016). Integrating language models into classifiers for BCI communication: A review. *Journal of Neural Engineering, 13*(3), 031002.
9. Kanaparthi, V. (2022). Examining natural language processing techniques in the education and healthcare fields. *International Journal of Engineering and Advanced Technology, 12*(2), 8–18.
10. Ray, P. P. (2023). ChatGPT: A comprehensive review on background, applications, key challenges, bias, ethics, limitations and future scope. *Internet of Things and Cyber-Physical Systems, 3*, 121–154.
11. Tosey, P., & Mathison, J. (2010). Neuro-linguistic programming as an innovation in education and teaching. *Innovations in Education and Teaching International, 47*, 317–326.
12. Rodriguez-Ruiz, J., Alvarez-Delgado, A., & Caratozzolo, P. (2021). Use of natural language processing (NLP) tools to assess digital literacy skills. In *2021 Machine Learning-Driven Digital Technologies for Educational Innovation Workshop* (pp. 1–8). IEEE.
13. Álvarez-Carmona, M. Á., Aranda, R., Rodríguez-Gonzalez, A. Y., Fajardo-Delgado, D., Sánchez, M. G., Pérez-Espinosa, H., & Díaz-Pacheco, Á. (2022). Natural language processing applied to tourism research: A systematic review and future research directions. *Journal of King Saud University–Computer and Information Sciences, 34*(10), 10125–10144.
14. Raj, S., & Paliwal, M. (2021). An analysis of application of natural language processing in enhancing education. *International Journal of Innovative Research in Computer Science & Technology, 9*(6), 184–187.
15. Abulibdeh, A., Zaidan, E., & Abulibdeh, R. (2024). Navigating the confluence of artificial intelligence and education for sustainable development in the era of Industry 4.0: Challenges, opportunities, and ethical dimensions. *Journal of Cleaner Production, 437*, 140527.
16. Kastrati, Z., Dalipi, F., Imran, A. S., Pireva Nuci, K., & Wani, M. A. (2021). Sentiment analysis of students' feedback with NLP and deep learning: A systematic mapping study. *Applied Sciences, 11*(9), 3986.
17. Alhawiti, K. M. (2014). Natural language processing and its use in education. *International Journal of Advanced Computer Science and Applications, 5*(12).
18. Pérez-Soler, S., Juarez-Puerta, S., Guerra, E., & Lara, J. D. (2021). Choosing a chatbot development tool. *IEEE Software, 38*(4), 94–103.
19. Radziwill, N., & Benton, M. (2017). Evaluating quality of chatbots and intelligent conversational agents. *arXiv*, abs/1704.04579.
20. Baha, T. A., El Hajji, M., Es-Saady, Y., & Fadili, H. (2023). The impact of educational chatbot on student learning experience. *Education and Information Technologies*, Advance online publication, 1–24.
21. Chaves, A. P., & Gerosa, M. A. (2021). How should my chatbot interact? A survey on social characteristics in human–chatbot interaction design. *International Journal of Human–Computer Interaction, 37*(8), 729–758.
22. Cobbe, J., Lee, M. S. A., & Singh, J. (2021). Reviewable automated decision-making: A framework for accountable algorithmic systems. In *Proceedings of the 2021 ACM Conference on Fairness, Accountability, and Transparency* (pp. 598–609).

23. Branco, R., Branco, A., Rodrigues, J., & Silva, J. (2021). Shortcutted commonsense: Data spuriousness in deep learning of commonsense reasoning. In *Proceedings of the 2021 Conference on Empirical Methods in Natural Language Processing* (pp. 1504–1521).
24. Roumeliotis, K. I., & Tselikas, N. D. (2023). ChatGPT and Open-AI models: A preliminary review. *Future Internet, 15*(6), 192.
25. Blodgett, S. L., Barocas, S., Daumé III, H., & Wallach, H. (2020). Language (technology) is power: A critical survey of "bias" in NLP. arXiv Preprint arXiv:2005.14050.
26. Ayyagari, R., Grover, V., & Purvis, R. (2011). Technostress: Technological antecedents and implications. *MIS Quarterly*, 831–858.
27. Hasan, R., Palaniappan, S., Mahmood, S., Shah, B., Abbas, A., & Sarker, K. U. (2019). Enhancing the Teaching and Learning Process Using Video Streaming Servers and Forecasting Techniques. *Sustainability*, *11*, 2049.
28. Pedro, F., Subosa, M., Rivas, A., & Valverde, P. (2019). *Artificial Intelligence in Education: Challenges and Opportunities for Sustainable Development*. United Nations Educational, Scientific and Cultural Organization.
29. Thakore, A. (2021). *AI Solution with Interactive Communication: AI-Enhanced Chat for Big Data in Education* (Doctoral dissertation, Colorado Technical University).
30. Dwivedi, Y. K., Hughes, L., Ismagilova, E., Aarts, G., Coombs, C., Crick, T., & Williams, M. D. (2021). Artificial intelligence (AI): Multidisciplinary perspectives on emerging challenges, opportunities, and agenda for research, practice and policy. *International Journal of Information Management, 57*, 101994.
31. Murtaza, M., Ahmed, Y., Shamsi, J. A., Sherwani, F., & Usman, M. (2022). AI-based personalized e-learning systems: Issues, challenges, and solutions. *IEEE Access, 10*, 81323–81342.
32. Paris, B., Reynolds, R., & McGowan, C. (2022). Sins of omission: Critical informatics perspectives on privacy in e-learning systems in higher education. *Journal of the Association for Information Science and Technology, 73*(5), 708–725.
33. Liu, M., Ren, Y., Nyagoga, L. M., Stonier, F., Wu, Z., & Yu, L. (2023). Future of education in the era of generative artificial intelligence: Consensus among Chinese scholars on applications of ChatGPT in schools. *Future in Educational Research, 1*(1), 72–101.
34. Romero-López, M., Pichardo, C., De Hoces, I., & García-Berbén, T. (2021). Problematic internet use among university students and its relationship with social skills. *Brain Sciences, 11*(10), 1301.
35. Grassini, S. (2023). Shaping the future of education: Exploring the potential and consequences of AI and ChatGPT in educational settings. *Education Sciences, 13*(7), 1–13.
36. Shin, D. (2020). User perceptions of algorithmic decisions in the personalized AI system: Perceptual evaluation of fairness, accountability, transparency, and explainability. *Journal of Broadcasting & Electronic Media, 64*(4), 541–565.
37. von Eschenbach, W. J. (2021). Transparency and the black box problem: Why we do not trust AI. *Philosophy & Technology, 34*(4), 1607–1622.
38. Smuha, N. A. (2022). Pitfalls and pathways for trustworthy artificial intelligence in education. In *The Ethics of Artificial Intelligence in Education* (pp. 113–145). Routledge.

39. Daniel, B. K. (2019). Big data and data science: A critical review of issues for educational research. *British Journal of Educational Technology, 50*(1), 101–113.
40. Patel, K. (2024). Ethical reflections on data-centric AI: Balancing benefits and risks. *International Journal of Artificial Intelligence Research and Development, 2*(1), 1–17.
41. Wang, Y., Liu, C., & Tu, Y. F. (2021). Factors affecting the adoption of AI-based applications in higher education. *Educational Technology & Society*, *24*(3), 116–129.
42. Ban, H., & Ning, J. (2021). Online English teaching based on artificial intelligence internet technology embedded system. *Mobile Information Systems*, *2021*(1), 2593656.
43. Yang, H., Goh, T. S., & Sormin, P. (2022). Computer anxiety and computer attitude in increasing staffs' interest in using the system through perceived usefulness and perceived ease of use. *Quantitative Economics and Management Studies, 3*(3), 298–309.
44. Atanasoff, L., & Venable, M. (2017). Technostress: Implications for adults in the workforce. *Career Development Quarterly, 65*, 326–338.
45. Nauta, C. A. (2020). *The Workload Impact of Technostress on the New Jersey School Nurse* (Doctoral dissertation, Kean University).
46. Wang, Q., & Yao, N. (2023). The impact of technostress creators on novice teachers' job satisfaction. *Journal of Education for Teaching, 49*(1), 104–119.
47. Alfalah, A. A. (2023). Factors influencing students' adoption and use of mobile learning management systems (m-LMSs): A quantitative study of Saudi Arabia. *International Journal of Information Management Data Insights, 3*(1), 100143.
48. Tagurum, Y., Okonoda, K., Miner, C., Bello, D., & Tagurum, D. (2017). Effect of technostress on job performance and coping strategies among academic staff of a tertiary institution in north-central Nigeria. *International Journal of Biomedical Research, 8*, 312–319.
49. Tarafdar, M., Pirkkalainen, H., Salo, M., & Makkonen, M. (2020). Taking on the "dark side"–Coping with technostress. *IT Professional, 22*(6), 82–89.
50. Gao, Y. (2023). *The Potential of Adaptive Learning Systems to Enhance Learning Outcomes: A Meta-Analysis* (Doctoral dissertation).
51. Linn, M. C., Donnelly-Hermosillo, D., & Gerard, L. (2023). Synergies between learning technologies and learning sciences: Promoting equitable secondary school teaching. In *Handbook of Research on Science Education* (pp. 447–498). Routledge.
52. Ahmad, S. F., Rahmat, M. K., Mubarik, M. S., Alam, M. M., & Hyder, S. I. (2021). Artificial intelligence and its role in education. *Sustainability, 13*(22), 12902.
53. Chen, L., Chen, P., & Lin, Z. (2020). Artificial intelligence in education: A review. *IEEE Access, 8*, 75264–75278.
54. Yang, W. (2022). Artificial intelligence education for young children: Why, what, and how in curriculum design and implementation. *Computers and Education: Artificial Intelligence, 3*, 100061.
55. Tenon, S. R., & Epler, P. (2020). *Evaluation of Principles and Best Practices in Personalized Learning*. IGI Global.
56. Porter, B., & Grippa, F. (2020). A platform for AI-enabled real-time feedback to promote digital collaboration. *Sustainability, 12*(24), 10243.

57. Joshi, M., & Brahmi, M. S. (2023). A mediation-based analysis of emotional intelligence effect on cognition and consumer decision-making. *International Journal of Public Sector Performance Management, 12*(1, 2), 223–251.
58. Joshi, M. (2023). A qualitative assessment of inter-organizational networks, organizational ecosystems, and joint venture associations. In *Exploring Business Ecosystems and Innovation Capacity Building in Global Economics* (pp. 1–25). IGI Global.
59. Joshi, M., Joshi, G., & Pathak, S. (2020). Awareness, entrepreneurial event theory and theory of planned behaviour as antecedents of student entrepreneurial intentions: An Indian perspective. *International Journal of Business and Globalization, 25*(2), 170–184.
60. Joshi, M. (2018). Workforce trends and challenges: A peek into the future. In *Management Techniques for a Diverse and Cross-Cultural Workforce* (pp. 39–53).
61. Dawar, G., Singh, S., Joshi, M., & Kumar, P. (2021). Effective corporate social responsibility in small and medium enterprises. In *Organizing Entrepreneurship and MSMEs Across India* (pp. 231–246).
62. Esposito, L., Brahmi, M., & Joshi, M. (2023). The importance of innovation diffusion in the renewable energy sector. In *Exploring Business Ecosystems and Innovation Capacity Building in Global Economics* (pp. 283–302). IGI Global.
63. Zhai, Y., & Du, X. (2020). Addressing collegiate mental health amid COVID-19 pandemic. *Psychiatry Research, 288*, 113003.
64. Priestley, M., Hall, A., Wilbraham, S., Mistry, V., Hughes, G., & Spanner, L. (2022). Student perceptions and proposals for promoting wellbeing through social relationships at university. *Journal of Further and Higher Education, 46*, 1243–1256.
65. Guzzardo, M. T., Khosla, N., Adams, A. L., Bussmann, J. D., Engelman, A., Ingraham, N., & Taylor, S. (2021). "The ones that care make all the difference": Perspectives on student-faculty relationships. *Innovative Higher Education, 46*(1), 41–58.
66. Le-Nguyen, H. T., & Tran, T. T. (2024). Generative AI in terms of its ethical problems for both teachers and learners: Striking a balance. In *Generative AI in Teaching and Learning* (pp. 144–173). IGI Global.
67. Phillips, P. J., Hahn, C. A., Fontana, P. C., Broniatowski, D. A., & Przybocki, M. A. (2020). Four principles of explainable artificial. *NIST Interagency/Internal Report (NISTIR)*. Gaithersburg, MD: National Institute of Standards and Technology.
68. Simbeck, K. (2023). They shall be fair, transparent, and robust: Auditing learning analytics systems. *AI and Ethics*, Advance online publication, 1–17.
69. Hassija, V., Chamola, V., Mahapatra, A., Singal, A., Goel, D., Huang, K., & Hussain, A. (2024). Interpreting black-box models: A review on explainable artificial intelligence. *Cognitive Computation, 16*(1), 45–74.
70. Rane, N. (2023). Enhancing mathematical capabilities through ChatGPT and similar generative artificial intelligence: Roles and challenges in solving mathematical problems.
71. Skowronek, M., Gilberti, R. M., Petro, M., Sancomb, C., Maddern, S., & Jankovic, J. (2022). Inclusive STEAM education in diverse disciplines of sustainable energy and AI. *Energy and AI, 7*, 100124.

72. George, A. S. (2023). Preparing students for an AI-driven world: Rethinking curriculum and pedagogy in the age of artificial intelligence. *Partners Universal Innovative Research Publication, 1*(2), 112–136.
73. Díaz Redondo, R. P., Caeiro Rodríguez, M., López Escobar, J. J., & Fernández Vilas, A. (2021). Integrating micro-learning content in traditional e-learning platforms. *Multimedia Tools and Applications, 80*, 3121–3151.
74. Gupta, S., Gupta, M., & Gupta, S. B. (2023). Analysis of AI-enhanced educational tools developed in India for linguistic minorities and disabled people. *Life Span & Disability, 26*(2), 221–243.
75. Tavakoli, M., Faraji, A., Vrolijk, J., Molavi, M., Mol, S. T., & Kismihók, G. (2022). An AI-based open recommender system for personalized labor market driven education. *Advanced Engineering Informatics, 52*, 101508.
76. Ali, S., Rubab, A., Jamshed, K., Sheikh, M. Z. A., Jamshaid, S., & Eman. (2023). Impact of techno stress on work engagement with mediating role of workload and moderating role of computer self-efficacy. *Journal of Xidian University, 17*(2), 515–540.
77. Rejeb, A., Rejeb, K., Appolloni, A., Treiblmaier, H., & Iranmanesh, M. (2024). Exploring the impact of ChatGPT on education: A web mining and machine learning approach. *The International Journal of Management Education, 22*(1), 100932.
78. Muzurura, O., Mzikamwi, T., Rebanowako, T. G., & Mpini, D. (2023). Application of artificial intelligence for virtual teaching assistance (Case study: Introduction to Information Technology). *International Research Journal of Engineering and Technology (IRJET), 10*(9), 276–283.
79. Narayan, S., & Gardent, C. (2022). *Deep Learning Approaches to Text Production.* Springer Nature.
80. Huang, X., Zou, D., Cheng, G., Chen, X., & Xie, H. (2023). Trends, research issues and applications of artificial intelligence in language education. *Educational Technology & Society, 26*(1), 112–131.
81. Forman, N., Udvaros, J., & Avornicului, M. S. (2023). ChatGPT: A new study tool shaping the future for high school students. *International Journal of Advanced Natural Sciences and Engineering Researches, 5*(6), 95–102.
82. Shaik, T., Tao, X., Li, Y., Dann, C., McDonald, J., Redmond, P., & Galligan, L. (2022). A review of the trends and challenges in adopting natural language processing methods for education feedback analysis. *IEEE Access, 10*, 56720–56739.
83. Akgun, S., & Greenhow, C. (2022). Artificial intelligence in education: Addressing ethical challenges in K-12 settings. *AI and Ethics, 2*(3), 431–440.
84. Díaz-Rodríguez, N., Del Ser, J., Coeckelbergh, M., de Prado, M. L., Herrera-Viedma, E., & Herrera, F. (2023). Connecting the dots in trustworthy artificial intelligence: From AI principles, ethics, and key requirements to responsible AI systems and regulation. *Information Fusion, 99*, 101896.
85. Holmes, W., Iniesto, F., Anastopoulou, S., & Boticario, J. G. (2023). Stakeholder perspectives on the ethics of AI in distance-based higher education. *International Review of Research in Open and Distributed Learning, 24*(2), 96–117.
86. Holt, K. (2021). Commentary: Technology, power and inequalities–Achieving a humane approach to the digital divide–A commentary on Aboujaoude and Gega (2021). *Child and Adolescent Mental Health, 26*(4), 378–380.

87. Torre, G. L., Esposito, A., Sciarra, I., & Chiappetta, M. (2019). Definition, symptoms and risk of techno-stress: A systematic review. *International Archives of Occupational and Environmental Health, 92*, 13–35.
88. Nisafani, A. S., Kiely, G., & Mahony, C. (2020). Workers' technostress: A review of its causes, strains, inhibitors, and impacts. *Journal of Decision Systems, 29*(sup1), 243–258.
89. Timms, M. J. (2016). Letting artificial intelligence in education out of the box: Educational cobots and smart classrooms. *International Journal of Artificial Intelligence in Education, 26*, 701–712.
90. Ma, X., & Jiang, C. (2023). On the ethical risks of artificial intelligence applications in education and its avoidance strategies. *Journal of Education, Humanities and Social Sciences, 14*, 354–359.
91. Peters, D., Vold, K., Robinson, D., & Calvo, R. A. (2020). Responsible AI—Two frameworks for ethical design practice. *IEEE Transactions on Technology and Society, 1*(1), 34–47.
92. Zhai, X., Chu, X., Chai, C. S., Jong, M. S. Y., Istenic, A., Spector, M., & Li, Y. (2021). A review of artificial intelligence (AI) in education from 2010 to 2020. *Complexity, 2021*, 1–18.
93. Joshi, M. (2019). Burnout and stressors as influencers on work engagement among law enforcement agents in selected cities. In *Management Techniques for Employee Engagement in Contemporary Organizations* (pp. 268–283). IGI Global.

CHAPTER 7

Designing a Sustainable Tourism Development Model Based on Blockchain Technology Using a Meta-Synthesis Approach

ELAHE HOSSEINI,[1,*] SOGOL SHAHIDI,[2] BAHRAM RAHMANI,[2] and MOHSEN BRAHMI[3]

[1]*Department of Business Management, Faculty of Economics, Management and Accounting, Yazd University, Yazd, Iran*

[2]*Department of Tourism Marketing Management, Faculty of Management and Accounting, Allameh Tabataba'i University, Tehran, Iran*

[3]*Faculty of Economics and Management (FEM), University of Sfax, Sfax, Tunisia*

*Corresponding author

ABSTRACT

Considering the importance of sustainable tourism development based on blockchain technology, no model for sustainable tourism development based on blockchain technology has been presented so far. Therefore, this study aims to present a comprehensive and efficient model for sustainable tourism development based on blockchain technology, which has tried to include all factors affecting the sustainable tourism development model based on blockchain technology. For this purpose, the meta-synthesis method with a qualitative approach was employed. The research model was proposed after reviewing 41 research papers in blockchain technology

Embracing the AI Frontier: Perspectives on Business and Organizational Development. Mihir Joshiand and Mohsen Brahmi (Eds.)

DOI: 10.1201/9781779641311-7

and tourism, published between 2017 and 2023. According to the findings, blockchain technology can help achieve economic goals by increasing the number of tourists and distributing tourism revenue directly among the local community. In addition, it can help promote transparency and reduce corruption to facilitate the achievement of social objectives of sustainable tourism development in Iran.

7.1 INTRODUCTION

In 2019, the United Nations World Tourism Organization (UNWTO) reported that international tourists comprised 1460 million individuals, leading to an overall revenue of $1481 billion. Accordingly, international tourism contributed to 7% of the world trade and 28% of the world service trade. It can be concluded that, following oil and chemical products, international tourism plays a crucial part in the global economy. Meanwhile, we should consider the substantial impact of uncontrollable external factors in this regard [1]. The COVID-19 pandemic had a severe impact on global tourism in 2020, with a 65% decrease in international tourist arrivals during spring and summer compared to the same period in 2019. However, there were indications that international tourism revenue could potentially recover to around 60% of pre-pandemic levels. Despite the alterations caused by the coronavirus pandemic and emergence of new technologies (e.g., blockchain), tourism development is inevitable. The tourism industry is considered a significant component of global development, which has evolved with the advent of new technologies [2]. Sustainability assessment is therefore an increasingly important area of research in the field of tourism [3]. Hence, the development of the tourism industry is crucial, particularly for developing countries [4], because they are dealing with various challenges, including poverty, unemployment, limited financial resources, and single-product economic background [1]. Accordingly, the tourism industry always appreciates technological advancements for sustainable development [5]. Blockchain technology is regarded as a recent innovation with promising potential in tourism. It can revolutionize this industry, affect functional profitability, promote competition among tourism organizations, and reduce poverty among the local population [6]. Blockchain technology can have a substantial impact on the tourism industry by removing intermediaries [7].

The globalization and digitalization of tourism have created a need for efficient international payment systems. Blockchain technology and cryptocurrencies offer a solution by eliminating intermediaries, reducing transaction costs, and enhancing privacy and security. This makes them an attractive alternative to traditional currencies for tourists, providing a safer and more convenient way to conduct international transactions [2]. Moreover, blockchain can help resolve double spending and liquidity [8]. As a result, the tourism industry evaluates and implements blockchain technology [9]. Given the growing appeal to use blockchain technology by industries, governments (as one of the major stakeholders in tourism) are also attracted to this technology and are planning extensive policy-making in this regard [10]. Moreover, blockchain technology builds trust. Therefore, tourism practitioners have become inclined to use it because of removing intermediaries and increasing the local population's income [11], which results in the allocation of more efficient resources and the decrease in economic inequalities [12]. Besides, cryptocurrencies can be considered as an international currency to provide tourism services and products [2].

Iran, as a developing country in the Middle East, faces unique challenges in its tourism industry due to political, social, and cultural factors. These challenges include corruption, lack of transparency, and unequal distribution of wealth. Additionally, the existing restrictions on financial transactions in Iran are considered a critical obstacle to international tourism. To address these challenges and facilitate financial transactions despite international sanctions, it is recommended to utilize various services provided by digital currency systems [13]. European debt crises (ESDC) between 2010 and 2013, as well as banking crises in Cyprus in 2012, are considered two instances of why cryptocurrencies have been efficient and appealing [14]. Blockchain technology is an innovation in the present era; many practitioners have sought the extensive analysis and exploration of appropriate approaches to implement it in the tourism industry [13]. For instance, blockchain technology in the international market can lead to the establishment of small businesses and facilitation of payment procedures, which will enhance the country's face and brand promptly.

Despite the extensive research on blockchain and tourism, only a few studies have investigated the impact of blockchain technology on sustainable tourism development [6]. This highlights a critical research gap, which is even more dramatic in the Iranian context because there are very few conceptual, review, experimental, and applied studies in Iran. Moreover, there is no research on the relationship between sustainable tourism and blockchain technology. In spite of the growing prominence of blockchain technology, there is no particular national model and no comprehensive and unified model at the international level in this regard. Thus, the present study aims to bridge this gap by designing a blockchain-based model for sustainable tourism development. This model can help cover respective theoretical gaps and propose empirical strategies and approaches to deal with international tourism challenges. Consequently, Iran will move away from a single-product economy toward ultimate progress.

7.2 LITERATURE REVIEW

7.2.1 CRYPTOCURRENCY

According to Nakamoto [15], transactions in the cryptocurrency mechanism are distributed within a peer-to-peer platform. It is equipped with timestamps and diverse cryptographic protocols, which do not require the presence of an institution or third-party and avoid double spending. Cryptocurrency is regarded as digital money, where encryption algorithms determine the production and validity of the transaction. It functions independently of a central resource, which is considered the opposite of focused banking systems [16]. Cryptocurrency refers to digital money that is produced based on cryptographic principles within a decentralized distributed ledger [17]. Hence, fraud or manipulation would seem fairly impossible. Cryptic controllers rule out the need for central authorities, which manipulate the transactions and create intervening risks in monetary transactions [18]. Given these definitions, cryptocurrencies refer to digital money within a decentralized distribution network using various encryption techniques in production, distribution, and trading. The reliability of cryptocurrency and related transactions is confirmed by blockchain technology and the transaction parties. Therefore, it is not necessary to include any third-party review.

7.2.2 BLOCKCHAIN

Researchers proposed a documentation approach for digital documents using timestamps, connection techniques, and various encryption approaches. As a result, the exact date of creation and modification is saved independent from the document content, and it is only observable to the users if necessary [19]. This approach can be regarded as the primary blockchain technology technique [2]. Researchers and practitioners have presented different definitions for blockchain, which share some similarities. Nonetheless, there is no distinctive definition for blockchain due to its complexity and novelty. Blockchain, a decentralized protocol, is broadly considered to have a huge innovation potential in all fields [20]. Blockchain technology is a decentralized system that securely stores transaction data in blocks linked together in a chain. It ensures data integrity through encryption and consensus among network members. The sequential linking of blocks makes data modifications transparent and resistant to tampering. This shared ledger system enhances data security and integrity by distributing the latest version among network participants [21]. Moreover, Treiblmaier [2] asserted that blockchain is regarded as a set of complicated and interrelated technologies in the form of a system with the aim of actual sharing among network members. New data is added to the database using an integration protocol, and various encryption approaches are employed for the security of the data. Blockchain technology offers transparency, security, solidity, and accountability of the data. Hence, everyone can trust its mechanism easily.

7.2.3 SUSTAINABLE TOURISM DEVELOPMENT

Tourism refers to a set of activities conducted by people in a place that is not their permanent residence, and it takes between 24 hours and 12 consecutive months for them to achieve their non-commercial objectives. Tourism is regarded as a substantial economic growth resource and a key to enhanced GDP for many countries, particularly developing countries [22]. This industry is actually popular, and countries, communities, and local residents consider it to be a promising instrument to development [23]. The development of the tourism industry has been introduced in Iran's Development Plan. Given the influential prospect, it can lead to enhanced economic growth and a higher quality of life by proposing an appropriate scenario. Moreover, global sustainable development has been recognized as the critical plan of the United Nations by 2030 [24]. The tourism industry has been referred to as the driving force of the global economy, resulting in sustainable development around the world [25].

In fact, sustainable development is the ideal prospect as well as the objective goals of the tourism industry in the present century. Sustainable tourism refers to a new approach in tourism, which prioritizes the preservation of the ecosystem and cultural heritage, enhancement of community economy, and social development [26]. According to the United Nations Brundtland Committee, "sustainability" is defined as the harmony of social, economic, and environmental goals to attain welfare, given that future generations will not face limitations in achieving welfare. Sustainable development should meet the present needs without restricting future generations' potential to supply their demands [27]. The sustainable tourism literature has expanded in terms of volume and scope of research [28]. Given that countries, non-governmental international organizations, local communities, and environmental activists have defined sustainable tourism differently, hence, there is no integrated definition for this concept [29]. The primary objectives of sustainable tourism are maximizing the benefits and minimizing the unfavorable impacts [30]. Thus, it is regarded as a growing trend in the tourism industry as well as a crucial component of sustainability in the global economy [26].

7.2.4 BLOCKCHAIN TECHNOLOGY AND TOURISM

The globalization and digitalization of tourism have increased the need for cost-effective international transactions and user-friendly payment systems. Blockchain technology offers a solution by streamlining exchange processes, cutting costs, and enhancing privacy. It enables tourists to potentially transition away from traditional currencies, reducing reliance on local money, eliminating intermediaries, and boosting privacy levels [32]. In addition, blockchain technology is not solely confined to payment procedures; it also includes creating exclusive tokens for particular purposes [32]. The extant knowledge is limited in this regard. Among the significant tourism destinations in the world, different countries (e.g., Singapore, Tunisia, Senegal, Marshal Islands, Uruguay, United Arab Emirates, Iran, Canada, Britain, Norway, Sweden, China, and Thailand) are researching the implementation of the blockchain industry. Despite all [33] the scientific efforts in this area, the tourism industry has recently employed this technology [34]. Existing models of accepting blockchain technology are generic and do not take into account the inherent features of this technology, positive or negative consequences, and abrupt technological changes [32]. Blockchain is regarded as an appropriate incentive to encourage demands in regional tourism [33], which has various benefits and disadvantages for clients and investors [7], where the most significant advantage of this technology is the unique code for each token that prevents fraud. Blockchain technology is decentralized with no locus of control. Therefore, transactions are conducted between the holders of the tokens, which enhances the transaction pace and reduces the costs [11].

Blockchain implementation can be influential when the production procedure is complicated. In other words, if different sectors need to transfer assets, there is shared responsibility for the products, and it is necessary to apply an automated and real-time platform for transactions and processes [35]. On the other hand, tourism is considered a complex industry, comprising interrelated sectors that aim to provide a tourism experience as their ultimate product. Blockchain technology is now recognized as an efficient interactional framework for business collaboration because of the extensive access to the internet [36]. If companies implement transparency in their transactions and provide the information on the spot, investors will be able to make more comfortable and solid decisions. It is crucial in international investment, particularly tourism, because it can lead to attracting multi-national companies to a particular destination and more capital, increasing competitiveness in each sector, and improving the quality of services. Furthermore, there will be more efficient collaboration among complementary businesses in the tourism industry [37, 38]. Consequently, cryptocurrencies will be considered a new payment mode in tourism that results in timely and secure modern services [7]. In addition to cryptocurrencies, blockchain technology can influence tourism development from another perspective. It can revise the business models in tourism. This technology can lead to the automation of various business processes based on smart contracts [39], which facilitates modifications and evolutions in booking processes, supply-chain, tourist interactions, and service delivery [40]. Moreover, extant studies reveal the lack of ample local and international research in proposing sustainable tourism development models based on cryptocurrency technology. There is also no comprehensive model in this regard. Hence, this qualitative study can help enrich the related literature. The following section reviews and summarizes the results of similar studies (Table 7.1).

TABLE 7.1 The Summary and Categorization of Studies in Blockchain Technology and Tourism

Sl. No.	Method	Results	References
1	Systematic review	Blockchain is considered a nascent technology with various challenges while being accepted in the tourism industry; Some of the guidelines to deal with these challenges are achieving a collaborative approach among stakeholders, deepening academic research in this field, assessing more models of blockchain-based systems (BC), and developing relevant policies.	[10]
2	Thematic analysis	The blockchain platform changes business models in tourism and leads to safe transactions in this industry through the creation of a secure network.	[40]
3	Conceptual	Blockchain technology can deal with some challenges of sustainable tourism development. Potential benefits of blockchain to achieve this goal: strengthening the local economy, managing the food supply chain and reducing food waste, achieving the tourists' satisfaction and addressing awareness raising.	[66]
4	Questionnaire	Tourists have a positive attitude to cryptocurrency in facilitating booking and payments for travel products and services, transportation, entertainment programs, shopping, and restaurants.	[67]
5	Exploratory	Blockchain technology can contribute to the development of local tourism in China by increasing the transparency of tourists' spending, improving the user evaluation system, and facilitating the increase of the local community's income by enabling direct payments with cryptocurrencies.	[26]
6	Thematic analysis	The decentralized blockchain-based destination recommends experimental system that increases the pace of information distribution and can handle a wider variety of information from more members.	[68]
7	Interview	Blockchain is regarded a proper technology to remove intermediaries from the supply chain of the tourism industry as well as an instrument to prevent new them from entering this industry.	[7]
8	Questionnaire	There are diverse applications and disadvantages of cryptocurrencies in the tourism industry. This technology is complex and difficult for the end consumer to understand, and the media plays a large role in shaping public attitudes toward cryptocurrency-based transactions.	[68]
9	Case study	The unchangeable nature of the Bitcoin blockchain leads to an unprecedented progress in dealing with corruption in developing countries, such as the Republic of Moldova. Besides, it can contribute to reduction of poverty based on a more equitable distribution of income and with the help of the tourism industry.	[36]

Source: Authors' contribution.

7.3 EXPERIMENTAL METHODS AND MATERIALS

We employed the meta-synthesis approach on the existing studies to design the sustainable tourism development model because it helps us in achieving the strengths and weaknesses of the research [41]. The meta-synthesis approach results in an integrated combination of the findings of target studies along with researchers' perceptions, which is used to develop a conceptual framework [42]. We used Barroso and Sandelowski's [43] framework to implement the meta-synthesis approach, which includes seven steps (Figure 7.1):

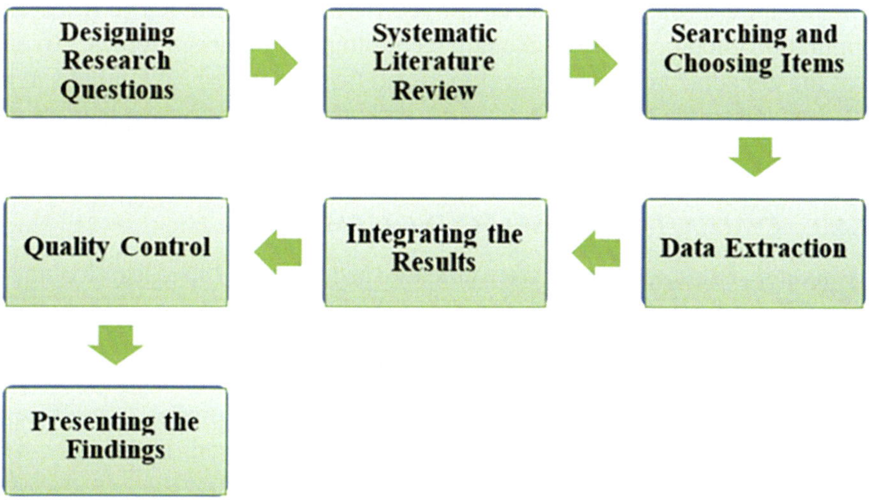

FIGURE 7.1 Framework the meta-synthesis approach.

Source: Reprinted with permission from Ref. [43]: Copyright © 2007 Wiley Periodicals, Inc.

7.4 RESULTS

The process of conducting this research was carried out with the meta-synthesis approach in seven stages, as follows:

7.4.1 DEVELOPING THE RESEARCH QUESTION

The papers published in scientific databases and reliable journals have been reviewed according to the strategies presented in Table 7.2.

TABLE 7.2 Research Strategy for Systematic Review of Published Papers

Sl. No.	Question	Response
1	What?	The impact of blockchain on the sustainable tourism development
2	Study population	Published papers in the Web of Science and Scopus journals
3	Time span	2017–2023
4	Data collection method	Content analysis of secondary information

Source: Authors' contribution.

7.4.2 SYSTEMATIC REVIEW OF THE LITERATURE

The library approach has been employed for data collection. The research population encompasses blockchain technology and tourism topics. Given that the concepts are newly developed and the literature is available since 2017, we used the terms "blockchain" and "tourism" to look up papers in Google Scholar. Finally, 124 papers were extracted from 2017 to 2023.

7.4.3 EVALUATING AND SELECTING ITEMS

In this step, extracted papers were assessed according to the research objectives. Given the few numbers of related studies, sampling was conducted along with the extraction process. All the unofficial transcripts, including review studies, reports, theses, book reviews, and so forth, were removed from the study population to improve the quality of the model. In addition, papers that were not published in English were removed. Eventually, 41 papers were selected for the meta-synthesis.

7.4.4 DATA EXTRACTION

The selected papers were analyzed meticulously to identify key concepts and themes related to the research objectives. Finally, a three-step coding process (open, axial, and selective) was conducted to obtain ultimate components.

7.4.5 DATA SYNTHESIS

The target codes were extracted from the samples based on the answers to the questions presented in step (1). In this regard, papers were examined meticulously. Then, coding was performed manually using the researcher-made checklist. Table 7.3 represents the summary of the results of step (1) and the implementation of the data synthesis.

TABLE 7.3 Open (Primary) Coding

Sl. No.	Variable	Open Coding
1	Token	Learn and acquire mechanics. Players can also earn NFTs and Tokens while learning and earn different points and seasonal rewards.
2.		It leads to new opportunities for the tourism industry because of a reliable platform for travel companies and tourists. Blockchain technology is regarded as a platform with the potential to connect tourists and attractions using a reliable approach. It increases the trust between travel companies and users. In tourism supply and demand chain ecology, different participants can share a new decentralized point-to-point travel experience.
3	Supply Chain	Singapore Airlines adopts such technologies to track the status and location of passengers' properties, the identity of crew members and passengers, or contracts with other participants in the supply chain.
4	Security	Promoting security and preserving tourism information

Source: Authors' contribution.

Consequently, the obtained open (primary) codes with similar meaning or conceptualization were combined; then, the selected codes were defined. The summary of classification is presented in Table 7.4.

TABLE 7.4 The Classification of Selected Codes

Sl. No.	Theme	Selective Coding	References
1	Security	• Tokenization of identity confirmation • Evaluation of the content of the blockchain-based system proposed by the users • Preserve the security of the users' and tourism businesses' data • Preserving users' privacy • Tokenization of medical tourism patients' documents	[10, 36]
2	Transparency	• Transparency of financial records of blockchain-based tourism organizations • Transparency of tourism organizations' commercial contracts • Transparent interaction among tourism organizations • Increasing constructive competition and reducing unbalanced distribution of the information	[36]

TABLE 7.4 *(Continued)*

Sl. No.	Theme	Selective Coding	References
3	Trust	• Tourists' trust in the comments on tourism services • Facilitating and expediting the selection of tourism services • Tourists' trust in the tourism services • Reducing the risk of internationalization of tourism organizations based on the blockchain technology commercial interactions • Tourism organizations can attract more investors based on stakeholders' trust. • Higher reliability of C2C products	[22, 37]
4	Sustainable supply chain	• Immediate synchronization of reliable data • Higher transaction pace using smart contracts • Higher liquidity of tourism SMEs using smart contracts • Modification of tourism supply chain by removing conventional intermediaries • Facilitating the identification of fraud in tourism supply chain • Reducing corruption in tourism supply chain • Improving the profitability of tourism system • Increasing collaboration among members of tourism supply chai • Reducing wastes	[7, 10, 44]
5	Intermediaries	• Decentralized blockchain networks lead to the reduction of intermediaries in tourism supply chain. • Blockchain technology facilitates removal of intermediaries and tourism costs. • Reduction of tourism costs by the adoption of blockchain	[10, 11]
6	Removing poverty	• Increasing local populations' income by the adoption of cryptocurrencies and reducing poverty	[36]
7	Tracking	• Real-time tracking of tourists' luggage while traveling and reducing respective dissatisfaction • Preventing from double spending and overbooking • Credibility check and tracking artifacts in the museums • Tracking and screening availability of tourism services and product	[7, 10]
8	Token	• Tokenization of travel insurance • Tokenization of tickets for tourism attractions and events • Tokenization of travel itinerary • Tokenization of medical tourism patients' records to preserve security and privacy • Providing standardized and tokenized certificates	[9, 45]

TABLE 7.4 *(Continued)*

Sl. No.	Theme	Selective Coding	References
9	Policies	• Responding to concerns about tourists' privacy in the blockchain platform • Facilitating cryptocurrency exchange in different countries • Enacting legislations to preserve individual property in blockchain platform	[36]
10	Competitive advantage	• Cryptocurrency as the innovative payment method for tourism products and services • Tokenization as the innovative payment method for tourism products and services • Cryptocurrency as the incentive for the blockchain-based loyalty club platform for tourism organizations • Tokenization as the incentive for the blockchain-based loyalty club platform for tourism organizations • Tokenized tickets for tourism attractions and events as the incentive for the blockchain-based loyalty club platform for tourism organizations • Saving tourists' time by proposing tokenized travel packages to expedite the payment and identity review processes and incentives using smart contracts • Modifying the business models based on blockchain technology, develop infrastructures at the national, regional, local, and industrial levels • Reducing costs of currency exchange based on blockchain technology	[10, 38, 40]

Source: Authors' contribution.

7.4.6 QUALITY CONTROL

In addition to highlighting the significance of the extracted concept, it is crucial to investigate the reliability and validity of the research instrument. Previous studies have employed various methods to ensure the validity of the research, such as reviewing by the research team, conducting the research from different perspectives, reflecting the extant reality, comparing the results with other research findings in terms of conceptual and content relatedness, and reviewing by the researcher [46]. In the present study, we aimed to reflect on extant reality and compare the conceptual and content-based relationship with the findings of other studies to ensure the validity of the research. We proposed a model for sustainable tourism development based on blockchain technology by synthesizing previous studies on blockchain and tourism. The implementation of this model in the Iran context may lead to an increase in local population business revenue and reducing poverty among these people by removing intermediaries, which is consistent with the findings of another study by Erol et al. [33]. This platform will also help attain a competitive advantage and improve tourism services in Iran, which is in line with the findings of studies by Aghaei et al. [40] and Dadkhah et al. [47] Moreover, the results are consistent with Pilkington et al.'s [36] study highlighting the impact of blockchain technology on dealing with corruption. Eventually, the transparency and trust in the implementation of blockchain platform in the tourism industry in Iran will result in enhanced supply chain sustainability, which is in line with the findings of another research by Thees et al. [38].

7.4.7 EVALUATION OF THE FINDINGS

The sustainable tourism development reflects on three major objectives, including economic, social, and environmental domains [48]. Given the detrimental impacts of cryptocurrency mining (e.g., Bitcoin) as well as ecologic effects of different functions of the blockchain technology [49], there is no reliable data on the environmental impact of this technology in sustainable tourism development. Nevertheless, comprehensive investigation of target studies reveals the noticeable role of blockchain technology in ensuring social and economic objectives of sustainable tourism development [7, 36].

Blockchain can provide various types of competitive advantage for tourism businesses [40] and improve economic profitability in the industry [7]. Cryptocurrencies are considered the most recognized function of blockchain technology [2], which leads to varied payment modes in the tourism industry [50]. Therefore, tourists can use cryptocurrency to pay for their tourism services, such as accommodation, tours, and so forth. [2]. Cryptocurrency-based transactions are considered immutable, which provides high security and privacy in trades and reduces tourists' expenses by removing currency exchange rates for international currencies [7]. In addition, cryptocurrencies are used as payment incentives to loyal customers of tourism firms [51]. Tourism businesses can remove the intermediaries and reduce costs by using cryptocurrencies to conduct financial transactions [52].

Blockchain technology facilitates the development of new business models or the modification of existing models [40]. The implementation of blockchain technology in hotels and airlines rules out the double-spending process, leading to overbooking [53]. Supply management can be enhanced by employing blockchain technology in hotels and accommodation service centers on an appropriately adequate scale. It also helps reduce extra costs and dissatisfaction [7, 10]. Different business sectors in the tourism industry can access the latest information required for the deployment of business transactions, collaborate on data among allies securely, and enhance trust in their transactions [7, 37, 54]. Moreover, with the expansion of the acceptance and implementation of blockchain technology, it is expected to observe modifications in the role of industry intermediaries [11]. Some researchers believe that blockchain technology will help provide different services irrespective of the presence of intermediaries. It can lead to the improvement of independence and reduction of business partner expenses [10, 55]. Meanwhile, other researchers claim that intermediaries will also comply with this technology and continue to grow in modern environments [11, 56]. Smart contracts based on blockchain technology can result in the automation of business processes, like paying employees, paying for services provided by other supply chain members in tourism, complying with business obligations, and so forth. [7, 40, 57].

The existing trust protocols in blockchain technology enable international financial supply in small and mid-size companies [5, 50]. Tourism firms can create an appropriate platform for tourists to share their opinions about tourism destinations and services. Besides, such information can help establish a recommender system, with acceptable accountability because the opinions are submitted using encryption protocol and blockchain's consensus [58]. In addition to the existing business products and processes, tourism companies can provide new products and services by implementing blockchain technology or follow business processes using different approaches. For instance, blockchain technology can result in loyalty programs for organizations [10]. Such communities can provide various incentives (in the form of non-fungible tokens and different cryptocurrencies) in response to customers' activities, including commenting on tourism destinations and services [38]. Thus, tourism organizations are able to provide a number of benefits to tourists by integrating the blockchain platform into their business models [7, 40]. For instance, airlines and hotels can track passengers' luggage during travel by employing appropriate hardware, internet of things (IoT), and blockchain technology. Hence, they can prevent potential damages and loss of their passengers' belongings and follow-up complaints and compensation expenses [10]. Blockchain technology has also evolved medical tourism processes, where patients' records are shared with physicians in a private and secure channel by the help of blockchain technology and data tokenization [9]. Therefore, blockchain technology can improve the security of data transfer among tourism organizations, tourists, and service providers (e.g., physicians and patients in medical tourism) because of consensus protocols, hashing process, encryption approaches, tokenization, trust building by removing the intermediaries [7, 9, 37]. Regarding economic perspectives, tourism can move toward more intelligent processes by implementing blockchain technology, which results in more efficient economic performance [59], business models [47], tourism supply chain [10, 50], and tourists' experiences [56].

The implementation of blockchain technology can also facilitate achieving social objectives along with ensuring economic goals of sustainable tourism development [60, 61]. Sustainable tourism development aims to reduce poverty in the destination local population; thus, blockchain technology and cryptocurrencies can result in improved quality of life and reduced poverty among the local population [36]. These two technologies will lead to the removal of commercial and governmental intermediaries from the interactions between tourists and the local population [6]. Consequently, local communities will have extensive profits from the tourism economic benefits and can improve their quality of life [36]. As a result of reduced poverty and improved welfare among local populations, they will have an increased purchase power. Accordingly, it will lead to a positive impact on tourism development [33].

Furthermore, blockchain technology can contribute to the transparency of tourism business processes and contracts among stakeholders in the social development of tourism [37]. Data that are recorded in the blockchain network remain intact using timestamps, so it is almost impossible to manipulate such data. This feature can be implemented in various sectors of tourism [7]. Besides, accommodation and tourism centers can ensure the acceptable condition of the foods by tokenizing the raw materials and tracking their preparation process. In addition to the transparency of the source and preparation of the raw materials, they can reduce the spread of potential infectious diseases [22]. Moreover, this method can lead to other benefits: recording the information, ease of tracking, and authenticating the artifacts in museums, which can help maintain originality in tourism [10]. This mechanism, along with tokenization and peer-to-peer synchronization, can result in the transparency of business measures and financial statements of tourism organizations, as well as improving the tourism stakeholders' access to national and international laws and treaties, and reducing the heterogeneity of the shared information. In addition to improving the tourism supply chain, building trust, attracting international investors, and gaining the tourists' trust, this technology helps promote the image of the tourism destination [7, 37].

Blockchain technology and tokenization of data are considered innovative approaches to authenticate tourists at entry gates and tourist attractions, which can tokenize and record tourist identity information in the blockchain network. Registered tokens remain intact and are provided to governments, organizations, and destination businesses in peer-to-peer networks. Thus, the authentication process of tourists can be conducted easily and securely [7, 10, 37, 47]. Tourism businesses can also improve the privacy of their clients and travelers by implementing appropriate protocols because of the extensive use of blockchain and the presence of tourists' information in this network [62]. Tourism organizations can also improve business relationships with their partners and enhance the tourists' experiences by developing secure peer-to-peer synchronization of travelers' preferences. Consequently, it leads to facilitation of business processes, preventing repetitive tasks, and preserving tourists' privacy [8, 63]. The safety and consensus mechanisms in blockchain technology can also be used to validate users' opinions about tourism destinations and services; therefore, service providers and government representatives cannot present a distorted and unrealistic image of the destination and its features and share inaccurate and unreliable information to the audience [10, 37, 50].

Despite the benefits of blockchain technology in realizing the economic and social objectives of tourism, there are still many challenges to be resolved [7]. There is a growing concern about the security and privacy of blockchain in spite of the decentralization and peer-to-peer based networks, as well as the implementation of consensus protocols and hashing and encryption mechanisms in such systems [7, 37, 47]. These challenges can lead to hesitation to adopting blockchain technology [10] and governments' wavering to enact legislations on blockchain and cryptocurrencies [10, 36]. Nevertheless, it is expected to observe improved knowledge of tourism stakeholders about this technology and the adoption and application of blockchain in the sustainable development of tourism over time [47, 50].

7.5 DISCUSSION

Iran is a developing country in the Middle East, with a variety of natural and cultural resources and capabilities to develop the tourism industry [64]. Blockchain is a well-distributed, peer-to-peer, decentralized platform for recording and tracking data [36]. The adoption of this technology can improve the commercial and legal structure of tourism in Iran. The blockchain platform can grant unbiased access to all business partners so that they can use such essential information, such as financial statements, contracts, regulations, government directives, and so forth. Eventually, it improves stakeholders' decision-making. Accordingly, it reduces the possibility of corruption and maximizing the benefits of one company at the expense of other partners by decentralizing and removing the unbalanced distribution of information. Thus, the tourism organizations' performance is clearly accessible to business partners, the government, shareholders, and users, which improves their decision-making procedure. In addition, local and international tourists can also receive reliable information about the popular tourist destinations and services by implementing the user review systems on the blockchain platform. Given the consensus protocol, tourism businesses cannot provide false information to their audience. On the other hand, the broadcasted image of Iran in the local and foreign media entails contradictions that may have a negative impact on the international tourists' intention to travel to Iran. The opinions of tourists who have traveled to Iran, which will be available to others within the blockchain platform, are regarded as valid and reliable because of blockchain technology's security protocols. Thus, tourists who intend to visit Iran can be encouraged to pursue their intentions.

Medical tourism is one of the most popular types of tourism in Iran [65]. According to the Ministry of Health and Medical Education report, around 1,200,000 individuals traveled to Iran for medical treatment purposes. Blockchain technology can help improve the quality of medical tourism services. Patients can easily pay for healthcare and medical services using cryptocurrencies; moreover, it prepares the ground to work with international partners and improve the quantity and quality of such services. In addition, it is possible to exchange patients' medical records with respective physicians in Iran while preserving security and privacy issues.

The Iranian government has adopted a policy to stall visa requirements for a significant number of countries in order to increase the number of international tourists. Therefore, it is necessary to improve the authentication processes at the entry gates and respective accommodations to enhance tourists' satisfaction. The implementation of blockchain technology and tokenization of the tourists' identity information can create a competitive advantage by expediting the arrival processes.

It is believed that tourism businesses in Iran can improve their service delivery to tourists by implementing blockchain technology. The establishment of loyalty programs that offer cryptocurrencies and non-fungible tokens to members can provide financial incentives for their audience to maintain their relationship with customers, even under sanctions. Hotels and airlines can also pursue the tokenization of vouchers and tickets to deliver them to their clients more comfortably and at a lower cost compared to conventional methods. Travel organizers can also provide travel insurance and other packages as tokens to the buyers.

Despite the facilitating impact of blockchain technology in achieving economic and social objectives of sustainable tourism development in Iran, they are faced with significant challenges in accepting and adopting this technology. Although technological infrastructures, like the Internet network, provide appropriate coverage, the service is not fast enough to implement the blockchain technology extensively. In addition, there is insufficient technical and even public awareness of the potential of blockchain technology in tourism development in the industrial and academic communities. The government does not have a clear agenda to enact necessary policies regarding blockchain and cryptocurrency. The adoption of blockchain technology by tourism organizations cannot lead to the realization of the economic and social objectives of sustainable tourism development without proper legislation, government support, stakeholders' awareness, and local communities' contribution (Figure 7.2).

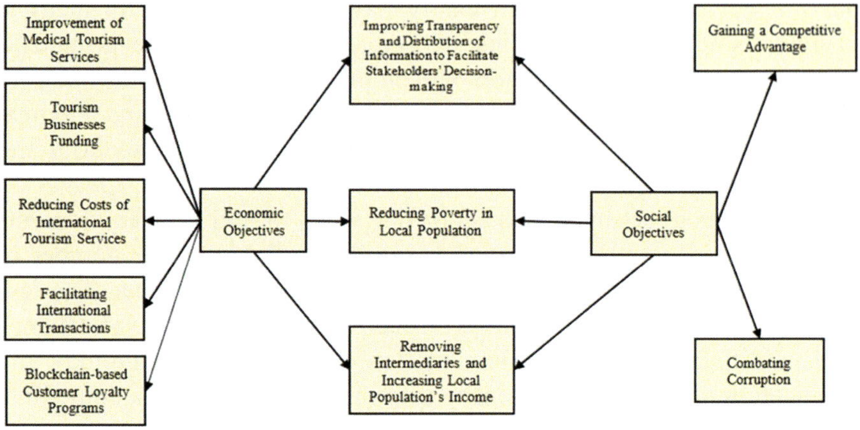

FIGURE 7.2 The final research model.

Source: Authors' Contribution.

7.6 CONCLUSION

The research focuses on proposing a model for sustainable tourism development in Iran using blockchain technology. Implementing blockchain in the Iranian tourism industry is expected to boost local businesses' income, reduce poverty by cutting out intermediaries, enhance competitiveness, improve tourism products, combat corruption, and increase transparency and trust in the supply chain. To achieve these goals, Iranian academic communities need to study blockchain's impacts on tourism, the government should develop policies based on feasibility assessments, and tourism businesses should collaborate with academia and the government. Media can also play a role in raising awareness about blockchain technology. Future research should explore blockchain's role in different tourism sectors in Iran, assess the acceptance of cryptocurrencies, estimate implementation costs, and address limitations like internet connectivity issues and the scarcity of academic articles on blockchain and tourism.

7.7 LIMITATIONS AND FUTURE RESEARCH

Although the researchers attempted to conduct the perfect study based on their capabilities, this study might have limitations. This study has only investigated articles that are essentially published in English.

The researchers should include a variety of factors within different cultures to perform an inclusive analysis. Future studies can improve the generalizability of these findings by reviewing the articles published in other languages. Moreover, we recommend that scholars perform similar studies on sustainable tourism development based on blockchain technology according to different economic, cultural, political, and social contexts to achieve proportionate, twofold objectives.

KEYWORDS

- **blockchain technology**
- **COVID-19**
- **cryptocurrency**
- **European debt crises**
- **globalization**

REFERENCES

1. Camilleri, M. A., & Camilleri, M. A. (2018). *The Tourism Industry: An Overview*. Springer.
2. Treiblmaier, H., Leung, D., Kwok, A. O., & Tham, A. (2021). Cryptocurrency adoption in travel and tourism: An exploratory study of Asia Pacific travelers. *Current Issues in Tourism, 24*(22), 3165–3181.
3. Sunkar, A., Lakspriyanti, A. P., Haryono, E., Brahmi, M., Setiawan, P., & Jaya, A. F. (2022). Geotourism hazards and carrying capacity in geosites of Sangkulirang-Mangkalihat Karst, Indonesia. *Sustainability, 14*(3), 1704.
4. Salamzadeh, A., Tajpour, M., & Hosseini, E. (2022). The impact of tourism events on destination selection: The mediating role of social media. *Media Management Review, 1*(1), 30–52.
5. Demirel, E., Karagöz Zeren, S., & Hakan, K. (2022). Smart contracts in tourism industry: A model with blockchain integration for post pandemic economy. *Current Issues in Tourism, 25*(12), 1895–1909.
6. Tyan, I., Yagüe, M., & Guevara-Plaza, A. (2020). Blockchain adoption in tourism: Grounded theory-based conceptual model. *Ara: Revita de Investigation en Turismo, 10*(1), 68–89.
7. Rashideh, W. (2020). Blockchain technology framework: Current and future perspectives for the tourism industry. *Tourism Management, 80*, 104125.

8. Chang, M., Walimuni, A. C., Kim, M. C., & Lim, H. S. (2022). Acceptance of tourism blockchain based on UTAUT and connectivism theory. *Technology in Society, 71*, 102027.
9. Pilkington, M. (2020). The relation between tokens and blockchain networks: The case of medical tourism in the Republic of Moldova. *The Journal of The British Blockchain Association.*
10. Rana, R. L., Adamashvili, N., & Tricase, C. (2022). The impact of blockchain technology adoption on tourism industry: A systematic literature review. *Sustainability, 14*(12), 7383.
11. Melkić, S., & Čavlek, N. (2020). The impact of blockchain technology on tourism intermediation. *Tourism: An International Interdisciplinary Journal, 68*(2), 130–143.
12. Tham, A., & Sigala, M. (2020). Road block (chain): Bit (coin) s for tourism sustainable development goals? *Journal of Hospitality and Tourism Technology, 11*(2), 203–222.
13. Seyedbagheri, F., Torabi Farsani, N., & Sadeghi, R. (2023). The identification of operational solutions for the application of blockchain technology in promoting of tourism in Iran. *Journal of Tourism and Development, 12*(1), 277–294.
14. Fauzi, M. A., Paiman, N., & Othman, Z. (2020). Bitcoin and cryptocurrency: Challenges, opportunities and future works. *The Journal of Asian Finance, Economics and Business (JAFEB), 7*(8), 695–704.
15. Nakamoto, S. (2008). Bitcoin: A peer-to-peer electronic cash system. *Decentralized Business Review.*
16. Patrick, S. (2017). *The Concise Fintech Compendium.* Fribourg: School of Management Fribourg/Switzerland.
17. Clark, J., Meiklejohn, S., Ryan, P. Y., Wallach, D., Brenner, M., & Rohloff, K. (2016). *Financial Cryptography and Data Security: FC 2016 International Workshops, BITCOIN, VOTING, and WAHC, Christ Church, Barbados, February 26, 2016, Revised Selected Papers (Vol. 9604).* Springer.
18. Gupta, A., & Gupta, S. (2018). Blockchain technology: Application in Indian banking sector. *Delhi Business Review, 19*(2), 75–84.
19. Haber, S., & Stornetta, W. S. (1991). *How to Time-Stamp A Digital Document.* Springer.
20. Jain, G., Shrivastava, A., & Brahmi, M. (2024). Consumer acceptance toward blockchain technology for anti-counterfeiting: Hype, credence or future? *International Journal of Business Innovation and Research, 34*(1), 90–108.
21. Yaga, D., Mell, P., Roby, N., & Scarfone, K. (2019). *Blockchain Technology Overview.* arXiv preprint arXiv:1906.11078.
22. Baralla, G., Pinna, A., Tonelli, R., Marchesi, M., & Ibba, S. (2021). Ensuring transparency and traceability of food local products: A blockchain application to a smart tourism region. *Concurrency and Computation: Practice and Experience, 33*(1), e5857.
23. Wijijayanti, T., Salleh, N., Hashim, N., Mohd Saukani, M., & Abu Bakar, N. (2023). The feasibility of rural tourism in fostering real sustainable development in host communities. *GeoJournal of Tourism and Geosites, 46*(1), 336–345.
24. Rasoolimanesh, S. M., Ramakrishna, S., Hall, C. M., Esfandiar, K., & Seyfi, S. (2023). A systematic scoping review of sustainable tourism indicators in relation to the sustainable development goals. *Journal of Sustainable Tourism, 31*(7), 1497–1517.

25. Buhalis, D., Leung, X. Y., Fan, D., Darcy, S., Chen, G., Xu, F., Wei-Han Tan, G., Nunkoo, R., & Farmaki, A. (2023). Tourism 2030 and the contribution to the sustainable development goals: The tourism review viewpoint. *Tourism Review, 78*(2), 293–313.
26. Shu, B., Li, J., & Pan, B. (2020). Exploring the implications of blockchain technology to the development of rural tourism in China: A future research agenda.
27. Vrontis, D., Christofi, M., Giacosa, E., & Serravalle, F. (2022). Sustainable development in tourism: A stakeholder analysis of the Langhe Region. *Journal of Hospitality & Tourism Research, 46*(5), 846–878.
28. Sharpley, R. (2020). Tourism, sustainable development and the theoretical divide: 20 years on. *Journal of Sustainable Tourism, 28*(11), 1932–1946.
29. Mzembe, A. N., Koens, K., & Calvi, L. (2023). The institutional antecedents of sustainable development in cultural heritage tourism. *Sustainable Development.*
30. Weaver, D. B., & Jin, X. (2016). Compassion as a neglected motivator for sustainable tourism. *Journal of Sustainable Tourism, 24*(5), 657–672.
31. Kim, J. J., Radic, A., Chua, B. L., Koo, B., & Han, H. (2022). Digital currency and payment innovation in the hospitality and tourism industry. *International Journal of Hospitality Management, 107*, 103314.
32. Treiblmaier, H. (2022). Blockchain and tourism: Paradoxes, misconceptions, and a research roadmap. *Tourism Economics, 28*(7), 1956–1960.
33. Erol, I., Neuhofer, I. O., Dogru, T., Oztel, A., Searcy, C., & Yorulmaz, A. C. (2022). Improving sustainability in the tourism industry through blockchain technology: Challenges and opportunities. *Tourism Management, 93*, 104628.
34. Kwok, A. O., & Koh, S. G. (2019). Is blockchain technology a watershed for tourism development? *Current Issues in Tourism, 22*(20), 2447–2452.
35. Valeri, M., & Baggio, R. (2021). A critical reflection on the adoption of blockchain in tourism. *Information Technology & Tourism, 23*, 121–132.
36. Pilkington, M., Crudu, R., & Grant, L. G. (2017). Blockchain and bitcoin as a way to lift a country out of poverty–Tourism 2.0 and e-governance in the Republic of Moldova. *International Journal of Internet Technology and Secured Transactions, 7*(2), 115–143.
37. Calvaresi, D., Leis, M., Dubovitskaya, A., Schegg, R., & Schumacher, M. (2019). Trust in tourism via blockchain technology: Results from a systematic review. In *Information and Communication Technologies in Tourism 2019: Proceedings of the International Conference in Nicosia, Cyprus, January 30–February 1, 2019.*
38. Thees, H., Erschbamer, G., & Pechlaner, H. (2020). The application of blockchain in tourism: Use cases in the tourism value system. *European Journal of Tourism Research, 26*, 2602–2602.
39. Polukhina, A., Arnaberdiyev, A., & Tarasova, A. (2019). Leading technologies in tourism: Using blockchain in TravelChain project. *3rd International Conference on Social, Economic, and Academic Leadership (ICSEAL 2019).*
40. Aghaei, H., Naderibeni, N., & Karimi, A. (2021). Designing a tourism business model on blockchain platform. *Tourism Management Perspectives, 39*, 100845.
41. Khoa, B. T., Hung, B. P., & Hejsalem-Brahmi, M. (2023). Qualitative research in social sciences: Data collection, data analysis and report writing. *International Journal of Public Sector Performance Management, 12*(1, 2), 187–209.

42. Malterud, K. (2019). *Qualitative Meta Synthesis: A Research Method for Medicine and Health Sciences*. Routledge.
43. Sandelowski, M., Barroso, J., & Voils, C. I. (2007). Using qualitative metasummary to synthesize qualitative and quantitative descriptive findings. *Research in Nursing & Health, 30*(1), 99–111.
44. Zhou, L., Tan, C., & Zhao, H. (2022). Information disclosure decision for tourism O2O supply chain based on blockchain technology. *Mathematics, 10*(12), 2119.
45. Wei, D. (2022). Gemiverse: The blockchain-based professional certification and tourism platform with its own ecosystem in the metaverse. *International Journal of Geoheritage and Parks, 10*(2), 322–336.
46. Finfgeld-Connett, D. (2018). *A Guide to Qualitative Meta-Synthesis*. Routledge.
47. Dadkhah, M., Rahimnia, F., & Filimonau, V. (2022). Evaluating the opportunities, challenges and risks of applying the blockchain technology in tourism: A Delphi study approach. *Journal of Hospitality and Tourism Technology, 13*(5), 922–954.
48. Hieu, V. M., & Nwachukwu, C. (2019). Perception of sustainable tourism development: Insights from stakeholders in Phu Quoc Island, Vietnam. *International Journal of Mechanical Engineering and Technology (IJMET), 10*(2), 1776–1788.
49. Wendl, M., Doan, M. H., & Sassen, R. (2023). The environmental impact of cryptocurrencies using proof of work and proof of stake consensus algorithms: A systematic review. *Journal of Environmental Management, 326*, 116530.
50. Nuryyev, G., Wang, Y. P., Achyldurdyyeva, J., Jaw, B. S., Yeh, Y. S., Lin, H. T., & Wu, L. F. (2020). Blockchain technology adoption behavior and sustainability of the business in tourism and hospitality SMEs: An empirical study. *Sustainability, 12*(3), 1256.
51. Sharma, M., Sehrawat, R., Daim, T., & Shaygan, A. (2021). Technology assessment: Enabling blockchain in hospitality and tourism sectors. *Technological Forecasting and Social Change, 169*, 120810.
52. Barrutia Barreto, I., Urquizo Maggia, J. A., & Acevedo, S. I. (2019). Cryptocurrencies and blockchain in tourism as a strategy to reduce poverty. *RETOS. Revita de Ciencia de la Administración y Economía, 9*(18), 287–302.
53. Varelas, S., Georgitseas, P., Nechita, F., & Sahinidis, A. (2019). Strategic innovations in tourism enterprises through blockchain technology. In *Strategic Innovative Marketing and Tourism: 7th ICSIMAT, Athenian Riviera, Greece, 2018*.
54. Li, D., Wang, H., Zheng, Y., & Li, K. (2021). Prospects for the impact of blockchain on the innovation and development of the tourism industry. *International Symposium on Intelligence Computation and Applications*.
55. Raluca-Florentina, T. (2022). The utility of blockchain technology in the electronic commerce of tourism services: An exploratory study on Romanian consumers. *Sustainability, 14*(2), 943.
56. Luo, L., & Zhou, J. (2021). BlockTour: A blockchain-based smart tourism platform. *Computer Communications, 175*, 186–192.
57. Bolici, F., Acciarini, C., Marchegiani, L., & Pirolo, L. (2020). Innovation diffusion in tourism: How information about blockchain is exchanged and characterized on Twitter. *The TQM Journal*.

58. Arif, Y. M., Nurhayati, H., Kurniawan, F., Nugroho, S. M. S., & Hariadi, M. (2020). Blockchain-based data sharing for decentralized tourism destinations recommendation system. *International Journal of Intelligent Engineering & System, 13*(6), 472–486.
59. Wei, C., Wang, Q., & Liu, C. (2020). Research on construction of a cloud platform for tourism information intelligent service based on blockchain technology. *Wireless Communications and Mobile Computing, 2020*, 1–9.
60. Özgit, H., & Adalıer, A. (2022). Can blockchain technology help small islands achieve sustainable tourism? A perspective on North Cyprus. *Worldwide Hospitality and Tourism Themes, 14*(4), 374–383.
61. Živanović, V., & Živanović, M. (2022). Blockchain as a methodology in the implementation of sustainable tourism. *PaKSoM*, 57.
62. Nam, K., Dutt, C. S., Chathoth, P., & Khan, M. S. (2021). Blockchain technology for smart city and smart tourism: Latest trends and challenges. *Asia Pacific Journal of Tourism Research, 26*(4), 454–468.
63. Puri, V., Mondal, S., Das, S., & Vrana, V. G. (2023). Blockchain propels tourism industry—An attempt to explore topics and information in smart tourism management through text mining and machine learning. *Informatics*.
64. Nikraftar, T., Karimizadeh, E., & Hosseini, E. (2024). Food and destination branding: Towards a conceptual model. *Environment, Development and Sustainability*, 1–24.
65. Ghasemi, M., Sahranavard, S. A., Alola, U. V., & Hassanpoor, E. (2022). Can cost and quality management-oriented innovation enhance patient satisfaction in medical tourist destination? *Journal of Quality Assurance in Hospitality & Tourism*, 1–30.
66. Tyan, I., Yagüe, M. I., & Guevara-Plaza, A. (2021, January). Blockchain technology's potential for sustainable tourism. In *Information and Communication Technologies in Tourism 2021: Proceedings of the ENTER 2021 eTourism Conference, January 19–22, 2021* (pp. 17–29). Springer International Publishing.
67. Rerkpichai, C., & Singporn, P. (2020). Digital currency in tourism markets in Thailand. *RICE Journal of Creative Entrepreneurship and Management, 1*(1), 54–66.
68. Arif, Y. M., Nurhayati, H., Kurniawan, F., Nugroho, S. M. S., & Hariadi, M. (2020). Blockchain-based data sharing for decentralized tourism destinations recommendation system. *International Journal of Intelligent Engineering & System, 13*(6), 472–486.

CHAPTER 8

Synergizing Human Resources Practices Toward the Employees' Safety Behavior at the Saudi Port Authority: The Theory of Planned Behavior

MOHAMED SAUD MIRA,[1,*] MOHSEN BRAHMI,[2] and MIHIR JOSHI[3,*]

[1]*Faculty of Management, Al Faisal University, Jeddah, Saudi Arabia*

[2]*Faculty of Economics and Management (FEM), University of Sfax, Sfax, Tunisia*

[3]*FMS WISDOM, Banasthali Vidyapith University, Rajasthan, India*

*Corresponding author

ABSTRACT

1. **Purpose:** The study aimed to identify the link between human resource practices and employees' safety behavior based on the expanded theory of planned behavior (TPB) at the Saudi Ports Authority, especially in the cargo section.
2. **Design/ Methodology:** The current research is conducted by using the positivism research philosophy, followed by a deductive approach. A research questionnaire was designed to collect data from the target population, selected using convenience sampling. Data were obtained from 285 employees working in the cargo section at the Saudi Ports Authority.
3. **Results:** The analysis was performed using SPSS version 25 and AMOS. Measurement model assessment confirms that the

Embracing the AI Frontier: Perspectives on Business and Organizational Development. Mihir Joshiand and Mohsen Brahmi (Eds.)

DOI: 10.1201/9781779641311-8

construct measures were reliable and valid. The structural model assessment was carried out to assess the hypotheses. The results show that intention, attitude, perceived behavioral control, and subjective norms are influenced by constructs of human resource practices. The findings of this study are useful for human resource policies and employability programs, specifically in public service sectors such as the Saudi Ports Authority, which could focus on stimulating the workplace to concurrently enhance employees' safety behavior.

4. **Originality:** The study provides a concise framework to expand the TPB. Public service sector organizations could rely on the framework when thinking about safety at work and the need for inculcating safety behavior in the workplace.

8.1 INTRODUCTION

Employees at organizations face different types of hazards, which could be based on health hazards and accidents. Hazards and injuries in the workplace could be a result of a lack of experience among the employees, work overload, and inadequate methods in the workplace. Employee injuries in the workplace present a method that reduces the level of well-being in the workplace. Although labor law was developed through the years to protect the workers, hazards still exist at work.

Most on-the-job injuries result from unsafe and unclear processes or instructions at the workplace. According to Haslam et al. [1], workshop/workplace accidents present through falls, loose goods, physical injury, and electrical hazards. Thus, it is an essential issue that could demean the company in their process or business [2]. Injuries and death at the workplace are unsolvable; it is present as an epidemic [3]. Employee well-being and work-setting conditions are considered the main issues within an organization. Though safety climates are a main goal to be achieved by organizations in different fields, however, hazards at the workplace could be presented at any time; in other words, it is inevitable. It could be present through high voltage or a shortage of electricity, gas, and oil leaks [2]. Thus, reducing the hazard at the workplace is a main goal for organizations to achieve a high level of safety behavior [4].

Neal and Griffin [5] argue that work setting safety minimizes work-related injuries or accidents. In addition, safety at the workplace can prevent unforeseen occurrences that can cause resource waste or damage to work-related equipment, or cause employee death or injury. On the other hand, safety in the workplace has a positive impact on enhancing employee productivity and behavior [5]. It is also reported that worker behavior is multifaceted and hard to predict, but it has been reported that with certain characteristics and conditions such as environmental, task, and equipment characteristics, work instructions, psychological and physiological stress, and individual factors, the behavior of an individual can be predicted [6]. The use of protective measures and adherence to safety measures is an indication of a deliberate action done to improve work output or productivity [7, 99, 100]. The safe work environment of an organization tends to promote the efficiency and effectiveness of employees at work. Thus, prior literature has extensively explored the importance of work safety and health practices to employees' safety behavior. Nonetheless, there is a lack of studies related to the public sector, especially the port authority sector. Therefore, this study intended to explore HRM practices as a predictor of employees' safety behavior at Saudi ports.

8.1.1 SIGNIFICANCE OF THE STUDY

The current study intends to contribute to the existing literature on the modified theory of planned behavior (TPB) by filling out the gap identified by researchers [8–10]. The previous researchers ignored including important factors such as human resource practices in terms of synergizing with the TPB in order to examine the employees' safety behavior. Practices such as T & D reward, recruitment and selection, social support, and empowerment. On the managerial benefit, managers can utilize knowledge from the findings of this study in order to implement employees' safety behavior practices from the different practices of human resources. Furthermore, the study offers a significant contribution in terms of confirming the modification of the TPB. Finally, the existing study offers outcomes based on analysis; the outcomes might help the managers and policymakers to plan a clear program of practices in order to lead the Saudi port authority to be an essential center of logistics and shipment in the world regarding the vision of 2030 of Saudi Arabia.

8.2 LITERATURE REVIEW

8.2.1 HUMAN RESOURCE PRACTICES

Berish and Kutllovci [11] illustrated the importance of human resource practices to gain overall competitive advantages and to overcome resource-related challenges in unstable and challenging markets and organizations. The method of HRP enhances the outcome, skills, knowledge, creation, synergy, and commitment of an organization and acts as a core for the achievement of organizational goals in different fields. In addition, it also sets up the behavior and attitude of workers besides building up the relationship between the employees and employers to spend more effort on innovation and creation towards the achievement of a goal. They also explained that as the field of business faced rapid changes and development, these challenges can be overcome by the practices of human resource practices. These practices increase the success of any organization by contributing to people.

Hassan [12] categorized human resource practices, for example, training and development, rewarding, recruitment and selection, employee empowerment, and social support, as the core elements practiced in most organizations. All of these practices build upon a coherent system to achieve a high level of safety behavior. In this regard, the connection between human resource practices and safety behavior is an important function in the context of a working organization. Consequently, organizations offer the right practices to the right person in terms of abilities and skills to gain the success of the working organization and reduce the hazard and injuries among employees [75–78].

8.2.2 REWARD

Accidents are prevalent at work and could translate into many other accidents of different grades [13]. The roles played by personnel in accident occurrence are indisputable. Inadequate processes of reward result in a low level of satisfaction, which leads to injury at work. According to Gooden and Wooldridge [14], the equity process of human resource practices could be presented as a main method to gain safe behavior.

Plessis et al. [15] argued that the system of reward management contains practices, policies, and processes of organizations to reward their employees according to their artifice, contribution, and abilities. This system is progressed further within the organization by policies, philosophies, and strategies and also includes arguments in the form of procedures, processes, practices, and structures which provide the appropriate level of benefits and pay levels, and other types of reward. In addition, the reward system includes both intrinsic (non-financial) and extrinsic (financial) rewards. Financial rewards include increments in perquisites, salary, and bonus systems, and intrinsic rewards include feedback, promotion, title, authority, responsibilities, education, appreciation, praise, and certificates. These two types of rewards might result in an increase in the level of employees' awareness at the workplace. According to Idemobi et al. [16], a reward system could offer a positive attitude to the employees, which leads them to follow up on the safety instructions at the workplace; thus, safety intention and behavior might be increased. The health and safety culture of a workplace is a result of individuals' or groups' values, attitudes, perceptions, and behaviors, which determine their involvement in health and safety in workplace management [17]. Many researchers have looked at the effect of workplace safety in terms of equity process [18, 19], safety behavior [20], knowledge, and motivation, and so forth. This study investigates reward as an antecedent of TPB. Therefore, it was hypothesized that:

- **H1:** Reward system has positively influence employees' attitude towards safety intention and safety behavior.

8.2.3 EMPLOYEE'S TRAINING AND DEVELOPMENT

Training and development are presented as a core function at each organization in terms of learning, increasing abilities, and skills. Training is presented as the main course that presents the function and basic idea of the subject; on the other hand, development is the second step that is used as a method to increase knowledge, skills, and abilities [21]. Accidents are prevalent at work and could translate into many other accidents of different grades [13]. The roles played by personnel in accident occurrence are indisputable. Inadequately trained personnel, lack of safety training, inadequate supervision, and insufficient safety skills are major contributors to injury at work [22]. Thus, training and development is a main method to offer a safe work environment. According to Albdour and Altarawneh [23], once employees increase their knowledge and skills, they might make the right decision in terms of dealing with the existing situation at the workplace; in other words, they might occupy or control their perceived behavioral control. Perceived behavioral control is the degree to which an individual feels that it is his choice to perform certain safety behaviors. At this stage, the individuals perform safe and healthy practices if they believe there are safety resources or equipment to perform safety behaviors but may not perform safety behaviors if there is no equipment, despite the formation of a positive attitude towards it, or believe that other important persons will approve it. Perceived behavioral control could lead to an increase in the level of safety intentions and safety behaviors through different practices such as training and development [24]. Each organization intends to reduce the level of hazard at the workplace, which results in increasing the level of productivity. Therefore, they intend to offer a safety culture. Safety culture presents two main factors, which are called safety intentions and safety behaviors; these two could be linked to different types of training and development programs. Behavioral control could be adjusted or changed based on the knowledge that is gained from the training and development programs regarding the need for a safety culture. Therefore, it was hypothesized that:

- ➢ **H2:** Training and Development has positively influence employees' Perceived behavioral control towards safety intentions and safety behavior.

8.2.4 RECRUITMENT AND SELECTION

Recruitment, selection, and safety practices can contribute immensely to the safety behavior of the workers and the organization [25]. The right process of recruitment and selection results engages in continuous role-making processes and exchange of safety resources with the workers [26]. The quality of the relationship that exists between the recruitment, selection, and safety practices is predictive of the outcomes to individual workers, department, and the organization [27]. The basic principle of the recruiter and selector is that the quality of the relationship affects the workers' and organization's attitude and behavior towards health and safety practices in the workplace [28].

Employees, as the method of achieving goals at the firm, explains the process of recruitment and selection conducted to attract and find qualified and suitable people for job vacancies. This process is a set of organizational activities which are used to attract candidates with the required attitude and abilities. The larger working organization tends to conduct a more sophisticated process of recruitment than the smaller one, as the smaller working organization relies upon advertising and referrals for their recruitment practices. Generally, the recruitment process provides a pool of the most suitable candidates, as the quality of any human resource organization depends upon the quality of selected candidates. The construction of the recruitment process is an entry point for the manpower into the working organization and also acts as a pathway followed by the organizations to make sure that they contain the right individuals for their vibes and cultures so they achieve overall strategic goals [25].

Sutanto and Kurniawan [29] emphasized the importance of adopting the appropriate employee retention, recruitment, and selection strategies, as these strategies are important to improve the performance of the organization while reducing the level of hazard at the workplace. The process of recruitment is the method of gathering all the available applicants within the organization and then deciding to employ the best-suited applicant. Selection usually involves choosing the applicants after satisfying the job requirements. Employee recruitment and selection is a psychological calculation or decision-making process of appropriateness. The working organizations that adopt the most appropriate process of selection are guaranteed to hire employees with confidence levels and specialized skills for the particular job. Prerogative selection and recruitment strategies imposed positive impacts on the performance of an organization. A positive and significant relationship exists between recruitment and selection, safety intentions, and safety behavior, which result in high performance of the firm. According to Bauer [30], safety intentions and safety behavior could be based on the right recruitment and selection process. Thus, once the organization offers a clear process of recruitment and selection, the level of safety intentions and safety behavior will be increased.

- **H3:** Recruitment and Selection positively influences employee's subjective norms towards Safety intentions and Safety behavior

8.2.5 SOCIAL SUPPORT

The concept of social support plays an important role in obtaining strategic objectives associated with human resource practices, as social support plays an instrumental role in improving and maintaining the well-being of the employees. Moreover, social support develops organizational commitments in order to encourage autonomy in the organization. Providing social support to the employees also develops the social network, formal volunteering, social capital, and a helping nature. Furthermore, social support plays an important role in the organization in terms of offering a positive attitude to the workers, which leads them to avoid mistakes or hazards. Social support could offer a positive attitude to the workers by offering help or assistance in order to cover a lack of knowledge or financial issues [95, 97]. When supervisors express concern for employee safety by proposing a critical perspective on how to improve safety, workers develop beliefs that their organization has a good attitude towards safety, which in turn improves the tendency for workers to participate in safety-related exchanges and participation in other safety-related activities [5]. In contrast, when security-related issues do not arise or are conflicting, employees are unwilling to share their ideas or be proactive about security. The supervisor's support based on safety knowledge is a key component in building safety practices among employees in the workplace. This knowledge includes the use of safety facilities, managing incidents, training workers, and understanding the safety conditions needed by workers to be efficient at work [101–105]. Hence, we hypothesize that:

- **H4:** Social Support positively influences employees' attitude towards Safety intentions and Safety behavior.

8.2.6 EMPLOYEES' EMPOWERMENT

With the development of knowledge and due to the changed working environment, an organization's view about human resources has shifted from traditional to modern. In a modern way, organizations are trying to implement practices that focus on the empowerment of employees rather than adopting job control measures. Empowerment of employees is the method implied in organizations where employees are given the right to present their views regarding important work and jobs. Empowerment refers to the perception of employees regarding the organization's policies, prevailing procedures, and practices as they relate to the value and importance of the safety culture within the organization [31, 86, 87]. The process of empowerment, identified as the core component of the safety climate in the institution, is the attitude, belief, and perceptions shared by the employee as defining norms and values [32]. Safety climate is a specific form of organizational climate that describes the individual perception of the value of safety in the work environment [5, 84, 85]. A robust institution's safety climate will enhance employees' safety compliance and participation in terms of offering decisions and sharing knowledge. Compliance with employee safety involves adhering to safety procedures and performing work safely, while involvement in safety involves supporting colleagues, promoting the workplace safety program, showing initiative, and striving to improve workplace safety [5]. In managing an institution's safety climate to yield low hazard casualties, Shannon et al. [108] suggested that institutions should promote safety officers to involve them in making decisions or sharing knowledge in safety activities, investigating accidents, hiring practices, displaying safety posters for identifying hazards, and daily communication between safety officers irrespective of rank.

- **H5:** Employees' Empowerment has positively influence employees' perceived behavioral control towards safety intention and safety behavior.

8.2.7 THEORY OF PLANNED BEHAVIOR (TPB)

The TPB is a theory that centers on behavior-based beliefs. The psychological theory has three cores, namely attitude, subjective norms, and perceived behavioral control. The intention of an individual's behavior can be determined by these three cores. The TPB has been applied in different fields of studies such as health-related behavior, entrepreneurial behavior [33], smoking behavior, mobile teaching [34], and academic dishonesty [35, 87–89, 94]. The existing theory is presented as an expansion of a previous theory called reasoned action; a new construct was added, perceived behavioral control [36, 88, 89, 93, 94]. The TPB considers that the three components, namely attitudes, subjective norms, and perceived behavioral control, could affect behavioral intention. Attitude presents the existing way of thinking or feeling about a current situation, which could appear in their behavior at the workplace. Subjective norms present the belief of workers in the society, knowledge, or the culture at the workplace, such as safety work behavior. Subjective norms could determine the behavior of workers in terms of safety behavior and motivation, which will comply with the regulation at the organization. Perceived behavioral control is presented as the decision that the workers or the employees intend to take in terms of the situation. Regarding a safety situation at the workplace, the workers will follow up on the instruction of following the safety process based on the methods or resources in order to gain a high level of safety behavior; thus, safety equipment or resources are essential at the workplace. Although a positive attitude could be present, however, without safety equipment or resources, safety behavior will be decreased.

TPB theory has been supported through different research as a main theory to predict behavior. However, a new construct could be added as a predictor to test the ability of the theory. In other words, the TPB theory could be modified [35].

The TPB has been modified by several researchers by adding different variables, direct or indirect, which could result in a positive or negative effect on the constructs of TPB. These variables could be present moral obligation, management safety attitude, entrepreneurial resources, family formation and fertility, traffic safety, speeding, distraction, socio – cognitive variables, monetary incentive [37] and other related variables. In literature, theoretical frameworks like C–TAM–TPB, C– VBN –TPB, C–TPB–EEM have been combined with the TPB model, which results in extending the model of TPB. Thus, the previous models present a solid relationship between the antecedents of TPB. The existing study added different independent variables with the TPB model in order to present the use of modified TPB in this study. Other exogenous variables were added with the TPB model, and these are: training and development, social support, reward, empowerment, recruitment, and selection. Based on the critical review of the safety behaviors,' it was hypothesized that:

- **H6:** Employees' safety intention negatively influences their Safety intentions and safety behavior.
- **H7:** Employees' safety attitude positively influences their intentions towards Safety intentions and safety behavior.
- **H8:** Employees' subjective norms positively influence their intentions towards Safety intentions and safety behavior.
- **H9:** Employees' perceived behavioral control positively influence their intentions towards Safety intentions and safety behavior

8.3 METHODOLOGY

8.3.1 RESEARCH PARADIGM

The research paradigm defines research as the strategy in which the study can be conducted to address the research problem and answer the research question. The positivist paradigm is objective in nature, while the constructivist paradigm is subjective. Furthermore, the realism paradigm combines the features of both the positivist and constructivist paradigms. The positivist approach is more scientific; positivism can be applied to the social world on the assumption that, first, the social world can be studied in the same way as the natural world; second, there is a value-free method of studying the social world; and third, explanations of a causal nature can be provided. Given the scope and primary goal of this research, the positivist paradigm seems more appropriate for this study. This is because the positivist paradigm allows the researcher to test proposed hypothetical relationships based on the assumptions of the existing theories. In addition, this research paradigm is also purely scientific and focuses on facts through implementing quantitative statistics analysis, which is the basis of this research. This approach is also suitable in such cases where the researcher does not interact with the subjects being observed [38].

8.3.2 RESEARCH DESIGN

Generally, research design can be defined as techniques or plans for conducting a research project. Creswell [39] recommends three stages for designing a research study, such as theoretical perspectives, the procedures, and data collection/analysis methods. Hence, this study adopts a fully quantitative design method as the study provides descriptive views of the respondents to investigate the basic skills and competencies required for employee work commitment. A quantitative survey is one of the most vital measurement areas in applying social science research.

According to Creswell [39], the survey method provides a clear description of trends and opinions of a particular population by studying a sample of that population. In addition, the quantitative paradigm is more popular among social science researchers. Creswell [39] posits that the quantitative method adopts a reductionist approach where the idea or knowledge is compacted into small, precise sets of testable variables in hypotheses and research questions. In addition, other researchers from similar fields also used the cross-sectional study design [106, 107].

8.3.3 SAMPLING PROCEDURE

The procedure related to sampling mainly consists of probability and non-probability sampling. Probability sampling is implied where the sample is known, whereas non-probability sampling is considered where the sample is unknown to researchers. This study used non-probability sampling techniques for data collection. Non-probability sampling methods can be put into three categories: convenience, quota, and judgmental sampling. The choice of a non-probability sampling strategy, such as convenience, is due to the absence of the exact sampling frame of employees at the Saudi Ports Authority [40, 72–75].

8.3.4 POPULATION AND SAMPLE SIZE

After determination of the procedure, it is imperative to categorize the population and determine the sample size. The population of the current study is the employees working in the freight department of the Saudi Port Authority. Nine ports are currently functioning in the KSA and selected as the target group for the study. After determination of the population, it is imperative to come up with a sample size either by using some formula or prevailing practices through identification of the relevant literature. Most of the methodological experts and researchers provided several guidelines to choose a sample size. By using the guidelines of prior literature, an appropriate sample size for the current study is selected from the population of interest. It has been reported that there are about 8,000 cargo workers in Saudi ports. The present study determines sample size selection based on a finite population based on the table of Krejcie and Morgan [41]. Therefore, according to Krejcie and Morgan [41], a sample size of 367 is chosen for this study. However, 285 of the 367 questionnaires were valid.

TABLE 8.1 Sample Size Selection

N	S	N	S	N	S	N	S	N	S
10	10	100	80	280	162	800	260	2800	338
15	14	110	86	290	165	850	265	3000	341
20	19	120	92	300	169	900	269	3500	346
25	24	130	97	320	175	950	274	4000	351
30	28	140	103	340	181	1000	278	4500	354
35	32	150	108	360	186	1100	285	5000	357
40	36	160	113	380	191	1200	291	6000	361
45	40	170	118	400	196	1300	297	7000	364
50	44	180	123	420	201	1400	302	8000	367
55	48	190	127	440	205	1500	306	9000	368
60	52	200	132	460	210	1600	310	10000	370
65	56	210	136	480	214	1700	313	15000	375
70	59	220	140	500	217	1800	317	20000	377
75	63	230	144	550	226	1900	320	30000	379
80	66	240	148	600	234	2000	322	40000	380
85	70	250	152	650	242	2200	327	50000	381
90	73	260	155	700	248	2400	331	75000	382
95	76	270	159	750	254	2600	335	1000000	384

Source: Author's contribution (survey).

8.3.5 WORKING CONSTRUCTS

The working constructs were mainly measured by the multiple-item scale (five-point Likert scale) proposed by Karatepe [109], dealing with five working constructs including training, reward, and empowerment. The social support questionnaire was adopted from Zimet et al. [42], the recruitment and selection questionnaire was adopted from Hsu [43], while the actual safety behavior and safety intention were adopted from Lyu et al. [44] and Brosseau et al. [45]. TNB constructions were measured through questionnaires that adapted from Venkatesh [46].

8.4 RESEARCH ANALYSIS

The main issue of offering an exploratory factor analysis is to present the effectiveness of the data collected in terms of validation. The principal component analysis was performed with a varimax rotation, suppressing small coefficients below 0.52. The rotation converged with an extraction of

9 factors, which present factor loadings as shown in Table 8.2. According to Lee [47], factor loadings are considered accepted once they pass the benchmark of 0.5, with Cronbach's alpha close to 1. The KMO statistic was 0.56, a value greater than 0.5, and the Bartlett's test is statistically significant at $p < 0.001$ [48]. Also, the off-diagonal value of the anti-image matrix is 0.5, with a peak value of 0.84 [49].

TABLE 8.2 Validity and Reliability Coefficients

Constructs	Items	Factor Loading	Cronbach Alpha (α)	CR	AVE	DV
	RW1	0.663				
	RW2	0.621				
RW	RW3	0.780	0.67	0.82	0.51	0.71
	RW4	0.785				
	RW5	0.681				
	SC1	0.691				
	SC2	0.583				
SC	SC3	0.766	0.64	0.81	0.46	0.68
	SC4	0.594				
	SC5	0.683				
	SC6	0.711				
	R&S1	0.697				
R&S	R&S2	0.786	0.61	0.72	0.49	0.7
	R&S3	0.596				
	T&D1	0.771				
T&D	T&D2	0.691	0.63	0.72	0.51	0.71
	T&D3	0.673				
	EMP1	0.531				
	EMP2	0.616				
	EMP3	0.603				
EMP	EMP4	0.732	0.64	0.85	0.47	0.69
	EMP5	0.721				
	ATT1	0.686				
ATT	ATT2	0.741	0.73	0.78	0.49	0.7
	ATT3	0.683				
	ATT4	0.697				
	SUN1	0.733				
SUN	SUN2	0.684	0.66	0.75	0.51	0.71
	SUN3	0.723				

TABLE 8.2 *(Continued)*

Constructs	Items	Factor Loading	Cronbach Alpha (α)	CR	AVE	DV
	PBC1	0.748				
PBC	PBC2	0.781	0.68	0.76	0.52	0.72
	PBC3	0.627				
	SAI1	0.717				
SAI	SAI2	0.655	0.72	0.75	0.51	0.71
	SAI3	0.766				
	SAB1	0.596				
SAB	SAB2	0.766	0.65	0.82	0.50	0.71
	SAB3	0.675				
	SAB4	0.696				
	SAB5	0.786				

SourWce: Author's calculation (survey).
CR – Composite reliability; AVE – Average variance expected; DV – Discriminant validity

RW: Reward, SC: Social Support, R&S: Recruitment and Selection, T&D: Training and Development,

EMP: Empowerment, ATT: Attitude, SUN: Subjective norms, PBC: perceived behavioral control, SAI: Safety intentions and SAB: Safety behavior.

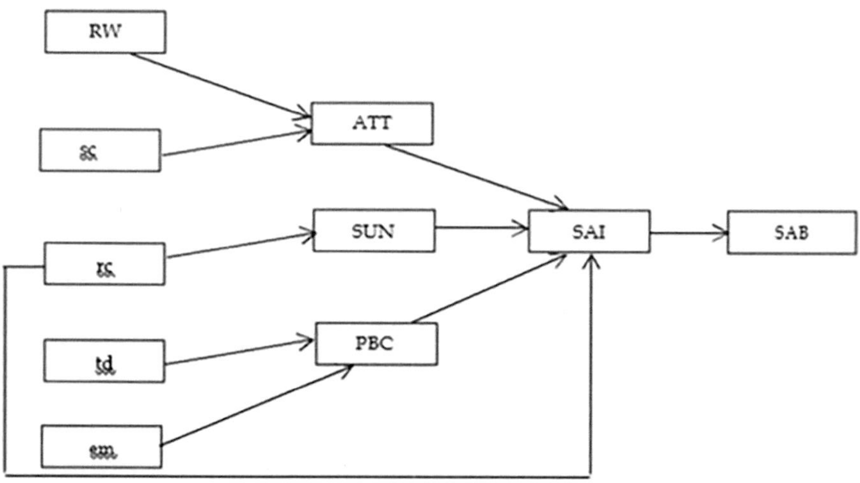

FIGURE 8.1 Modified theory of planned behavior.

Note: RW: Reward, SC: Social support, R&S: Recruitment and selection, T&D: Training and development, EMP: Empowerment, ATT: Attitude, SUN: Subjective norms, PBC: Perceived behavioral control, SAI: Safety intentions, SAB: Safety behavior.

According to Hair et al. [50], the internal consistencies of the constructs should be close to 1. In addition, the internal consistency and the composite reliability could be related or interlinked. The composite reliability of the constructs is based on the reliabilities of all the measured variables; thus, internal consistency among measured variables in a latent variable could be presented. Chang et al. [51] mentioned that the higher the composite reliability, the higher the internal consistency.

The square root of the average variance extracted (AVE) was applied in order to determine the discriminant validity as presented in Table 8.1. On the other hand, Table 8.3 indicates the comparison with the correlations between the constructs. It results in the square root of the AVE being larger than the correlation of the constructs [52]. Thus, each construct is stronger with its measure than others. Validity of data is sufficient to be used as a measurement of the model. The mean, standard deviation, and correlations between the variables in the structural model are presented in Figure 8.1. The study showed a positive and stronger relationship with reward. However, there was a negative relationship with social support, training and development, and subjective norms.

TABLE 8.3 Correlation Matrix, Mean and Standard Deviation of constructs

Constructs	1	2	3	4	5	6	7	8	9	10
RW	**1**									
SC	0.275**	1								
R&S	0.002	–.067**	1							
T&D	0.002	–0.047	0.045	1						
EMP	0.169**	0.175**	–.04	–.109**	1					
ATT	0.05	–.05	0.151**	–.007	0.023	1				
SUN	0.093**	0.063*	–.027	–.003	0.017	0.054	1			
PBC	0.159**	0.159**	0.015	–.006	0.016	–.011	–.028	1		
SAI	0.031	–.006	0.06*	0.05	0.021	0.038	–.017	0.055	1	
SAB	0.074*	0.011	0.092**	–.098**	0.049	0.037	0.043	0.05	–.132**	1
X	4.07	4.11	4.30	4.38	3.55	3.76	3.89	3.97	3.86	3.79
SD	0.347	0.343	.254	0.249	0.652	0.375	0.344	0.33	0.328	0.349

Source: Author's calculation (survey).

RW: Reward, SC: Social Support, R&S: Recruitment and Selection, T&D: Training and Development, EMP: Empowerment, ATT: Attitude, SUN: Subjective norms, PBC: perceived behavioral control, SAI: Safety intentions and SAB: Safety behavior Note *p< 0.05; **p< 0.01; N = 285.

8.4.1 CONFIRMATORY FACTOR ANALYSIS

The statistics programs that were used to analyze the hypothesis were AMOS and SPSS 25. These programs were applied to evaluate the model, and these tests were used to offer the function of evaluation: Chi-square to degrees of freedom ratio (χ^2/df), Goodness-of-fit index (GFI), Normed-fit-index (NFI), Comparative-fit-index (CFI), Tucker-Lewis index (TLI), Bollen's fit index (IFI), and the Root mean square error of approximation (RMSEA). According to Byrne [110], these tests are essential to indicate the fitness and evaluation of the model.

The constructs indicated $\chi^2(1080) = 124.25$ and $\chi^2/df = 4.97$, $p < 0.001$ [53], GFI = 0.978, RMR = 0.005 [54], AGFI = 0.951, NFI = 0.911 [55], CFI = 0.938 [56], IFI = 0.912 [57], TLI = 0.921 [58], RMSEA = 0.061 [56], PCLOSE = 0.046 [59]. With adequate measure of the structural equation as indicated in Figure 8.2 and illustrated above it can be concluded that the model fits the data adequately.

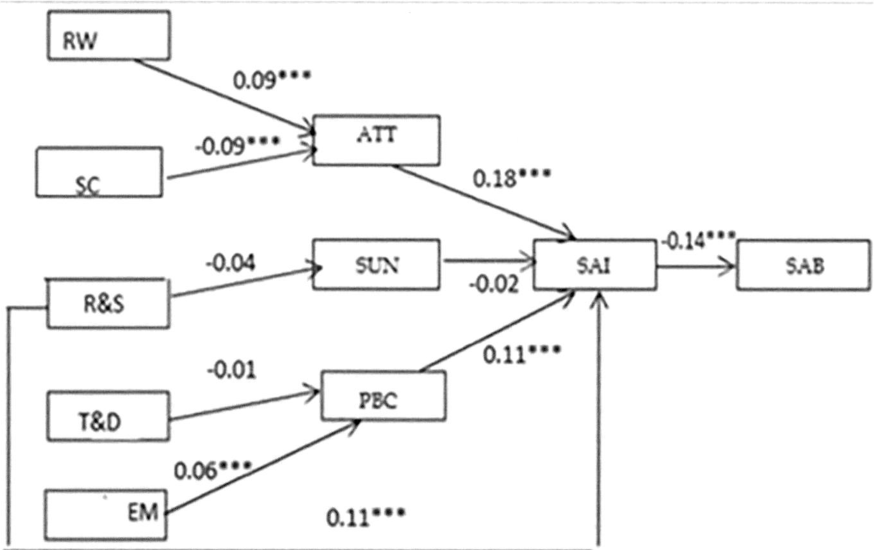

FIGURE 8.2 Estimated structure model of the hypotheses.

Note: RW: Reward, SC: Social support, R&S: Recruitment and selection, T&D: Training and development, EMP: Empowerment, ATT: Attitude, SUN: Subjective norms, PBC: Perceived behavioral control, SAI: Safety intentions, SAB: Safety behavior.

8.4.2 EVALUATION OF STRUCTURAL EQUATION MODEL

The outcome of the analysis based on the path coefficients (estimated structural model) present that the number of accepted hypotheses was 7 in term of critical ratio value ± 2.58. P value indicate that each path where ***, which means that it is significant (p – value is below 0.01) [60].

TABLE 8.4 Hypothesis Testing and Path Coefficient

HYP	Model Path			Estimates	S.E	C.R	P	Decision
1.	SAB	<---	SAI	–0.140	0.032	–4.359	***	Accepted
2.	SAI	<---	ATT	0.181	0.045	4.026	***	Accepted
3.	SAI	<---	SUN	–0.015	0.029	–0.509	0.611	Rejected
4.	SAI	?-	PBC	0.113	0.03	3.780	***	Accepted
5.	ATT	<---	RW	0.091	0.034	2.691	***	Accepted
6.	ATT	<---	SC	–0.09	0.035	–2.688	***	Accepted
7.	SUN	<---	RC	–0.037	0.041	–0.889	0.374	Rejected
8.	SAI	<---	RC	0.108	0.039	2.785	***	Accepted
9.	PBC	<---	T&D	–0.006	0.041	–0.140	0.889	Rejected
10.	PBC	<---	EM	0.056	0.016	3.519	***	Accepted

Source: Author's calculation.

RW: Reward, SC: Social Support, R&S: Recruitment and Selection, T&D: Training and Development, EM: Empowerment, ATT: Attitude, SUN: Subjective norms, PBC: perceived, Behavioral control, SAI: Safety intentions and SAB: Safety behavior

8.5 DISCUSSION

The existing study evaluated different validities to find out the level of fitness of the data with the proposed model. On the other hand, this study found out that human resource practice constructs have a significant influence on employees' safety behavior. The outcome presents as support for previous studies or literature that used exploratory analysis. In addition, the results indicate a robust modified TPB with the inclusion of human resource practices. In this practice, several revelations were made that will serve as an eye-opener to many safety managers, public service sectors, and employers.

The results indicate that safety intentions present a negative impact on safety behavior. Thus, safety culture at the workplace could or could not be affected by adequate safety methods that could be offered to the workers to change their habit. However, the mindset of workers at the workplace could determine the habit of safety. Therefore, hypothesis 1 is accepted. This outcome is in line with previous studies [61, 62, 94, 95].

The result of the finding shows that there is a positive and significant influence between employees' safety intentions, their attitude, and perceived behavioral control, but not on their subjective norms. This points to the fact that the employees' attitude and what they think about themselves, but not what others think about their level of safety skills, will influence their safety intentions towards safety practices in the workplace. Hence, hypotheses 2 and 4, but not 3, will be accepted. This result is in alliance with other previous studies that, other than subjective norms, show a positive attitude towards safety practice and better perceived behavioral control [37, 63, 64, 90, 91].

The result of the findings presents that employees' attitude to safety at the workplace has been significantly influenced by reward and social support. Although reward has a positive significant influence, social support has a negative significant influence on employees' attitude towards safety in the workplace. Therefore, hypotheses 5 and 6 are accepted. The result of the finding concurs with previous literature that the constructs of the TPB model [65, 66, 90, 91].

The result of the finding shows that social support, knowledge/skills, and safety practices at the workplace have a positive and significant influence on the employees' safety intentions, but not on their subjective norms. This indicates that the safety culture adopted, motivations, and enforcement on the use of safety equipment by the supervisors/managers is not limited, but stirs the employees' towards the intentions of health and safety practices at work, not minding what they think about him. Hence, hypothesis 7 is rejected, but not hypothesis 8. Such kinds of results are consistent with the findings of prior studies where it was indicated and identified that subjective norms have a strong relationship with intentions. On the basis of the results, empirical evidence e.g., Lewis et al., [67] and Burns and Roberts [8] suggested that the influence from external parties had a significant effect on whether an individual intends to engage, or not engage, in protective behaviors. The engagement tendencies are an important factor of an employee's attitude, and it is dependent upon the external factors that are prevailing in the environment. The results of the current study are also validating the available literature with the similar variables.

The result of the finding shows that the Saudi Port Authority has a negative and insignificant influence on the employees' perceived behavioral control, while safety programs carried out in the workplace have a positive and significant influence on the technician's perceived behavioral control. Therefore, hypothesis 9 is rejected, but not hypothesis 10. The result of this finding is in concordance with [20]. Since institutional climate involves human resources, it will have a positive influence on perceived behavioral control, as found in previous literature [68, 71, 82]. Therefore, the management role in the provision of health and safety facilities through human resource practices in the workplace should be evident. They are responsible for planning health and safety systems, examining health and safety problems, constituting safety committees, developing safety public sector programs, and establishing safety policies that drive the institution [69, 83].

8.5.1 THEORETICAL CONTRIBUTION

The existing study has contributed to the knowledge of employees' safety behavior. First, the study presents the link of different practices of human resources based on the assumption of TPB theory. TPB theory is an essential method to ensure and increase the organization's growth through the behavior of workers, which could be shaped by attitude, subjective norms, perceived behavioral control, and intention [67, 73–75]. Thus, the organization intends to apply the assumption of the existing theory by offering high-level requirements and designs at the workplace. However, the outcome of the study indicates that a high level of intention among the workers could lead them to be committed and motivated; in addition, modifying the theory results in a positive outcome [90–95].

8.5.2 PRACTICAL IMPLICATIONS

The outcome of the study indicates that human resource practices could lead the organization to gain a high level of competitive advantage. These practices motivate employees and enhance the level of safety intention, which results in safety behavior. Thus, each organization should pay close attention to these practices in terms of applying them through appropriate methods and designs.

Secondly, the literature review that relates to the TPB in terms of applying, modifying, and linking it to different practices needs to be reviewed [70, 92, 93, 96]. Third, the Saudi government intends to achieve the vision of 2030, which concerns developing citizenship in order to increase the outcome of the public sector, resulting in gaining a high level of competition in the global market. Thus, different human resource practices have been offered from different sectors in order to achieve the vision of 2030 based on safety behavior. However, due to the lack of human resource practices, which presents a main challenge at Saudi ports author. The outcome of the study offers a clear understanding regarding human resource practices and their effect on safety intention and behavior, which leads the organization to achieve vision 2030 in terms of a developed nation and a high level of competition among firms.

8.5.3 MANAGERIAL IMPLICATIONS

The present study indicates managerial implications. The outcome presents that human resource practices are related to safety intention and behavior. Therefore, safety intention offers a significant role in safety behavior. Thus, managers at Saudi ports, especially in the cargo section, should pay high attention to human resource practices and apply them as a method to gain the assumption of the theory. Moreover, the study could add more information regarding the influence of human resource practices on safety behavior in terms of making more precise decisions in order to increase the awareness of management design at Saudi ports.

Since training and development, recruitment, and selection towards perceived behavioral control and subjective norms were found to have an insignificant impact, Saudi ports should build a correct design of training and development and recruitment and selection programs to be used as a method in terms of positive affect towards behavioral control and subjective norms. In addition, since subjective norms have an insignificant impact toward safety intention, Saudi ports should pay high attention regarding subjective norms among workers by offering different practices, designs, and evaluations.

8.5.4 LIMITATIONS AND RECOMMENDATION

The study also proposed limitations, such as the proposed model being applied in the public sector and synergizing with human resource practices. Thus, further study might be applied in the banking sector in terms of expanding the TPB in order to measure satisfaction and engagement.

8.6 CONCLUSION

Ports are usually the focal point used for the industrial transition and trading between people and different states, and they receive the largest proportion of import and export movements all around the world. Port operators are not only interested in just measuring, reporting, and comparing productivity, which, no doubt, are the crucial steps in any effort towards raising productivity. Thus, HRM is essential to set out the objectives, including development and motivation of the working force, maintaining and creating a harmonious working climate to maximize effort and commitment, and promoting productive relationships to improve overall productivity through the people. The TPB's applications are associated with implementing practices. TPB acts as a framework to determine the behavioral intentions towards the safety of behavior. The concept of Human Resource practices includes social support, empowerment, training and development, reward, recruitment, and selection. All of these practices are built on a coherent system in order to achieve a high level of worker safety behavior. All of these important factors necessary for organizational performance can be further assisted by understanding the behavior of employees towards their work and studied by implementing the modified TPB.

KEYWORDS

- **average variance extracted**
- **comparative-fit-index**
- **goodness-of-fit index**
- **methodology**
- **theory planned behavior**

REFERENCES

1. Haslam, S. A., O'Brien, A., Jetten, J., Vormedal, K., & Penna, S. (2005). Taking the strain: Social identity, social support, and the experience of stress. *British Journal of Social Psychology, 44*(3), 355–370. https://doi.org/10.1348/014466605X37468 (accessed on 29th August 2025).
2. Janicak, C. A. (2008). Occupational fatalities due to electrocutions in the industry. *Journal of Safety Research, 39*, 617–621. https://doi.org/10.1016/j.jsr.2008.10.007 (accessed on 29th August 2025).
3. Dodge, R. B. (2012). Patterns of root cause in workplace injury. *International Journal of Workplace Health Management, 5*(1), 31–43. https://doi.org/10.1108/17538351211215375 (accessed on 29th August 2025).
4. Williamson, A., & Feyer, A. (1998). Rules or trust; Ensuring compliance. In A. Feyer & A. Williamson (Eds.), *Occupational Injury: Risk, Prevention and Intervention* (pp. 215–217). London, UK: Taylor & Francis.
5. Neal, A., & Griffin, M. A. (2006). A study of the lagged relationships among safety climate, safety motivation, safety behavior, and accidents at the individual and group levels. *Journal of Applied Psychology, 91*(4), 946.
6. Brauer, R. L. (2016). *Safety and Health for Engineers*. John Wiley & Sons.
7. Rundmo, T. (1994). Associations between safety and contingency measures and occupational accidents on offshore petroleum platforms. *Scandinavian Journal of Work, Environment & Health*, 128–131.
8. Burns, S., & Roberts, L. (2013). Applying the theory of planned behavior to predicting online safety behavior. *Crime Prevention and Community Safety, 15*(1), 48–64.
9. Nelson, A., Modeste, N. N., Marshak, H. H., & Hopp, J. W. (2014). Using the theory of planned behavior to predict infant restraint use in Saudi Arabia. *Saudi Medical Journal, 35*(9), 959.
10. Albuluwi, A. S., Alteraiqi, N. A., Alotaibi, N. M., & Alsuhaibani, S. (2020). Predicting the intention to practice physical activity among high school female students in Riyadh, Saudi Arabia. *Saudi Journal of Sports Medicine, 20*(3), 77.
11. Berisha Qehaja, A., & Kutllovci, E. (2015). The role of human resources in gaining competitive advantage.
12. Hassan, S. (2016). Impact of HRM practices on employee's performance. *International Journal of Academic Research in Accounting, Finance and Management Sciences, 6*(1), 15–22.
13. Cameron, I., Hare, B., & Davies, R. (2008). Fatal and major construction accidents: A comparison between Scotland and the rest of Great Britain. *Safety Science, 46*(6), 692–708. https://doi.org/10.1016/j.ssci.2007.06.007 (accessed on 29th August 2025).
14. Gooden, S. T., & Wooldridge, B. (2007). Integrating social equity into the core human resource management course. *Journal of Public Affairs Education, 13*(1), 59–77.
15. Plessis, A. D., Douangphichit, N., & Dodd, P. (2015). HRM in relation to employee motivation and job performance in the hospitality industry. *International Business Conference (IBC)*.

16. Idemobi, E., Ngige, C. D., & Ofili, P. N. (2017). Relationship between organization reward system and workers' attitude to work. *Journal of Business and Economic Development, 2*(4), 247.
17. Mearns, K., & Flin, R. (1995). Risk perception and attitudes to safety by personnel in the offshore oil and gas industry: A review. *Journal of Loss Prevention in the Process Industries, 8*(5), 299–305.
18. Flynn, M. A., Check, P., Steege, A. L., Sivén, J. M., & Syron, L. N. (2022). Health equity and a paradigm shift in occupational safety and health. *International Journal of Environmental Research and Public Health, 19*(1), 349.
19. Livingston, R. (2020). How to promote racial equity in the workplace. *Harvard Business Review, 98*(5), 64–72.
20. Ceren, A., & Ali, Y. (2014). Examining safety behavior with the safety climate and theory of planned behavior. *International Journal of Arts and Sciences (IJAS)*. International Conference for Academic Disciplines, Venice, Italy.
21. Latham, G. P. (2003). Goal setting: A five-step approach to behavior change. *Organizational Dynamics, 32*(3), 309–318.
22. Guerin, R. J., Toland, M. D., Okun, A. H., Rojas-Guyler, L., & Bernard, A. L. (2018). Using a modified theory of planned behavior to examine adolescents' workplace safety and health knowledge, perceptions, and behavioral intentions: A structural equation modeling approach. *Journal of Youth and Adolescence, 47*(8), 1595–1610.
23. Albdour, A. A., & Altarawneh, I. I. (2014). Employee engagement and organizational commitment: Evidence from Jordan. *International Journal of Business, 19*(2), 192.
24. Tangthong, S., Trimetsoontorn, J., & Rojniruntikul, N. (2014). HRM practices and employee retention in Thailand. *International Journal of Trade, Economics and Finance, 5*(2), 86–92.
25. Osemeke, M. (2012). The impact of human resource management practices on organizational performance: A study of Guinness Nigeria Plc. *International Journal of Arts and Humanities, 1*(1), 79–94.
26. Ghinea, V. M., Rus, M. A., & Ghinea, M. (2010). Possible effects of the recruitment process on the occupational health and safety. In *7th WSEAS International Conference on Engineering Education* (p. 137).
27. Vredenburgh, A. G. (2002). Organizational safety: Which management practices are most effective in reducing employee injury rates? *Journal of Safety Research, 33*(2), 259–276.
28. Berta, W., Laporte, A., Perreira, T., Ginsburg, L., Dass, A. R., Deber, R., & Neves, P. (2018). Relationships between work outcomes, work attitudes and work environments of health support workers in Ontario long-term care and home and community care settings. *Human Resources for Health, 16*(1), 1–11.
29. Sutanto, E. M., & Kurniawan, M. (2016). The impact of recruitment, employee retention and labor relations to employee performance on batik industry in Solo City, Indonesia. *International Journal of Business and Society, 17*(2), 375–390.
30. Bauer, T. N. (2010). *Maximizing Success*. SHRM Foundation's Effective Practice Guidelines Series.
31. Geller, E. S. (1994). Ten principles for achieving a total safety culture. *Professional Safety, 39*(9), 18.

32. Wiegmann, D. A., Zhang, H., Von Thaden, T. L., Sharma, G., & Gibbons, A. M. (2004). Safety culture: An integrative review. *The International Journal of Aviation Psychology, 14*(2), 117–134.
33. Singh, K. D., & Onahring, B. D. (2019). Entrepreneurial intention, job satisfaction and organization commitment—Construct of a research model through literature review. *Journal of Global Entrepreneurship Research, 9*(1), 1–18.
34. Cheon, J., Lee, S., Crooks, S. M., & Song, J. (2012). An investigation of mobile learning readiness in higher education based on the theory of planned behavior. *Computers & Education, 59*(3), 1054–1064.
35. Alleyne, P., & Phillips, K. (2011). Exploring academic dishonesty among university students in Barbados: An extension to the theory of planned behavior. *Journal of Academic Ethics.* https://doi.org/10.1007/s10805-011-9144-1 (accessed on 29th August 2025).
36. Trifiletti, L. B., Gielen, A. C., Sleet, D. A., & Hopkins, K. (2005). Behavioral and social sciences theories and models: Are they used in unintentional injury prevention research? *Health Education Research, 20*(3), 298–307.
37. Locke, E., Ted, A., Liz, J., & Terri, F. (2016). Identifying determinant to predict intention to complete a health risk assessment. *International Journal of Workplace Health Management, 9*(1), 63–83. https://doi.org/10.1108/IJWHM-11-2014-0053 (accessed on 29th August 2025).
38. Burns, E., & Groove, W. (2014). Research method. *Ergonomics, 32*(3), 237–248.
39. Creswell, J. W. (2012). *Educational Research: Planning, Conducting, and Evaluating, 260*, 375–382.
40. Sekaran, U., & Bougie, R. (2016). *Research Methods for Business: A Skill Building Approach*. John Wiley & Sons.
41. Krejcie, R. V., & Morgan, D. W. (1970). Determining sample size for research activities. *Educational and Psychological Measurement, 30*(3), 607–610.
42. Zimet, G. D., Powell, S. S., & Farley, G. K. (2012). Multidimensional scale of perceived social support (MSPSS).
43. Hsu, Y. R. (1999). Recruitment and selection and human resource management in the Taiwanese cultural context.
44. Lyu, S., Hon, C. K., Chan, A. P., Wong, F. K., & Javed, A. A. (2018). Relationships among safety climate, safety behavior, and safety outcomes for ethnic minority construction workers. *International Journal of Environmental Research and Public Health, 15*(3), 484.
45. Brosseau, L. M., & Li, S. Y. (2005). Small business owners' health and safety intentions: A cross-sectional survey. *Environmental Health, 4*(1), 1–9.
46. Venkatesh, V. (2000). Determinants of perceived ease of use: Integrating control, intrinsic motivation, and emotion into the technology acceptance model. *Information Systems Research, 11*(4), 342–365.
47. Lee, C. F. (2004). *Advances in Quantitative Analysis of Finance and Accounting.*
48. Hill, B. D. (2011). *The Sequential Kaiser-Meyer-Olkin Procedure as an Alternative for Determining the Number of Factors in Common-Factor Analysis: A Monte Carlo Simulation* (Doctoral dissertation, Oklahoma State University).

49. Beavers, A., Lounsbury, J., Richards, J., Huck, S., Skolits, G., & Esquivel, S. (2013). Practical considerations for using exploratory factor analysis in educational research. *Practical Assessment, Research & Evaluation, 18*(2), 1–13.
50. Hair, J. F., Anderson, R. E., Tatham, R. L., & Black, W. (1998). *Multivariate Data Analysis* (5th ed.). Prentice-Hall, Englewood Cliffs, NJ.
51. Chang, C. C., Yan, C. F., & Tseng, J. S. (2012). Perceived convenience in an extended technology acceptance model: Mobile technology and English learning for college students. *Australasian Journal of Educational Technology, 28*(5), 809–826.
52. Kerlinger, F. N., & Lee, H. B. (2000). *Foundations of Behavioral Research* (4th ed.). Harcourt College Publishers.
53. Tabachnick, B., & Fidell, L. (2007). Multivariate analysis of variance and covariance. In *Using Multivariate Statistics*, *3*(2), 402–407.
54. Hu, L., & Bentler, P. M. (1999). Cutoff criteria for fit indexes in covariance structure analysis: Conventional criteria versus new alternatives. *Structural Equation Modeling: A Multidisciplinary Journal, 6*(1), 1–55.
55. Lomax, R. G., & Schumacker, R. E. (2012). *A Beginner's Guide to Structural Equation Modeling*. Routledge Academic, New York, NY.
56. Hair, J. F., Black, W. C., Babin, B. J., & Anderson, R. E. (2010). *Multivariate Data Analysis: A Global Perspective* (7th ed.). New Jersey, USA: Pearson Education Inc.
57. Shahbaz, H., Hafia, H. N., Farrukh, S., Zeeshan, F., & Zainul, A. (2014). An empirical investigation of entrepreneurial intentions among business students of Pakistan. *Economic Studies Babes–Bolyai University, 59*(2), 68–80.
58. Prudon, P. (2015). Confirmatory factor analysis as a tool in research using questionnaire: A critique. *Comprehensive Psychology, 4*(10), 1–19.
59. MacCallum, R. C., Browne, M. W., & Sugawara, H. M. (1996). Power analysis and determination of sample size for covariance structure modeling. *Psychological Methods, 1*(2), 130–139.
60. Byrne, B. M. (2001). *Structural Equation Modeling with AMOS: Basic Concepts, Applications, and Programming*. Mahwah, NJ: Erlbaum, Inc.
61. Hinsz, V. B., & Nickell, G. S. (2015). The prediction of workers' food safety intentions and behavior with job attitudes and the reasoned action approach. *Journal of Work and Organizational Psychology, 31*(2), 91–100.
62. Elkind, P. D. (2008). Perception of risk, stressors and locus of control influence intentions to practice safety behavior in agriculture. *Journal of Agromedicine, 12*(4), 1–25.
63. Koo, K. E., Nurulazam, M. D. A., Rohaida, M. S. Z., Teo, T. G., & Salleh, Z. (2014). Examining the potential of safety knowledge as extension construct for theory of planned behavior: Explaining safety practices of young adults at engineering laboratories and workshops. *Procedia–Social and Behavioral Sciences, 116*(10), 1513–1518.
64. Mullan, B. A., & Wong, C. L. (2009). Hygienic food handling behavior: An application of the theory of planned behavior. *Appetite, 52*(3), 757–761. https://doi.org/10.1016/jappet.2009.01.00t (accessed on 29th August 2025).
65. Şimşekoğlu, Ö., & Lajunen, T. (2008). Social psychology of seat belt use: A comparison of theory of planned behavior and health belief model. *Transportation Research Part F: Traffic Psychology and Behavior, 11*(3), 181–191.

66. Ohanu, I. B., & Shodipe, O. T. (2021). Influence of the links between resources and behavioral factors on the entrepreneurial intentions of electrical installation and maintenance work students. *Journal of Innovation and Entrepreneurship, 10*(13), 123–132.
67. Lewis, K., Kaufman, J., & Christakis, N. (2008). The taste for privacy: An analysis of college student privacy settings in an online social network. *Journal of Computer-Mediated Communication, 14*(1), 79–100. https://doi.org/10.1111/j.1083-6101.2008.01432.x (accessed on 29th August 2025).
68. Ajzen, I. (1991). The theory of planned behavior. *Organizational Behavior and Human Decision Processes, 50*(2), 179–211.
69. Bingöl, D. (2013). *Human Resources Management*. İstanbul: Beta.
70. Bahrami, L., Safaie, N., & Hamidi, H. (2021). Effect of motivation, opportunity and ability on human resources information security management considering the roles of attitudinal, behavioral and organizational factors. *International Journal of Engineering, 34*(12), 2624–2635.
71. Al-Nughimshi, A. M. (1998). *Port Employment in Eastern Saudi Arabia: Problems and Prospects* (Doctoral dissertation, Durham University).
72. Alsuwaigh, M. A., Mohd Noor, A. B., & Abdullah Othman, A. H. (2020). The importance of the accounting disclosure as a mediator factor between the shareholders of the cash Waqf in the Kingdom of Saudi Arabia: The theory of planned behavior. *International Journal of Business Ethics and Governance, 3*(1), 15–24.
73. Andrew, D. P. S., & Kent, A. (2007). The impact of perceived leadership behaviors on satisfaction, commitment, and motivation: An expansion of the multidimensional model of leadership. *International Journal of Coaching Science, 1*(1), 35–56.
74. Brown, P. (2005). The evolving role of strategic management development. *Journal of Management Development, 24*(3), 209–222.
75. Chandler, G. N., & McEvoy, G. M. (2000). Human resource management, TQM, and firm performance in small and medium-size enterprises. *Entrepreneurship Theory and Practice, 25*(1), 43–57.
76. Christian, M. S., Garza, A. S., & Slaughter, J. E. (2011). Work engagement: A quantitative review and test of its relations with task and contextual performance. *Personnel Psychology, 64*(1), 89–136.
77. Dawar, G., Singh, S., Joshi, M., & Kumar, P. (2021). Effective corporate social responsibility in small and medium enterprises. In *Organizing Entrepreneurship and MSMEs Across India* (pp. 231–246).
78. Elentably, A. (2015). Strategic and operational plan implementation of seaports (Utilization Jeddah Port). *TransNav: International Journal on Marine Navigation and Safety of Sea Transportation, 9*(4).
79. Esposito, L., Brahmi, M., & Joshi, M. (2023). The importance of innovation diffusion in the renewable energy sector. In *Exploring Business Ecosystems and Innovation Capacity Building in Global Economics* (pp. 283–302). IGI Global.
80. Fornell, C., & Larcker, D. F. (1981). Evaluating structural equation models with unobservable variables and measurement error. *Journal of Marketing Research, 18*(1), 39–50.

81. Gberevbie, D. E. (2010). Strategies for employee recruitment, retention and performance: Dimension of the federal civil service of Nigeria. *African Journal of Business Management, 4*(8), 1447–1456.
82. Hair, J., Hult, G. T. M., Ringle, C., & Sarstedt, M. (2014). *A Primer on Partial Least Squares Structural Equation Modeling (PLS-SEM)*. Los Angeles: SAGE Publications, Incorporated.
83. Hallberg, U. E., & Schaufeli, W. B. (2006). "Same same" but different? Can work engagement be discriminated from job involvement and organizational commitment? *European Psychologist, 11*(2), 119–127.
84. Hansez, I., & Chmiel, N. (2010). Safety behavior: Job demands, job resources, and perceived management commitment to safety. *Journal of Occupational Health Psychology, 15*(3), 267–278.
85. Hee, O. C., & Jing, K. R. (2018). The influence of human resource management practices on employee performance in the manufacturing sector in Malaysia. *International Journal of Human Resource Studies, 8*(2), 129–147.
86. Heslin, P. A., & VandeWalle, D. (2011). Performance appraisal procedural justice: The role of a manager's implicit person theory. *Journal of Management, 37*(6), 1694–1718.
87. Hofmann, D. A., Morgeson, F. P., & Gerras, S. J. (2003). Climate as a moderator of the relationship between leader–member exchange and content-specific citizenship: Safety climate as an exemplar. *Journal of Applied Psychology, 88*(1), 170–178. https://doi.org/10.1037/0021-9010.88.1.170 (accessed on 29th August 2025).
88. Javadi, M., Kadkhodaee, M., Yaghoubi, M., Maroufi, M., & Shams, A. (2013). Applying theory of planned behavior in predicting of patient safety behaviors of nurses. *Materia Socio-Medica, 25*(7), 52–55.
89. Jones, G., & George, J. (2008). *Contemporary Management* (5th ed.). McGraw Hill/ Irwin, The United States.
90. Joshi, M. (2018). Workforce trends and challenges: A peek into the future. In *Management Techniques for a Diverse and Cross-Cultural Workforce* (pp. 39–53).
91. Joshi, M. (2019). Burnout and stressors as influencers on work engagement among law enforcement agents in selected cities. In *Management Techniques for Employee Engagement in Contemporary Organizations* (pp. 268–283). IGI Global.
92. Joshi, M. (2023). A qualitative assessment of inter-organizational networks, organizational ecosystems, and joint venture associations. In *Exploring Business Ecosystems and Innovation Capacity Building in Global Economics* (pp. 1–25). IGI Global.
93. Joshi, M., & Brahmi, M. S. (2023). A mediation-based analysis of emotional intelligence effect on cognition and consumer decision-making. *International Journal of Public Sector Performance Management, 12*(1, 2), 223–251.
94. Joshi, M., Joshi, G., & Pathak, S. (2020). Awareness, entrepreneurial event theory and theory of planned behavior as antecedents of student entrepreneurial intentions: An Indian perspective. *International Journal of Business and Globalization, 25*(2), 170–184.
95. Jouili, T., & Allouche, M. A. (2016). Investment in seaports and economic growth. *International Journal of Transport Economics = Rivista Internazionale di Economia dei Trasporti, 43*(4).

96. Lee, M. K. O., Cheung, C. M. K., & Chen, Z. (2007). Understanding user acceptance of multimedia messaging services: An empirical study. *Journal of the American Society for Information Science & Technology, 58*(13), 2066–2077.
97. McLaws, M. L., Maharlouei, N., Yousefi, F., & Askarian, M. (2012). Predicting hand hygiene among Iranian healthcare workers using the theory of planned behavior. *Journal of Infection Control, 40*(3), 336–339.
98. Morris, M. L., & Madsen, S. R. (2007). Issue overview: Advancing work–life integration in individuals, organizations, and communities. *Advances in Developing Human Resources, 9*(2), 439–454.
99. Neal, A., Griffin, M. A., & Hart, P. M. (2000). The impact of organizational climate on safety climate and individual behavior. *Safety Science, 34*(1–3), 99–109. https://doi.org/10.1016/S0925-7535(00)00008-4 (accessed on 29th August 2025).
100. Ozbilgin, M. (2020). *International Human Resource Management: Theory and Practice*. Bloomsbury Publishing.
101. Paul, A. K., & Anantharaman, R. N. (2003). Impact of people management practices on organizational performance: Analysis of a causal model. *The International Journal of Human Resource Management, 14*(7), 1246–1266.
102. Soomro, Y. A., Hameed, I., Bhutto, M. Y., Waris, I., Baeshen, Y., & Al Batati, B. (2022). What influences consumers to recycle solid waste? An application of the extended theory of planned behavior in the Kingdom of Saudi Arabia. *Sustainability, 14*(2), 998.
103. Williamson, A. (n.d.). Occupational injury, risk, prevention and intervention (pp. 215–217). London, UK: Taylor & Francis.
104. Yuriev, A., Boiral, O., & Guillaumie, L. (2020). Evaluating the determinants of employees' pro-environmental behavioral intentions. *International Journal of Manpower, 41*(7), 1005–1019.
105. Zhao, C., Chang, Q., Zhang, X., Wu, Q., Wu, N., He, J., & Zhao, Y. (2019). Evaluation of safety attitudes of hospitals and the effects of demographic factors on safety attitudes: A psychometric validation of the safety attitudes and safety climate questionnaire. *BMC Health Services Research, 19*, 836, 1–11. https://doi.org/10.1186/s12913-019-4682-0 (accessed on 29th August 2025).
106. Zikmund, W. (2003). *Business Research Methods*. Thomson Learning: Singapore.
107. Zikmund, W. G., Babin, B. J., Carr, J. C., & Griffin, M. (1997). Sampling designs and sampling procedures. In *Exploring Marketing Research* (p. 411). Thomson South-Western.
108. Shannon, H. S., Mayr, J., & Haines, T. (1997). Overview of the relationship between organizational and workplace factors and injury rates. *Safety Science, 26*(3), 201–217.
109. Karatepe, O. M. (2013). High-performance work practices and hotel employee performance: The mediation of work engagement. *International Journal of Hospitality Management, 32*, 132–140.
110. Byrne, Z. S., & LeMay, E. (2006). Different media for organizational communication: Perceptions of quality and satisfaction. *Journal of Business and Psychology, 21*(2), 149–173.

CHAPTER 9

Harnessing the Power of Artificial Intelligence in Medicine: Current Trends and Future Directions

SHRESHTHA SHARMA* and ISHITA SHIVPURI

FMS WISDOM, Banasthali Vidyapith University, Rajasthan, India

*Corresponding author

ABSTRACT

Artificial intelligence (AI) in medicine has transformed the way that healthcare is delivered by providing innovative methods for patient care, diagnosis, and treatment. This study offers a thorough analysis of the obstacles, opportunities, and current developments in AI in medicine. First, we clarify the many uses of AI in healthcare, such as medication development, medical imaging analysis, predictive analytics, and customized medicine. We demonstrate the amazing potential of AI algorithms in boosting patient outcomes, optimizing treatment plans, and increasing diagnostic accuracy through the examination of multiple studies and real-world applications. Additionally, we go over the difficulties and restrictions that come with implementing AI in clinical practice, including issues with data privacy, algorithm bias, legal barriers, and the requirement for interdisciplinary cooperation. In order to guarantee the moral and responsible application of AI technology in medicine, it is essential to address these issues. We also examine new developments and potential paths for AI research.

Embracing the AI Frontier: Perspectives on Business and Organizational Development. Mihir Joshiand and Mohsen Brahmi (Eds.)

DOI: 10.1201/9781779641311-9

9.1 INTRODUCTION

A breakthrough in artificial intelligence (AI) is anticipated in every aspect of human existence. The field of AI has advanced in several directions: speech recognition, computer vision, and natural language processing (NLP) synthesis. All of them are associated with Narrow AI, which is capable of completing a single set of tasks. Narrow AI is in line with what scientists have already accomplished in the present. In the typical hierarchy of AI creation, three categories of study can be distinguished [1].

A new technical field called AI studies and develops the theory, method, technique, and application system for simulating, extending, and expanding human intelligence using computer technology. New AI technologies have brought about significant changes to the traditional medical setting. For instance, a patient's diagnosis derived from biochemical, endoscopic, radiographic, and ultrasonographic investigations has been successfully advanced with reduced human workload and increased accuracy. Improved surgical outcomes have led to a major improvement in perioperative medical therapies, including preoperative education, surgery, and postoperative recuperation.[2] A variety of instruments that can help medical professionals give patients and society a higher quality of life by facilitating early diagnosis, lowering complications, optimizing treatment and/or offering less invasive options, and shortening hospital stays are collectively referred to as "medical technology." Prior to the emergence of smartphones, wearables, sensors, and communication systems, medical technologies were primarily known as classic medical devices (such as implants, stents, and prosthetics). However, with the advent of these devices and their ability to contain AI-powered tools (such as applications) in extremely small sizes, medical technologies have revolutionized medicine [3].

AI in medicine has created completely new environments for both physicians and patients. You may call the healthcare system of the future unstructured; it will be filled with rapid Big Data feeds, algorithms, judgments, and modifications. Interpersonal communications between "humans" should be resistant to AI in order to avoid a scenario wherein medical professionals lose control over the course of therapy and their capacity to interact with patients in the absence of AI. Without AI support, medical professionals should be able to do manual patient examinations, emergency care, and cardiac resuscitation. In a world of technology and AI, it's also critical to uphold the proper ethical and emotional components of communication between a doctor and patient [4]. One important area of innovation is the study of AI applications in healthcare and in hospitals. Due to particular obstacles in the field, smart healthcare with the assistance of AI technologies, such as Machine Learning (ML), is required to provide medical assistance throughout the world, not just in European nations [5]. This is coupled with the fact that illnesses and medical treatment are getting more complicated. Smaller hospitals typically cannot adequately accommodate the increasingly specialized medical staff due to the complexity of medicine in rural regions. In addition, Europe is already experiencing a demographic shift; for example, the percentage of people over 80 in the EU27 will double from 6.1% in 2020 to 12.5% in 2060 [6]. As a result, the healthcare system will be used by more elderly people who have their particular health issues. On the other hand, fewer young, highly qualified medical professionals are being employed, and several European countries are already experiencing a scarcity of competent workers, including physicians and nurses [7].

AI in medicine has created completely new environments for both physicians and patients. You could call the healthcare system of the future unstructured; it will be filled with rapid Big Data feeds, algorithms, judgments, and modifications. For this reason, the most in-demand abilities will be analytical ones. Simultaneously, as AI replaces doctors more and more, the human aspect will become more and more necessary—not the other way around [8]. AI has shown to be especially useful in fields where diagnostic data has already been digitally converted. These include the following: identifying strokes from computed tomography scans; classifying skin lesions from skin images; finding indicators of diabetic retinopathy in eye images; detecting cancers based on molecular, genomic, and radiological data; making individual prognosis in psychiatry using neuroimaging [9, 10] and identifying strokes from computed tomography scans [11]. Today's healthcare systems are significantly better equipped to handle the ongoing economic, sociodemographic, and epidemiological constraints thanks to the shift in clinical practice brought about by technology innovation [12–16].

9.2 MACHINE LEARNING (ML)

Additionally, a key component in the creation of learning healthcare systems will be ML. Systems that integrate research, informatics, incentives, and culture to support innovation and ongoing improvement are referred to as learning healthcare systems. Practically speaking, these systems will integrate many data sources with sophisticated ML algorithms. They might be implemented on any size, ranging from small group practices to major national providers. As a consequence, there will always be access to data-driven insights to improve public health, biomedical research, and healthcare quality [17].

Algorithms are collections of mathematical operations that characterize the relationships between variables, and they are the foundation of ML techniques. Despite the fact that algorithms vary in how they function based on what kind they are, there are some obvious similarities in how they are created. Even while ML algorithms can seem sophisticated, they frequently have a lot in common with traditional statistical analysis.

Many correlations of importance to the medical industry are rather simple, such as the one between tobacco use and lung cancer risk or body mass index and diabetes risk. This means that, with relatively simple models, their interaction can typically be explained fairly effectively. In numerous widely used ML applications, such as document translation, object recognition in movies, and navigation optimization, comprehending the correlation between features and results is not as crucial. This makes it possible to use sophisticated non-linear algorithms. Given this crucial distinction, researchers may find it helpful to think of algorithms as existing on a continuum between those that are simple to understand [18].

9.3 MEDICAL ROBOTS

Medical robots were initially created to enable surgeons to operate on patients more precisely and/or remotely. The field's history is extensively recorded in the literature [19–21]. Applications in orthopedic surgery [22] and neurosurgery [23] date back to the early attempts. 20 years ago, a transatlantic cholecystectomy was carried out, which was the first long-distance telesurgery [24]. As is to be expected with the introduction of any completely new technology, the field of medical robotics saw some erratic early progress, but it has now attained a maturity that has prompted the healthcare industry to invest heavily in research and development.

9.4 MACHINE LEARNING ALGORITHMS AND TECHNIQUES

The integration of ML algorithms and techniques in medicine has revolutionized healthcare delivery by enabling data-driven decision-making and personalized patient care. The diverse applications of ML span various domains of healthcare, including medical imaging analysis, clinical decision support, predictive modeling, drug discovery, and personalized medicine. Through the analysis of numerous studies and real-world implementations, it highlights the remarkable capabilities of ML algorithms in improving diagnostic accuracy, treatment efficacy, and patient outcomes.

The applicability of several ML methods for tasks involving prescription recommendation has been studied. Both traditional methods like collaborative filtering and cutting-edge strategies like reinforcement learning, deep learning models, and NLP have been used. Scholars have compared the effectiveness of these algorithms and talked about how they could be used in various healthcare environments while taking things like interpretability and scalability into consideration [25].

9.5 PERSONALIZATION AND PATIENT-CENTERED APPROACHES

One of the primary objectives of intelligent medication recommendation systems is personalization. Researchers have explored strategies to tailor medication recommendations to individual patient characteristics, preferences, and medical histories. This includes the use of patient clusters, phenotype-genotype associations, and shared decision-making frameworks to ensure that the prescribed medications align with patient needs and goals [26].

9.6 FUTURE RESEARCH

To further investigate the potential avenues for future research aimed at utilizing AI in medical settings, the following areas warrant additional investigation:

1. **Explainable AI in Clinical Decision Support:** Look into ways to improve the clinical decision support systems powered by AI in terms of interpretability and transparency so that medical professionals can have a better understanding of, and confidence in, the recommendations that the AI generates. This could entail creating methods for producing justifications or illustrations of the fundamental characteristics and thought processes of AI models.

2. **Personalized Treatment Optimization:** Investigate cutting-edge AI algorithms to optimize treatment regimens based on unique patient attributes such as genetic composition, medical background, lifestyle choices, and preferences. In order to customize interventions for every patient, future research might concentrate on creating algorithms for reinforcement learning or hybrid strategies that combine deep learning with techniques for causal inference.
3. **AI-Enabled Drug Development and Development:** Examine how AI might be used to speed up the preclinical and clinical trial stages of the drug development process, as well as target identification and lead optimization. Future studies may examine how to create innovative medicines with improved safety and efficacy profiles by utilizing virtual screening methods, reinforcement learning, and generative models.
4. **Examine Techniques for Combining Various Patient Data Sources**, such as genetic information, wearable sensor data, medical imaging, electronic health records, and environmental variables, to produce multimodal data integration for thorough patient profiles. In order to facilitate comprehensive patient care and illness management, future research may concentrate on creating AI-driven methods for data fusion, feature extraction, and predictive modeling.
5. **Regulatory and Ethical Considerations:** Examine the moral ramifications and legal difficulties posed by the growing use of AI in medical technology. Future studies should examine methods for resolving concerns with data privacy, bias, and algorithmic discrimination, as well as frameworks for guaranteeing justice, accountability, and transparency in AI-driven healthcare interventions.
6. **AI for Healthcare Equity and Accessibility:** Investigate how AI might help reduce healthcare inequalities and increase marginalized people's access to high-quality medical care. Subsequent investigations may concentrate on creating AI-powered approaches for early health condition identification, disease risk prediction modeling, and focused interventions catered to the requirements of marginalized populations.

7. **Real-time Tracking of Patient Health Indicators and Early Disease Progression Identification:** Examine the application of AI-powered monitoring systems for real-time tracking and early disease identification. In order to facilitate ongoing monitoring and prompt actions, especially in critical care settings, future research could examine the integration of wearable technology, Internet of Things (IoT) sensors, and AI algorithms.
8. **The Implementation of Longitudinal Studies** can be employed to evaluate the long-term effects of AI-driven treatments on healthcare utilization, cost-effectiveness, and patient outcomes. On the basis of longitudinal patient data, future research may concentrate on creating predictive models for predicting treatment response, disease trajectories, and the distribution of healthcare resources.

9.7 CONCLUSION

AI in medicine has the potential to completely transform patient treatment, enhance community health, and improve patient outcomes. It is clear from this examination of present trends, directions for the future, and possible research routes that AI has the power to drastically alter how we identify, treat, and manage illnesses. It is critical to acknowledge AI's enormous potential as well as the difficulties in implementing it as technology advances. While AI-driven technologies present previously unheard-of possibilities for predictive analytics, precision healthcare, and personalized treatment, they also bring up issues with data privacy, algorithmic bias, ethical considerations, and regulatory compliance. Strong regulatory frameworks, interdisciplinary cooperation, and continuous stakeholder communication will be needed to address these issues. Future studies should concentrate on improving the readability and transparency of AI algorithms, streamlining individualized treatment plans, quickening the process of finding and developing new drugs, merging multimodal patient data for all-encompassing care, and guaranteeing accessibility and equity in AI-driven medical interventions. To guarantee the ethical and fair application of AI technologies in medicine, regulatory requirements and ethical issues must also be properly managed.

KEYWORDS

- **algorithms**
- **artificial intelligence**
- **computer technology**
- **machine learning**
- **medical robots**

REFERENCES

1. Arbabshirani, M. R., Plis, S., Sui, J., & Calhoun, V. D. (2017). Single subject prediction of brain disorders in neuroimaging: Promises and pitfalls. *NeuroImage, 145*, 137–165.
2. Awan, S. E., Sohel, F., Sanfilippo, F. M., Bennamoun, M., & Dwivedi, G. (2018). Machine learning in heart failure: Ready for prime time. *Current Opinion in Cardiology, 33*, 190–195.
3. Bzdok, D., & Meyer-Lindenberg, A. (2018). Machine learning for precision psychiatry: Opportunities and challenges. *Biological Psychiatry: Cognitive Neuroscience and Neuroimaging, 3*, 223–230.
4. Suryadevara, C. K. (2022). Towards personalized healthcare–An intelligent medication recommendation system. *International Engineering Journal for Research & Development*, 22–30.
5. Esteva, A., Kuprel, B., Novoa, R. A., Ko, J., Swetter, S. M., Blau, H. M., & Thrun, S. (2017). Dermatologist-level classification of skin cancer with deep neural networks. *Nature, 542*, 115–118.
6. Friedman, C. P., Wong, A. K., & Blumenthal, D. (2010). Achieving a nationwide learning health system. *Science Translational Medicine, 2*(57), 57–29.
7. Gulshan, V., Peng, L., Coram, M., Stumpe, M. C., Wu, D., Narayanaswamy, A., Venugopalan, S., Widner, K., Madams, T., Cuadros, J., et al. (2016). Development and validation of a deep learning algorithm for detection of diabetic retinopathy in retinal fundus photographs. *JAMA, 316*, 2402–2410.
8. Halawa, F., Madathil, S. C., Gittler, A., & Khasawneh, M. T. (2020). Advancing evidence-based healthcare facility design: A systematic literature review. *Health Care Management Science, 23*, 453–480.
9. Hampe, N., Wolterink, J. M., Van Velzen, S. G. M., Leiner, T., & Išgum, I. (2019). Machine learning for assessment of coronary artery disease in cardiac CT: A survey. *Frontiers in Cardiovascular Medicine, 6*, 172. https://doi.org/10.1161/CIRCULATIONAHA.115.001593 (accessed on 29th August 2025).

10. Eurostat. (n.d.). Increase in the share of the population aged 65 years or over between 2009 and 2019. https://ec.europa.eu/eurostat/statistics_explained/index.php?title=Population_structure_and_ageing (accessed on 29th August 2025).
11. Marescaux, J., Leroy, J., Gagner, M., Rubino, F., Mutter, D., Vix, M., Butner, S. E., & Smith, M. K. (2001). Transatlantic robot-assisted telesurgery. *Nature, 413*, 379–380.
12. Joshi, M. (2019). Burnout and stressors as influencers on work engagement among law enforcement agents in selected cities. In *Management Techniques for Employee Engagement in Contemporary Organizations* (pp. 268–283). IGI Global.
13. Joshi, M., & Brahmi, M. S. (2023). A mediation-based analysis of emotional intelligence effect on cognition and consumer decision-making. *International Journal of Public Sector Performance Management, 12*(1, 2), 223–251.
14. Joshi, M. (2023). A qualitative assessment of inter-organizational networks, organizational ecosystems, and joint venture associations. In *Exploring Business Ecosystems and Innovation Capacity Building in Global Economics* (pp. 1–25). IGI Global.
15. Joshi, M., Joshi, G., & Pathak, S. (2020). Awareness, entrepreneurial event theory and theory of planned behaviour as antecedents of student entrepreneurial intentions: An Indian perspective. *International Journal of Business and Globalization, 25*(2), 170–184.
16. Joshi, M. (2018). Workforce trends and challenges: A peek into the future. In *Management Techniques for a Diverse and Cross-Cultural Workforce* (pp. 39–53).
17. Dawar, G., Singh, S., Joshi, M., & Kumar, P. (2021). Effective corporate social responsibility in small and medium enterprises. In *Organizing Entrepreneurship and MSMEs Across India* (pp. 231–246).
18. Esposito, L., Brahmi, M., & Joshi, M. (2023). The importance of innovation diffusion in the renewable energy sector. In *Exploring Business Ecosystems and Innovation Capacity Building in Global Economics* (pp. 283–302). IGI Global.
19. Lee, E. J., Kim, Y. H., Kim, N., & Kang, D. W. (2017). Deep into the brain: Artificial intelligence in stroke imaging. *Journal of Stroke, 19*, 277–285.
20. Liu, P. R., Lu, L., Zhang, J. Y., et al. (2021). Application of artificial intelligence in medicine: An overview. *Current Medical Science, 41*, 1105–1115. https://doi.org/10.1007/s11596-021-2474-3 (accessed on 29th August 2025).
21. McKinney, S. M., Sieniek, M., Godbole, V., Godwin, J., Antropova, N., Ashrafian, H., Back, T., Chesus, M., Corrado, G. S., Darzi, A., et al. (2020). International evaluation of an AI system for breast cancer screening. *Nature Cell Biology, 577*, 89–94.
22. Michal, J., & Ecarnot, F. (2020). The shortage of skilled workers in Europe: Its impact on geriatric medicine. *European Geriatric Medicine, 11*, 345–347.
23. Mishima, H., Suzuki, H., Doi, M., Miyazaki, M., Watanabe, S., Matsumoto, T., Morifuji, K., Moriuchi, H., Yoshiura, K. I., Kondoh, T., et al. (2019). Evaluation of Face2Gene using facial images of patients with congenital dysmorphic syndromes recruited in Japan. *Journal of Human Genetics, 64*, 789–794.
24. Simaan, N., Yasin, R. M., & Wang, L. (2018). Medical technologies and challenges of robot-assisted minimally invasive intervention and diagnostics. *Annual Review of Control, Robotics, and Autonomous Systems, 1*, 465–490.

25. Varlamov, O. O., Chibirova, M. O., Khadiev, A. M., Antonov, P. D., Sergushin, G. S., Shoshev, I. A., & Nazarov, K. V. (2016). *Manual of the MIVAR Expert Systems Creation* (p. 180). Moscow, Russia: White Wind.
26. Varlamov, O. O., Chuvikov, D. A., Adamova, L. E., Petrov, M. A., Zabolotskaya, I. K., & Zhilina, T. N. (2019). Smart multi-agent architecture for control of knowledge extraction in educational process. *International Journal of Machine Learning and Computing, 9*(6), 626–631.

CHAPTER 10

Entrepreneurial Ecosystems and AI Contribution: A Systematic Literature Review and an Agenda for Future Research

MUHAMMAD NAWAZ TUNIO,[1,*] SAMREEN TUNIO,[2]
MOHSEN BRAHMI,[3] and MIHIR JOSHI[4]

[1]*University of Klagenfurt, Austria*

[2]*Department of Political, Economic and Social Sciences, University of Milan, Italy*

[3]*Faculty of Economics and Management (FEM), University of Sfax, Sfax, Tunisia*

[4]*FMS WISDOM, Banasthali Vidyapith University, Rajasthan, India*

*Corresponding author

ABSTRACT

There is growing attention on the potential of artificial intelligence (AI) regarding its impact on the growth of entrepreneurship. There is a lack of systematic literature; therefore, this study pours a new perspective on AI and entrepreneurship into the literature. This study seeks to understand how AI influences entrepreneurship as an enabler for entrepreneurs, considering the application of AI within technological paradigms such as the Internet of Things (IoT), augmented reality (AR), and blockchain. In this study, a systematic literature review approach was used to analyze and interpret the closely related literature on entrepreneurship and AI. This study acknowledges that AI has great implications regarding entrepreneurship

Embracing the AI Frontier: Perspectives on Business and Organizational Development. Mihir Joshiand and Mohsen Brahmi (Eds.)

DOI: 10.1201/9781779641311-10

and that it has a strong impact on entrepreneurship in three major ways: opportunity, decision-making, and performance. This study can be useful for entrepreneurs who want to unfold new opportunities through AI.

10.1 INTRODUCTION

We are experiencing a new era of the Industrial Revolution. Meanwhile, in the third revolution, the computer is launched with new paradigms, and technological evolution takes place with digitalized production modes and methods. However, the industry refers to the transformation of the manufacturing paradigm of self-monitoring, collaborating autonomously [1]. Industrial growth is triggered by accelerating manufacturing productivity and quality production with more efficient and effective processes [2]. In the departure phase of Artificial Intelligence (AI), complex problems are easily tackled by digital computers and algorithms that exceed human intelligence, which changed the circumstances [3].

By the way, this resolution needs changes that affect organizational dimensions and new perspectives of a firm, such as through AI processes. People can work more humanely and less automatically. AI has the power to support acts with superhuman abilities [4, 5]. However, AI sustains critical consequences as well for organizations experiencing more pressure regarding productivity and competitiveness. This condition may cause unemployment and inequality, as it happened during the first wave of mechanical automation and the second wave of digital innovation [6].

Resultantly, the great challenge is related to utilizing the benefits of AT technologies regarding new opportunities and productivity; however, ignoring the drawbacks in terms of unemployment, job losses, and financial inequalities [7]. AI has both advantages and disadvantages for society, but entrepreneurs have an important role and responsibility to use these technologies for social and economic benefit [8]. Several approaches, situations, and related findings entail the academic debate around AI related to entrepreneurship. Thus, we intend to conduct a systematic literature review on the new combination of entrepreneurship and AI, which proposes new directions for further research [9].

There are many potential reasons why this investigation is important, appropriate, and timely. We have scanned academic literature which drives the results and systematization. To the best of our understanding, this is a rare study of its kind to contribute to the literature [10]. The contribution of the chapter is twofold: at a theoretical level, this is a rare study to systematize extant literature on entrepreneurship and AI. This chapter contains three clusters showing the positive impact of AI on entrepreneurship in terms of opportunity, decision-making, and performance. We explored each thematic cluster by scanning relevant and extant literature [11, 12].

Secondly, the framework is created which helps to interpret the impact of AI on entrepreneurship and the entrepreneurial ecosystem. This chapter may prove beneficial for researchers and aspirant entrepreneurs who want to harness the potential of AI. The chapter is structured as follows: In the coming section, a combination of entrepreneurship and AI is presented, and the following methodology is discussed. Subsequently, cluster analysis results are demonstrated, and in the fifth section, a framework is proposed to translate the impact of AI on entrepreneurship and suggestions on the agenda for future research. The last section contains the conclusion and limitations of the study.

10.2 AI-DRIVEN ENTREPRENEURSHIP AND PIONEERING NEW FRONTIERS

The concept of Industry 4.0 was launched by Kagermann [13], merging the virtual and real-world concerning engineering applications like robotics, digitalization, and automation. Scholars have experience dealing with automation using AI technology since the 1950s with theoretical machine learning (ML) models; however, recent developments due to the revolution 4.0 have furnished a platform to actualize these theoretical models [14].

In such a revolution, AI is treated as a leading research domain, and its use is expected to expand into business and social domains based on human intelligence [15]. AI is core to all industrial and technological paradigms [16]. AI application exists in smart factories to connect the manufacturing system without interference from humans. It aids in operating different operations based on the data for production. AI keeps intelligent control of the system and mechanism in scheduling interventions for the automated machines, setting workflow of operations, quality outcomes, and performing major activities [17].

Simultaneously, AI is interconnected to the IoT for the network of physical devices and their interactions. For AoI, AI facilitates the large volume of data to make productive outcomes, connecting software languages that IoT devices enforce [18]. AI is also useful for the augmented reality (AR) paradigm, which is a form of human-computer interaction that blends real and virtual 2D objects in real time. AI enhances the accuracy and robustness of image processing and correlated tasks. However, AI is twisted with blockchain to distribute chain to keep records of digital assets.

AI merely depends on the data to learn and decide and perform certain operations, which lead to more trusted and reliable outcomes [19]. Such incremental innovation transforms technological entrepreneurship regarding new venture creation. AI plays a crucial role in the entrepreneurial process, creating new opportunities, and introducing new products and services [20].

Further, AI techniques aid in the decision-making process of entrepreneurs, which focuses on effectiveness and efficiency. AI appreciates small and medium enterprises to embark on AI-based solutions and developing business models concerning AI. Thus, the arrival of AI has paved the way for immense entrepreneurial opportunities [21].

10.3 METHODOLOGY

The systematic literature review approach is used to unfold the combination of entrepreneurship and AI as an emerging research field based on the extant literature. This inquiry process of systematic literature review was initiated by focusing on two streams: entrepreneurship and AI, and sub-areas coming under the same umbrella [22].

This review was limited to peer-reviewed journal articles published in the English language across two leading databases, Scopus and Web of Science, while searching in the article's title, abstracts, and keywords. At the first stage, 400 papers were discovered using the keywords, 250 in the Scopus database and 150 in the Web of Science database. In the second stage, we used the filtration process in which 30 relevant articles were retained and 370 irrelevant articles were removed. As mentioned in Figure 10.1, there were 30 articles: 15 theoretical articles, 10 empirical (quantitative), and 5 empirical (qualitative) papers.

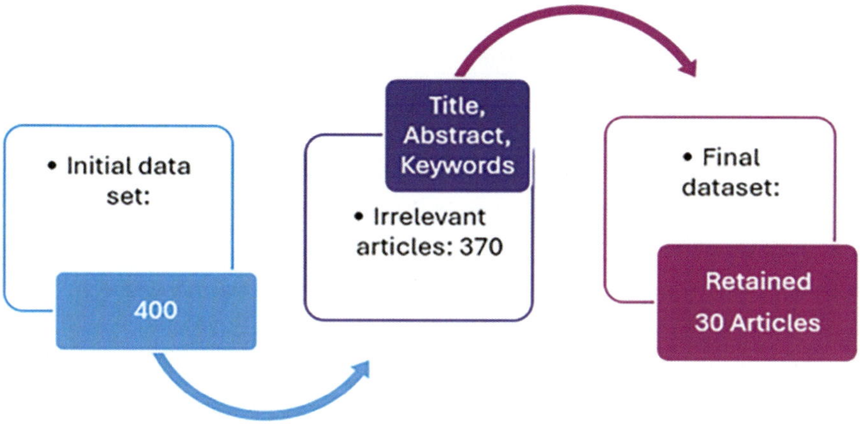

FIGURE 10.1 Filtration of dataset study.

10.4 RESULTS AND DISCUSSION OF THE SYSTEMATIC LITERATURE REVIEW

The selected papers considered in the systematic literature review are categorized into three clusters, showing the differences in the impact of AI on entrepreneurship using the extensive filtration process (*cf.* Table 10.1). Those clusters are: 1: Opportunity, composed of 10 articles focusing on AI as an enabler for entrepreneurs for translating new business opportunities; 2: Decision-making cluster, which consists of 10 articles focusing AI as an enabler for entrepreneurs for better predictions and decisions; and 3: Performance cluster, based on the 10 articles regarding AI role in firm performance.

Every cluster developed from this study can be supposed to be a step in what we have called the AI-enabled entrepreneurial process. This mechanism is presented in Figure 10.2, in which opportunity, decision-making, and performance are three steps of the process.

10.4.1 CLUSTER: OPPORTUNITY

This cluster evolves from the study, depicting new products, new services, and business models. AI and big data can be considered external enablers of entrepreneurial initiatives. This is the precedence of radical external changes that support new economic activities, which disclose new products and new services through an entrepreneurial way [23]. This is a very interesting and important implication about how entrepreneurs develop,

TABLE 10.1 Papers Included in SLR

Opportunity	Decision Making	Performance
Brown (2017)	Ahmad et al. (2019)	Alotaibi et al. (2020)
Chalmers et al. (2021)	Antretter et al. (2019)	Brynjolfsson and Mitchell (2017)
Ehret and Wirtz (2017)	Baldegger et al. (2020)	Calvo (2018) Khalid (2020)
Elia et al. (2020)	Dellermann et al. (2019)	Darwish et al. (2020)
Garbuio and Lin (2019)	Duan et al. (2020)	Dubey et al. (2020)
Makridakis (2017)	Dubey et al. (2020)	Guerzoni et al. (2020)
Mamedov et al. (2018)	Evans et al. (2017)	Huibers (2020)
Mariani (2019)	Fish and Ruby (2009)	Kamishima et al. (2018)
Obschonka and Audretsch (2020)	Glupker et al. (2019)	Kraus et al. (2020)
Palmie et al. (2020)	Ivashchenko et al. (2020)	Ratten (2020)

Source: Author's contribution.

design, and expand their enterprises. Emerging technology may influence individuals' interest to establish new enterprises [24].

The potential of AI lies in its propensity to unlock new opportunities for nascent entrepreneurs when technologies are plugged into business and moved to the marketplace [25]. Developments in AI are supposed to have a high influence on industrial as well as small businesses in the next years. The rapid diffusion of technology will cause and create new entrepreneurial opportunities which can contribute to social and economic development [26].

10.4.2 CLUSTER: DECISION-MAKING

In this cluster of decision-making, AI supports entrepreneurs in using available data for predictions and decisions. Humans and machines both have strengths and weaknesses in their activities and operations. Human performance is better when data is scarce, while when data is huge, machines perform efficiently and effectively [24].

Large organizations produce more data, while small enterprises produce less or limited data; however, in available capacity, there is a need to have predictive analytics. This improves the decision-making mechanism at all levels and develops support for the entrepreneurs in the decision-making process [27]. Modern data science techniques help us to comprehend the critical decisions taken by the entrepreneurs, such as investment decisions.

The leading domain of the social signal process uses AI, which contains the potential to automatically detect and analyze signals being communicated in human-to-human interactions [28]. Such datafication is very important in developing innovation, entrepreneurship analytics, trend prediction, and decision support for entrepreneurs [29]. Thus, there is a dire need to apply big data to entrepreneurship [30].

10.4.3 CLUSTER: PERFORMANCE

After identifying opportunities and deciding to pursue them, entrepreneurs should focus on improving performance and adopting new AI tools and techniques to expand their business. Entrepreneurs are allied alongside intelligent machines to take advantage and get the best results.

Emerging technologies have accelerated routine operations, which have become automated. Simultaneously, AI systems create threats to medium-skilled professional jobs. Thus, entrepreneurship should be empowered and promoted as an alternative option to employment, where a huge population of youth can be accommodated [19, 31]. In fact, deep learning networks support enhanced performance and provide an effective method to counteract predation and improve performance from data analytic models [27].

Further, AI-based solutions offer high productivity and resource efficiency through the adoption of the technology. AI-based activities help growth for three reasons: they focus on higher average local unit value; they help in the intensification of foreign-owned companies; and they diversify the factors and drivers of growth [32].

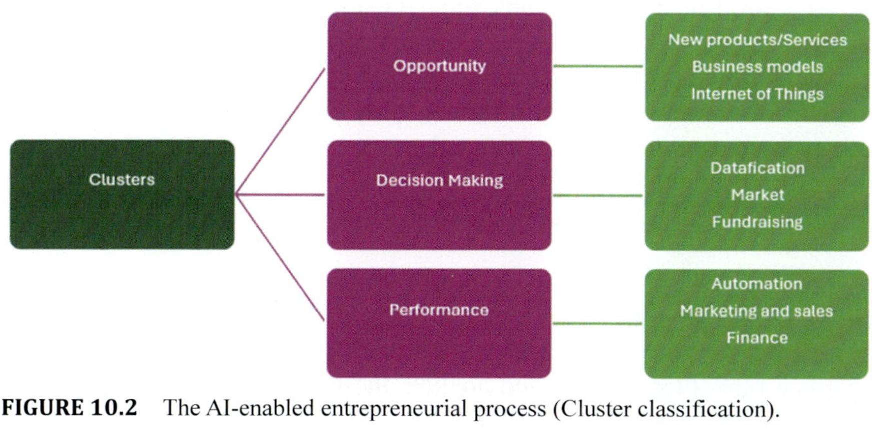

FIGURE 10.2 The AI-enabled entrepreneurial process (Cluster classification).

10.4.4 ORIGINALITY VALUE AND CONTRIBUTION TO LITERATURE REVIEW

It is believed that AI systems will gradually replace humans in all sectors one by one, which may reduce employment opportunities but may trigger new entrepreneurial opportunities for entrepreneurs. AI has the potential to complement and enhance human abilities. Human strengths like creativity, improvisation, dexterity, judgment, and skills are closely relevant to the strengths of emerging technologies like speed, accuracy, repetition, predictive skills, and scalability [33].

Hence, it is believed that such reasoning is beneficial for entrepreneurship as a process through which young entrepreneurs can identify new business opportunities [34, 35]. AI helps us to understand the entrepreneurial cognitive process of identifying, evaluating, and exploiting new entrepreneurial opportunities. AI in combination with neuroscience allows entrepreneurs to understand the entrepreneurial process to identify entrepreneurial opportunities and translate them into a feasible business. Thus, AI has the potential to aid humans in progressing in creativity and stimulate an entrepreneurial mindset through the use of data [36].

AI can be useful in decision-making in the entrepreneurial process [37]. There can be different ways to make and implement decisions. AI could be helpful for entrepreneurs' communication, which can help them to generate more funds. Entrepreneurs can engage their investors easily if they are better convinced by the miracles of AI. Performance is concerned with the exploiting of new opportunities. In this regard, AI and the blockchain may enable automation and scaling. Blockchain supports the validation of data and helps smart factories to automate the process more, using limited resources and low cost [38].

The combination of blockchain with AI can transform the traditional ways of collecting data and information. It is believed blockchain technology increases its use in financial matters and thus, has become an integral part of every organization. However, future study may focus on how to deal with the risks and vulnerabilities of blockchain.

10.5 CONCLUSION

This is a rare study to map and analyze the latent and relevant literature regarding entrepreneurship and AI. In order to fill a research gap, a systematic literature review of 30 articles was conducted, in which AI as an enabler of entrepreneurs was focused on, and AI-based entrepreneurial processes were discussed. AI aids in checking opportunities, enables entrepreneurs to identify new opportunities, make better decisions based on the available data through AI, and improve performance to show distinction and to achieve goals.

KEYWORDS

- **artificial intelligence**
- **augmented reality**
- **entrepreneurship**
- **innovation technology**
- **Internet of Things**

REFERENCES

1. Agrawal, A., Gans, J., & Goldfarb, A. (2018). *Prediction Machines: The Simple Economics of AI*. Harvard Business Review Press, Boston, MA.
2. Afshan, G., Shahid, S., & Tunio, M. N. (2021). Learning experiences of women entrepreneurs amidst COVID-19. *International Journal of Gender and Entrepreneurship, 13*(2), 162–186.
3. Ahmad, A. M., bin Masri, R., & Chong Aik, L. (2019). Future challenges to the entrepreneur in relation to the changing business environment. *Global Business and Management Research, 11*(2), 197–205.
4. Alotaibi, B., Abbasi, R. A., Aslam, M. A., Saeedi, K., & Alahmadi, D. (2020). Startup initiative.
5. Tunio, M. N., Chaudhry, I. S., Shaikh, S., Jariko, M. A., & Brahmi, M. (2021). Determinants of the sustainable entrepreneurial engagement of youth in developing country—Empirical evidence from Pakistan. *Sustainability, 13*(14), 7764.
6. Amankwah-Amoah, J., Khan, Z., Wood, G. R., & Knight, G. A. (2021). COVID-19 and digitalization: The great acceleration. *Journal of Business Research, 136*, 602–611.
7. Antretter, T., Blohm, I., Grichnik, D., & Wincent, J. (2019). Predicting new venture survival: A Twitter-based machine learning approach to measuring online legitimacy. *Journal of Business Venturing Insights, 11*, 1–8.

8. Luigi, A., Mohsen, B., Xihui, C., & Concetto, P. V. (2021). Knowledge spillovers and technical efficiency for cleaner production: An economic analysis from agriculture innovation. *Journal of Cleaner Production, 320*, 128830. https://doi.org/10.1016/j.jclepro.2021.128830 (accessed on 29th August 2025).
9. Aoun, A., Ilinca, A., Ghandour, M., & Ibrahim, H. (2021). A review of Industry 4.0 characteristics and challenges, with potential improvements using blockchain technology. *Computers and Industrial Engineering, 162*.
10. Ashton, K. (2009). That 'Internet of Things' thing. *RFID Journal, 22*(7), 97–114.
11. Azuma, R., Baillot, Y., Behringer, R., Feiner, S., Julier, S., & MacIntyre, B. (2001). Recent advances in augmented reality. *IEEE Computer Graphics and Applications, 21*(6), 34–47.
12. Baldegger, R., Caon, M., & Sadiku, K. (2020). Correlation between entrepreneurial orientation and implementation of AI in human resource management (HRM). *Technology Innovation Management Review, 10*(4), 72–79.
13. Kagermann, H., Lukas, W. D., & Wahlster, W. (2011). Industrie 4.0: Mit dem Internet der Dinge auf dem Weg zur 4. industriellen Revolution. *VDI Nachrichten.*
14. French, A. M., Shim, J. P., Risius, M., & Jain, H. K. (2021). The 4th industrial revolution powered by the integration of 5G, AI, and blockchain. *Communications of the Association for Information Systems, 49*(6).
15. Oztemel, E., & Gursev, S. (2018). Literature review of Industry 4.0 and related technologies. *Journal of Intelligent Manufacturing, 31*(1), 127–182.
16. Brahmi, M., & Zouari, S. (2014). TIC, innovation et impacts sur analyses concurrentielle: Leader Firme du Bassin Minier Tunisien. *International Journal of Innovation and Applied Studies, 10*(1), 195–217. https://issr-journals.org/xplore/ijisr/0010/001/IJISR-14-230-05.pdf (accessed on 29th August 2025).
17. Bogoviz, A. V., Lobova, S. V., Karp, M. V., Vologdin, E. V., & Alekseev, A. N. (2019). Diversification of educational services in the conditions of Industry 4.0 on the basis of AI training. *On the Horizon, 27*(3, 4), 206–212.
18. Brown, T. E. (2017). Sensor-based entrepreneurship: A framework for developing new products and services. *Business Horizons, 60*(6), 819–830.
19. Brynjolfsson, E., & Mitchell, T. (2017). What can machine learning do? Workforce implications: Profound change is coming, but roles for humans remain. *Science, 358*(6370), 1530–1534.
20. Cadena, A., & Ferrari-Haines, F. (2020). Saving our livelihoods from COVID-19: Toward an economic recovery. https://www.mckinsey.com/industries/public-and-social-sector/our-insights/saving-our-livelihoods-from-covid-19-toward-an-economic-recovery (accessed on 29th August 2025).
21. Calvo, J. (2018). High-tech start-ups in Japan: Cogent Labs, AI-OCR solutions for automated business process outsourcing. *International Journal of Entrepreneurial Knowledge, 6*(2), 12–31.
22. Bui, T. K., Bui Phu, H., & Mohsen, B. (2022). Qualitative research in social sciences: Data collection, data analysis and report writing. *International Journal of Public Sector Performance Management, 12*(1/2), 187–209. https://doi.org/10.1504/IJPSPM.2023.132247 (accessed on 29th August 2025).
23. Obschonka, M., & Audretsch, D. B. (2020). AI and big data in entrepreneurship: A new era has begun. *Small Business Economics, 55*(3), 529–539.

24. Chalmers, D., MacKenzie, N. G., & Carter, S. (2021). AI and entrepreneurship: Implications for venture creation in the fourth industrial revolution. *Entrepreneurship Theory and Practice, 45*(5), 1028–1053.
25. Garbuio, M., & Lin, N. (2019). AI as a growth engine for healthcare startups: Emerging business models. *California Management Review, 61*(2), 59–83.
26. Makridakis, S. (2017). The forthcoming artificial intelligence (AI) revolution: Its impact on society and firms. *Futures, 90*, 46–60.
27. Kraus, M., Feuerriegel, S., & Oztekin, A. (2020). Deep learning in business analytics and operations research: Models, applications and managerial implications. *European Journal of Operational Research, 281*(3), 628–641.
28. Liebregts, W., Darnihamedani, P., Postma, E., & Atzmueller, M. (2020). The promise of social signal processing for research on decision-making in entrepreneurial contexts. *Small Business Economics, 55*(3), 589–605.
29. Mohsen, B., & Adala, L. (2015). The strategic choices of small medium-sized enterprises integration: Evidence from specific economic territory. *ŒCONOMICA, 11*(2), 254–272. https://www.ceeol.com/search/article-detail?id=521810 (accessed on 29th August 2025).
30. Nie, X. (2020). Research on economic function data and entrepreneurship analysis based on machine learning and computer interaction platform. *Journal of Intelligent and Fuzzy Systems, 39*(4), 5635–5647.
31. Zemtsov, S., Barinova, V., & Semenova, R. (2019). The risks of digitalization and the adaptation of regional labor markets in Russia. *Foresight and STI Governance, 13*(2), 84–96.
32. Szalavetz, A. (2019). AI-based development strategy in dependent market economies—Any room amidst big power rivalry? *Central European Business Review, 8*(4), 40–54.
33. Daugherty, P., & Wilson, J. (2018). *Human + Machine: Reimagining Work in the Age of AI.* Harvard Business Review Press, Boston, MA.
34. Tajpour, M., Hosseini, E., & Brahmi, M. (2022). Effect of international entrepreneurship indicators on innovative performance: The mediating role of motivation. *International Journal of Technology Transfer and Commercialization, 19*(1), 142–162. http://www.inderscience.com/storage/f731124561812910.pdf (accessed on 29th August 2025).
35. Shane, S., & Venkataraman, S. (2000). The promise of entrepreneurship as a field of research. *Academy of Management Review, 25*(1), 217–226.
36. Nicolaou, N., Lockett, A., Ucbasaran, D., & Rees, G. (2019). Exploring the potential and limits of a neuroscientific approach to entrepreneurship. *International Small Business Journal, 37*(6), 557–580.
37. Hamrouni, B., Bourouis, A., Koricho, A., & Brahmi, M. (2021). Explainable ontology-based intelligent decision support system for business model design and sustainability. *Sustainability, 13*, 9819. https://doi.org/10.3390/su13179819 (accessed on 29th August 2025).
38. Wang, K., Dong, J., Wang, Y., & Yin, H. (2019). Securing data with blockchain and AI. *IEEE Access, 7*, 77981–77989.

CHAPTER 11

Application of Robotics in Medical Sector and Healthcare

PUSHPA LOHANI,[1] DEVESH PATHAK,[1] MEGHA BHATT,[1] and KARTIK LOHANI[2,*]

[1]MBGE-CBSH, G. B. Pant University of Agriculture and Technology, Uttarakhand, India

[2]College of Medical Sciences, Teerthanker Mahavir University, India

*Corresponding author

ABSTRACT

The first industrial-grade robot was introduced in the 1960s. Since then, robotic technologies have made a significant contribution to overcoming the physical limitations of human beings in terms of durability, accuracy, and repeatability in many fields of industrialization, including the automobile, electronics, broadcasting, and metal industries. In the 21st century, robots have seen great advancement and are further used in the field of healthcare and medicine, which requires techniques that are accurate, precise, repetitive, robust, and safe for the users. Fueled by rapid improvements in medical engineering and equipment techniques, robots have gained acceptability in nearly all medical procedures by therapists and surgeons. The article highlights the different ways robotics is used in the healthcare sector and describes its application. We study the technological advancement and the progress made in the field of robotics in the medical sector during the last 10 years. Finally, we summarize the limitations of medical robots as assistive machines for medical personnel.

Embracing the AI Frontier: Perspectives on Business and Organizational Development. Mihir Joshiand and Mohsen Brahmi (Eds.)

DOI: 10.1201/9781779641311-11

11.1 INTRODUCTION

Robots can be seen everywhere, from science fiction movies to local supermarkets. Robots are also in your local hospital, where they are changing healthcare and making a huge impact on the field of medicine. Robots are of great utility to medical professionals in performing their daily routine duties, thus freeing them to perform their more demanding roles. The use of robots in healthcare is safe and, at times, makes treatment affordable. Robots are capable of performing delicate surgeries accurately in tiny places and transporting dangerous substances that are toxic for humans with ease. Health robotics enables an extreme level of patient care and accurate process settings in medical procedures.

Biomedical advancements make it possible for robotic medical assistants to monitor patient vital statistics, keep track of records, and alert medical personnel when a human presence is required in the ward, allowing them to monitor a large number of patients at once. Robotic medical assistants keep track of patients' health details and store the information into electronic devices [1–3]. Robotic carts may be seen shipping medical equipment and medicines. Robots are also capable of assisting doctors and surgeons in surgery, allowing them to conduct surgery through a tiny incision instead of a long one. Robotics is making a huge impact in other areas of medical sciences as well.

Robotic medical assistants are used to disinfect the rooms of patients and operating suites, reducing the risk of contamination and spread of any lethal disease to both patients and medical personnel. Robots are used in laboratories for the transportation, analysis, and storage of lab samples. In huge facilities, robots are used for hospitality purposes to transport bed linens and meals for patients floor to floor in the building. Sometimes robots may also help as medical assistants to support paraplegics, move, and help in physical therapy. Over time, AI, amalgamated with computer science and statistical analysis, has boosted the application of robotics in the healthcare industry, expanding into many areas of medical and biomedical fields.

11.2 USE OF ROBOTICS IN HEALTHCARE

Surgery is the most common robotic application in the field of medicine, and also the most successful. Surgical assistance has become even more precise after the integration of AI [2, 4, 5].

As motion control technologies have advanced, robots are capable of performing tasks independently and providing enriched support to doctors during remote surgeries. The capability of medical robots to record and display a video live from an operation theatre to a nearby ward and other locations helps surgeons to understand and learn from consultations of other surgeons leading in their respective field of practice. Robotics plays a major role in surgery practice and training too. *The Mimic Stimulation Platform* uses AI and virtual reality (VR) for creating a virtual arena, where new surgeons can practice surgery. In the field of surgery, robotics is evolving by making great use of AI. Computer vision is now able to differentiate between the different types of tissues within their field of view and assist the surgeons by avoiding nerves and muscles during medical procedures. Subsequently, doctors will oversee robots performing surgeries besides providing directions. But it is not the only way robotics is implemented in the field of healthcare. Robots have started to show their presence in different spaces of the healthcare sector, including medical equipment delivery and shipment, sanitization, telepresence, rehabilitation, and prescription dispensing.

1. **Modular Robots:** Modular robots connected with integrated systems can be developed to carry out different functions. In the healthcare sector, this includes prosthetic body parts and therapeutic robots.

   Therapeutic robots help a human to recover from traumatic brain strokes, mental strokes, paralysis, and various scleroses. Therapeutic robots are equipped with 3D cameras and AI vision, which help these robots to analyze the shape, form, and degree of motion of a patient over a period of time and track progress more precisely as compared to its human counterpart. These are also capable of interacting with patients to provide mental assistance and encouragement.

2. **Service Robots:** These robots relieve the routine burden of healthcare personnel by monitoring and handling routine logistical duties. A few robots perform duties autonomously and send a detailed report to their specific handling medical personnel when they accomplish their assigned tasks [1, 6–8]. These robots set up operating rooms, patient wards, medicine orders and shipments, restock medical supplies, transport bed linens, track supplies,

and file purchase orders. Having a large number of sideline tasks handled provides health workers more time to look after the immediate health of the patient.

3. **Social Robots:** As the name suggests, social robots are capable of interacting with patients directly. These robots are friendly and can be used to create a lively environment for children and senior citizens, providing social interaction and analysis [5, 7–9]. They encourage patients to comply with treatment procedures and provide cognitive engagement, keeping patient morale positive and encouraged. They are often used to offer navigation to visitors and patients inside healthcare premises. In short, social robots are used to reduce the workload of medical personnel and caregivers and boost the well-being of patients.
4. **Mobile Robots:** Mobile robots navigate inside the hospital premises and clinics, following a predefined track. They are capable of performing a variety of tasks, such as sanitizing rooms, transporting patients, and moving heavy medical equipment. Cleaning mobile robots is done using UV light to help minimize contamination to the vulnerable environment.
5. **Autonomous Robots:** Autonomous robots are equipped with a robust range of depth and 3D cameras and are capable of navigating to patients in the operation ward, thus allowing interaction of patients and healthcare personnel from afar. Robots controlled remotely are capable of accompanying doctors as they make routine rounds of inspection. These robots are self-sufficient and keep a track record of their battery status.

11.3 IMPACT OF ARTIFICIAL INTELLIGENCE IN HEALTHCARE

If AI could establish a direct connection between the human mind and technology, bypassing traditional output devices such as keyboards or mice, it would have a transformative impact on healthcare, particularly for patients with neurological disorders or traumatic injuries. This technology could significantly improve the lives of those who have suffered strokes, nervous system diseases, or locked-in syndrome. By enabling patients to interact with technology using their thoughts, AI could help restore lost abilities, thereby improving their quality of life and promoting independence. Imagine a patient who has lost the ability to move or communicate due to a neurological condition—AI could allow them to control devices, communicate, and perform daily tasks, offering them newfound autonomy.

AI also has the potential to automate numerous routine healthcare processes, reducing the burden on both patients and healthcare professionals. For example, patients could request medications, schedule appointments, and report symptoms through messages or calls via AI systems. Such automation would save time, reduce errors, and ensure that patients receive timely interventions. By streamlining these tasks, AI can significantly enhance the efficiency of healthcare delivery and improve patient satisfaction [10–13]. In regions with limited resources, AI can play a critical role in providing quality healthcare. The use of AI-powered diagnostic tools can make disease detection and management much more accessible. Through mobile applications, individuals living in remote or underserved areas could have access to diagnostic capabilities comparable to those found in well-equipped hospitals. This means that conditions could be detected early, and treatment could be started sooner, reducing the need for physical diagnostic centers and highly trained personnel. This not only brings healthcare closer to communities in need but also reduces the cost and complexity of medical care in these regions.

One of the major challenges in healthcare today is the overuse of antibiotics, which has led to the development of antibiotic-resistant superbugs. These resistant strains are a growing threat globally, as they can cause severe infections that are difficult to treat and lead to high mortality rates. AI can be instrumental in combating this issue by analyzing infection data and identifying patterns that indicate an emerging risk of antibiotic resistance. AI systems can detect potential outbreaks and identify individuals at high risk before symptoms become apparent, allowing for timely intervention and prevention. Such predictive capabilities could save countless lives by curbing the spread of multi-drug-resistant infections in hospitals and communities.

Smart devices are becoming increasingly important in monitoring patients in critical care units (ICUs) and other healthcare settings. These devices, when integrated with AI, can enhance the early detection of complications such as sepsis or organ failure. Sepsis is a life-threatening condition that requires rapid intervention, and AI-powered tools can monitor vital signs and alert healthcare providers before the condition worsens. By embedding AI algorithms into monitoring devices, healthcare professionals can reduce their cognitive load and make better-informed decisions. This ensures that patients receive the necessary care as quickly as possible, potentially preventing hospital-acquired complications and reducing associated costs. AI in medical monitoring not only improves outcomes but also helps in optimizing healthcare resources by minimizing unnecessary interventions.

The proliferation of wearable devices and smartphones equipped with sensors has revolutionized the collection of health-related data. From step trackers to heart rate monitors, these gadgets generate an enormous amount of valuable information that can provide insights into both individual and population health trends. When combined with patient-reported data through apps and other monitoring tools, these devices can paint a comprehensive picture of a person's health status. AI plays a crucial role in analyzing this vast dataset, extracting relevant insights, and providing personalized recommendations for health improvement. By leveraging machine learning (ML) algorithms, AI can identify patterns in the data that may indicate a potential health issue, allowing individuals to take preventive action before the condition becomes serious.

Furthermore, AI-driven insights can contribute to population health management by identifying risk factors, predicting outbreaks, and guiding public health interventions. For example, AI could analyze the health data of a population to identify early warning signs of an epidemic, enabling authorities to take proactive measures to contain the spread. This kind of data-driven approach can lead to more targeted and efficient public health strategies, ultimately improving health outcomes on a larger scale.

In conclusion, AI holds immense promise for transforming healthcare in numerous ways. From enabling direct brain-technology interfaces that can help restore lost functions to patients with neurological disorders, to automating routine processes that make healthcare more efficient and accessible, AI has the potential to improve the quality of care significantly. For people living in resource-limited areas, AI can bring quality healthcare to their doorsteps, reducing the need for trained diagnostic centers and improving early disease detection. AI's role in combating antibiotic resistance, enhancing patient monitoring, and deriving meaningful insights from health data is critical in addressing some of the biggest challenges faced by the healthcare industry today. As AI technologies continue to evolve, they will likely play an even greater role in promoting health, preventing disease, and improving the quality of life for people around the world.

11.4 FUTURE OF ROBOTS IN HEALTHCARE

Robots were first introduced in hospitals in the 1980s, resembling machinery from a car assembly line repurposed for medical use, specifically aiding in brain biopsies. Since then, these AI-powered assistants have evolved significantly alongside technological advancements. Modern robotic arms can be remotely controlled by surgeons, enabling them to perform delicate and precise surgeries in a highly sterile environment, benefiting both the patient and the medical team. Additionally, robots are used for handling hazardous materials, thereby enhancing worker safety. Although traditional robots may not resemble humans, researchers are striving to create more human-like robots to make them appear friendlier and more approachable. In Japan, advancements in robotics have produced robots that closely resemble humans in appearance, complete with lifelike "skin" and "tissue." These robots can analyze and respond to human voices, offering social interaction and emotional comfort to patients.

Medical robots are instrumental in assisting with surgeries, providing care and monitoring for patients with chronic conditions, ensuring timely administration of medication, and engaging with elderly patients to improve their well-being. In healthcare settings where there is a risk of disease transmission, robots are employed to transport supplies and linens, helping to protect healthcare workers. Cleaning and disinfection robots also play a crucial role in reducing hospital-acquired infections by minimizing the exposure of hospital staff to harmful pathogens. Many hospitals and healthcare centers now rely on these robots for enhanced safety. Robots are also utilized to lift heavy equipment, such as beds and medical devices, or even to assist in transporting patients between different hospital floors, thereby reducing the physical strain on healthcare staff [10, 11, 14, 15]. Surgical-assistance robots have become more accurate as motion control technology has advanced. Surgeons can now perform complex micro-surgeries with minimal incisions using these robots, significantly improving patient outcomes. As AI continues to develop, surgical robots will likely incorporate computer vision, allowing them to navigate precisely to targeted areas of the body while avoiding critical structures like nerves. In the future, some surgical robots might even be capable of independently performing tasks, with physicians overseeing the procedure remotely.

Modular robots can be integrated with other systems and programmed to perform a variety of tasks. In healthcare, this includes therapeutic exoskeleton robots and prosthetic limbs. These devices aid in the rehabilitation of patients recovering from strokes, paralysis, brain injuries, or multiple sclerosis. Therapeutic robots equipped with AI can monitor patients' movement as they perform exercises, tracking their progress more accurately than the human eye can. They can also interact with patients, providing guidance and motivation throughout their rehabilitation [6, 14, 16, 17]. Self-navigating robots, equipped with various cameras, can move independently to reach patients in examination rooms or hospital wards, enabling healthcare providers to communicate remotely. Physicians may also use remotely controlled robots to accompany them on hospital rounds, providing on-screen consultations and aiding in diagnosis and treatment planning. These robots manage their own power needs, returning to charging stations as required. Social robots, designed to interact with humans, offer companionship and assistance in long-term care facilities. They can engage patients cognitively, encourage adherence to treatment plans, and keep them active and positive. Social robots also help direct visitors and patients within healthcare facilities, reduce caregivers' workloads, and contribute to the emotional well-being of patients.

The field of robotics in healthcare will continue to advance, driven by improvements in ML, data analytics, VR, and other technologies. As robotic technologies evolve, they will become increasingly autonomous, efficient, and accurate, further transforming the healthcare landscape.

11.5 LIMITATION OF ROBOTICS IN HEATHCARE

While there are numerous advantages to using robots to conduct errands in healthcare, there is also the possibility of errors and malfunctions. With these powerful robots, there is always the possibility of human error or mechanical failure. A single mechanical failure can result in human death. Small hazards of infection and bleeding must be overlooked when using surgical robots.

Another significant downside is the cost. Surgical robots are only used in industrialized countries, research institutes, and advanced multispecialty hospitals. Patients, too, may find that robotic surgery is out of their financial grasp in some circumstances. Also, the healthcare sector needs to invest a lot of initial investment money and time to train the workforce to handle robotic equipment; besides, their lifetime maintenance cost is another problematic factor for the healthcare sector.

11.6 EXAMPLES OF ROBOTS IN HEATHCARE

The Da Vinci System is a general surgical robot facilitating a variety of surgical procedures in urology and gynecology. Apart from it, the MAKO System from Stryker specializes in orthopedic surgery with specialization in partial and complete knee replacements.

Paro, one of their machines, responds to human speech and appears to be a non-threatening baby seal. Other humanoid robotic technology is utilized to assist with personal care, socialization, and training. One used in trauma training for emergency responders, for example, resembles a victim who yells, bleeds, and even responds to treatment.

Robots can help with rehabilitation and surgery. Cyberdyne's Hybrid Assistive Limb (HAL) exoskeleton, for example, is designed to help patients recover from conditions that lead to lower limb disorders, such as spinal cord injuries and strokes, by using sensors placed on the skin to detect small electrical signals in the patient's body and responding with movement at the joint [12, 18, 19].

One of the fastest expanding categories in robotics is exoskeletons. Airport and warehouse employees would benefit from bio-feedback waistband lumbar support, which is currently prevalent in Japan. The evolution of exoskeletons will be influenced by advances in brain-machine connectivity. Cyberdyne, ReWalk Robotics, and Esso Bionics are the main businesses in the sector [7, 8, 12, 20].

Robots can provide much needed support and care to the elderly as well as patients with deformities. Unfortunately, at present, the number of such robots is very low, but it may rise dramatically over the next decade, especially in countries like Japan, where a shortage of available caretakers is forecast. These care robots may carry out relatively simple roles such as assisting people in getting in and out of bed, supporting them in walks, and so forth. Challenging jobs for the robots will be to remind patients of the timings of medicines and sometimes provide them emotional support by interacting with them as a replacement for human beings. Another important job the robots can do is to provide support to nursing staff in different activities like collection of blood, documenting temperature, ensuring cleanliness of patients, and so forth. In this way, nursing staff would have sufficient time to pay attention to customized patient care and treatment plans.

11.7 CONCLUSION AND FUTURE PROSPECTS

The final question with healthcare robotics is whether they will eliminate human jobs. There are various reasons why machines will not be able to take the place of humans. For starters, the majority of hospitals have fewer than 300 beds. They simply do not have the financial means to invest in technology. The autonomous driven vehicles will require tracks laid on the floor and an efficient navigation system housed in the hospital area. Other carts use AI-drawn navigation tools of the hospital that include elevators, turns, and automated doors that are programmed into them. That procedure is also very costly. However, robotic helpers will never be able to completely replace human interaction.

VR is being combined with rehabilitation robots in order to broaden the scope of therapy exercises while also enhancing motivation and improving physical treatment outcomes. Nanoparticles and nanomaterials are being used to make exciting discoveries. Nanoparticles, for example, can cross the "blood-brain barrier." Nanodevices could be loaded with "treatment payloads" of medicine in the future, which could be injected into the body and autonomously steered to specific target spots. Ingestible, broadband-enabled smart instruments that use wireless technology to monitor internal reactions to drugs will be available soon.

KEYWORDS

- **artificial intelligence**
- **critical care units**
- **hybrid assistive limb**
- **Internet of Things**
- **virtual reality**

REFERENCES

1. Patel, A. R., et al. (2017). Vitality of robotics in healthcare industry: An Internet of Things (IoT) perspective. In *Internet of Things and Big Data Technologies for Next Generation Healthcare* (pp. 91–109).

2. Fischinger, D., et al. (2016). Hobbit, a care robot supporting independent living at home: First prototype and lessons learned. *Robotics and Autonomous Systems, 75*, 60–78.
3. Pérez-Vidal, C., et al. (2012). Steps in the development of a robotic scrub nurse. *Robotics and Autonomous Systems, 60*(6), 901–911.
4. Ashrafian, H., Darzi, A., & Athanasiou, T. (2015). A novel modification of the Turing test for artificial intelligence and robotics in healthcare. *The International Journal of Medical Robotics and Computer Assisted Surgery, 11*(1), 38–43.
5. Martínez-López, M. V., et al. (2024). Exploring the ethics of interaction with care robots. In *Ethics of Artificial Intelligence* (pp. 149–167). Springer Nature Switzerland.
6. Garmann-Johnsen, N., Mettler, T., & Sprenger, M. (2014). Service robotics in healthcare: A perspective for information systems researchers?
7. Lipp, B. (2023). Caring for robots: How care comes to matter in human–machine interfacing. *Social Studies of Science, 53*(5), 660–685.
8. Chan, H. Y., & Muralidharan, A. (2024). Care robots for the elderly: Legal, ethical considerations and regulatory strategies. In *Developments in Intellectual Property Strategy: The Impact of Artificial Intelligence, Robotics and New Technologies* (pp. 129–156). Springer International Publishing.
9. Torras, C. (2024). Ethics of social robotics: Individual and societal concerns and opportunities. *Annual Review of Control, Robotics, and Autonomous Systems, 7*.
10. Gelderblom, G. J., De Wilt, M., Cremers, G., & Rensma, A. (2009). Rehabilitation robotics in robotics for healthcare; a roadmap study for the European Commission. In *2009 IEEE International Conference on Rehabilitation Robotics* (pp. 834–838). IEEE.
11. Silvera-Tawil, D., Rye, D., & Velonaki, M. (2015). Artificial skin and tactile sensing for socially interactive robots: A review. *Robotics and Autonomous Systems, 63*, 230–243.
12. Sharkey, A., & Sharkey, N. (2012). Granny and the robots: Ethical issues in robot care for the elderly. *Ethics and Information Technology, 14*, 27–40.
13. Lin, P., Abney, K., & Bekey, G. A. (2014). *Robot Ethics: The Ethical and Social Implications of Robotics*. MIT Press.
14. Guntur, S. R., Gorrepati, R. R., & Dirisala, V. R. (2019). Robotics in healthcare: An Internet of Medical Robotic Things (IoMRT) perspective. In *Machine Learning in Bio-Signal Analysis and Diagnostic Imaging* (pp. 293–318). Academic Press.
15. Sparrow, R., & Sparrow, L. (2006). In the hands of machines? The future of aged care. *Minds and Machines, 16*, 141–161.
16. Sánchez, A., et al. (2014). A design framework for surgical robots: Example of the Araknes robot controller. *Robotics and Autonomous Systems, 62*(9), 1342–1352.
17. Coeckelbergh, M. (2013). E-care as craftsmanship: Virtuous work, skilled engagement, and information technology in healthcare. *Medicine, Health Care and Philosophy, 16*, 807–816.
18. Coeckelbergh, M. (2011). Human development or human enhancement? A methodological reflection on capabilities and the evaluation of information technologies. *Ethics and Information Technology, 13*, 81–92.
19. Coeckelbergh, M. (2011). Are emotional robots deceptive? *IEEE Transactions on Affective Computing, 3*(4), 388–393.

20. Decker, M., & Fleischer, T. (2008). Contacting the brain–Aspects of a technology assessment of neural implants. *Biotechnology Journal: Healthcare Nutrition Technology, 3*(12), 1502–1510.

Index

D

H

I

V

W

Y